AF529814

Hinduism
On Its Own Terms

Hinduism
On Its Own Terms

Arvind Sharma

DK PRINTWORLD
Publishers of Indian Traditions

Cataloging in Publication Data — DK
[Courtesy: D.K. Agencies (P) Ltd. <docinfo@dkagencies.com>]

Sharma, Arvind, author.
Hinduism and its own terms / Arvind Sharma.
pages cm
ISBN: 9788124608395

1. Hinduism. 2. Hinduism — Dictionaries. I. Title.

DDC 294.5 23

ISBN: 978-81-246-0839-5
First published in India in 2016
© Arvind Sharma

All rights reserved. No part of this publication may be reproduced or transmitted, except brief quotations, in any form or by any means, electronic or mechanical, including photocopying, recording, or any information storage or retrieval system, without prior written permission of the copyright holder, indicated above, and the publishers.

Printed and published by:
D.K. Printworld (P) Ltd.
Regd. Office: Vedaśrī, F-395, Sudarshan Park
(Metro Station: Ramesh Nagar), New Delhi - 110 015
Phones: (011) 2545 3975, 2546 6019; *Fax*: (011) 2546 5926
e-mail: indology@dkprintworld.com
Website: www.dkprintworld.com

Preface

This book consists of two parts, the second being more substantial than the first. The first part provides a general survey of Hinduism. Many of the terms which appear in this survey, along with some additional terms, are then elaborated in the second part. The preponderance of these terms in the book is reflected in the title *Hinduism : On Its Own Terms*.

A survey of Hinduism can only be suggestive, given the vast area to be covered, and the terms can only be illustrative, given the large number of items which could potentially be included.

We hope that, despite these limitations, the reader will find the book useful.

Arvind Sharma

Contents

Abbreviations

AitUp	*Aitareya Upaniṣad*
ĀpDhSū	*Āpastamba-Dharmasūtras*
BṛUp	*Bṛhadāraṇyaka Upaniṣad*
ChāUp	*Chāndogya Upaniṣad*
MS	*Manu-Smṛti*
MuṇḍUp	*Muṇḍaka Upaniṣad*
ṚV	*Ṛg-Veda*
ŚataBrā	*Śatapatha Brāhmaṇa*
ŚvetUp	*Śvetāśvatara Upaniṣad*
VDhSūP	*Vāsiṣṭha-Dharmasūtras*
Viṣṇu	*Viṣṇu Purāṇa*
YS	*Yoga-Sūtra*

I
General Introduction to Hinduism

1

Definition : Primary Sources

History : Trends in Scholarly Study

What Is Hinduism?

THOUGH now accepted by Hindus, the word Hindu is not a Hindu word.[1] It gained international currency in the eighteenth century, mercifully over an earlier form Gentoo, as an omnibus term to describe an adherent of the major religious tradition of India, with which the West was coming into increasing contact after the establishment of British Raj over India. The word itself goes back at least to the sixth century BCE, and, after various philological adventures, now seems fairly well-established as indicating an Indian citizen or a person of Indian origin who is not a Muslim, Christian, Zoroastrian or Jew, and at a second order of negation, not a Jaina, Buddhist or Sikh. The ultimate reality is often described via negativa by the Hindus; it seems that the reality about the Hindus themselves may also have to be so described. The fact that, at least initially, one identifies a Hindu as an Indian who is not a non-Hindu, serves to indicate the close bond that exists between the Hindu religion, as a religious entity, and India, as a geographical entity, which virtually makes Hinduism an ethnic religion. Over 90 per cent of the Hindus of the world reside in the Republic of India and over 80 per cent of the citizens of this Republic itself are classified as Hindus, though there also exist significant Hindu communities in

---

1 See Arvind Sharma, 2002, "On Hindu, Hindustān, Hinduism and Hindutva", *Numen,* 49: 1-36.

Sri Lanka, Bangladesh, Bali, South-East Africa, and in the islands of the Caribbean and Oceania. But these have resulted from migration rather than conversion, though this is less clear in the case of Bali. The Hindus do not seek converts as such, but now accept them, so that a Hindu may be identified finally as a person of Indian origin who does not claim to be non-Hindu, and a person of non-Indian origin who claims to be one.

The reader would have noted that the use of the word Hinduism has hitherto been avoided, and for a good reason. Scholars have long given up the attempt to define Hinduism, as an ism, on account of its doctrinal proteanness, and because it is more a way of life rather than a creed. Instead, they feel more confident of identifying a Hindu (as the Hindu Marriage Act of 1955 tries to). Once the Hindu has been identified, Hinduism may then be defined as the religion of the Hindus.[2]

Primary Sources

It is the corpus of literature known either collectively in the singular as the Veda, or in the plural as the Vedas, which must be regarded as the earliest accessible primary literary source for the study of Hinduism, as the inscriptions on the seals of the Indus Valley have not yet been deciphered.[3] The Hindu tradition recognizes the Vedas as its foundational scripture, Hinduism itself being indigenously known as Vaidika Dharma.[4]

What are the Vedas? Like the Bible or the Qur'ān, the Vedas are the sacred books of the Hindus. The word itself means knowledge or perhaps better still, wisdom, the latter word sharing with the

---

[2] For more on the problematique of defining Hinduism, see J.E. Llewellyn, ed., 2005, *Defining Hinduism: A Reader,* New York: Routledge.

[3] Thomas J. Hopkins, 1971, *The Hindu Religious Tradition,* Belmont, CA Dickenson Publishing Company, p. 4; also see Asko Parpola, 1994, *Deciphering the Indus Script,* Cambridge: Cambridge University Press.

[4] T.M.P. Mahadevan, 1971, *Outlines of Hinduism,* Bombay: Chetana, pp. 12-13.

word *veda* the Indo-European root (*vid* in Sanskrit, which means "to know"). In the abstract, the word means wisdom or spiritual wisdom par excellence; in the concrete it refers to the four collections which bear the names of *Ṛg-*, *Sāma-*, *Yajur-* and *Atharva-Veda*. Of these *Ṛg-Veda* is the oldest, also supplying, in varying degrees, the source material for the other three. The *Atharva-Veda* is qualitatively different from the other three Vedas, being concerned with household rather than sacrificial religion.[5]

Not only are the Vedas four in number, it is useful to look upon each as possessing a fourfold division, which seems to correspond roughly to the evolution of Vedic religion, as it passed through different phases of growth. The first phase (*c.* 1500–1200 BCE), which corresponds to the Mantra or Saṁhitā division, was marked by simple hymnal prayers addressed to the various gods. In the second phase, which corresponds to the Brāhmaṇa division (*c.* 1200 – 1000 BCE), these hymns came to be accompanied by complex ritual. The third phase (*c.* 1000–800 BCE), which corresponds to the Āraṇyaka division, marks the beginnings of that investigation into the meaning of ritual which initiated a trend towards philosophical speculation, of which we get intimations even in the *Ṛg-Veda* (*ṚV*), as when the question is asked: What was the wood, what was the tree out of which they fashioned heaven and earth? (*ṚV* X.31.7). This reached its climax in the Upaniṣads, the last section of the Vedas (*c.* 800 BCE). The dates here are only shrewd guesses, but the sequence of the development of religious priorities is reasonably clear.[6]

The emergence of the Upaniṣads represents a decisive moment

---

5 James A. Santucci, 1976, *An Outline of Vedic Literature,* Missoula, MT: Scholars Press, p. 1; Michael Witzel, 2003, "Vedas and Upaniṣads", in Gavin Flood ed. *The Blackwell Companion of Hinduism,* Oxford: Blackwell Publishing, pp. 68-101.

6 Wm. Theodore de Bary, ed., 1958, *Sources of Indian Tradition,* New York: Columbia University Press, vol. 1, pp. 1-34; also see Ainslie T. Embree, ed., 1988, *Sources of Indian Tradition* (2nd edn), New York: Columbia University Press, part 1.

in the history of Hinduism. Gradually, by way of informal consensus, the tradition felt that the answers to the probing questions raised early in the hymns of the *Ṛg-Veda* were to be found in this class of literature — the Upaniṣads — and Vedic development was seen as fulfilled. Such an understanding of the development also came to be conveyed, in due course, by the term *vedānta,* as a synonym of the Upaniṣads. As pointed out earlier, the word *veda* has the twofold meaning of (1) a literary corpus, and (2) spiritual knowledge. The word *vedānta* is formed by combining the word *anta* with *veda,* which carries the twofold meaning in Sanskrit, of (1) end, and (2) conclusion (perhaps because a conclusion comes at the end of a discussion or disquisition). The word *vedānta* then, in all its fullness, means conclusions about spiritual knowledge contained in the last section of the Vedas, i.e. the Upaniṣads.

The Hindus themselves classify the main primary sources of their own religion into two categories:

1. Śruti — or that which is heard, and
2. Smṛti — that which is remembered.[7]

The first term connotes the Vedas and stands for revelation, as distinguished from the second category, which stands for tradition. The Śruti, in theory, is believed to have been heard divinely by the sages and is therefore not a work of human authorship, but rather the result of human reception. The Smṛti, by contrast, is of human authorship, and unlike the Śruti, fallible. It is clear, then, that Śruti has primacy over Smṛti; tradition is supposed to follow in the footsteps of revelation. But though Śruti is primary in theory, it is Smṛti which really constitutes the popular religious literature in practice, partly because the study of the Śruti was restricted by considerations of caste, and later, language.

The Smṛti literature of Hinduism is less clearly organized than the Śruti, and, by comparison, is also more vast. The word Smṛti itself, as a category of literature, has two distinct senses. It means

---

[7] Louis Renou, ed., 1961, *Hinduism*, New York: George Braziller, p. 7.

a law book, laying down the rules of right living for the Hindus. Of these over forty are listed, among which the *Manu*-Smṛti is accorded pride of place. In its widest application, the word *smṛti* has been used to include, apart from the law books, at least the two great *itihāsas* (national epics), the *Rāmāyaṇa* and the *Mahābhārata*, the eighteen Purāṇas, the Āgamas (Vaiṣṇava, Śaiva and Śākta), the Darśana literature or the treatises of the philosophical schools and sometimes even Buddhist and Jaina works, apart from works in regional languages. A brief description and enumeration of this literature is well-nigh impossible but no account of the primary sources for the study of Hinduism can be concluded without further word on the two great epics and the Purāṇas.

The *Rāmāyaṇa* deals with the life and adventures of Rāma, the hero of the epic, who is recognized therein as an incarnation of the God Viṣṇu. The story of the birth of Rāma, his marriage to Sītā, of his exile, of the abduction of Sītā by Rāvaṇa, the demon-king of Laṅkā, and of her recovery with an army of monkeys led by Hanumān, is known in every Hindu home. The word Rāma has become a synonym for God Himself; it was the last word to escape the lips of Mahatma Gandhi, when he was felled by the assassin's bullets. Similarly, the story of the fratricidal struggle for the throne between the Kauravas and the Pāṇḍavas, which forms the nucleus of the *Mahābhārata*, perhaps the second longest epic in the world, is also known to every Hindu. The popular Hindu text, the *Bhagavad-Gītā*,[8] forms a miniscule part of this epic, but has acquired a status of its own. This text of 700 verses, couched in the form of a dialogue between Kṛṣṇa, also an incarnation of God Viṣṇu, and Arjuna, on the eve of the battle between the opposing armies of 100 Kaurava brothers on the one hand and the five Pāṇḍava brothers on the other, of whom Arjuna is one, is now virtually looked upon as a revealed text. In it Hinduism comes closest to possessing a universal scripture. The

---

8 See Franklin Edgerton, 1972, *The Bhagavadgītā,* Cambridge: Harvard University Press; Barbara Stoler Miller, 1986, *The Bhagavadgītā: Krishna's Counsel in Time of War,* New York: Columbia University Press.

Vedas are known only to a few, though revered by all, but the stories of the *Rāmāyaṇa* and the *Mahābhārata* are known to virtually every Hindu, as also the stories of the Purāṇas. These relate to the main gods of the Hindu pantheon, the kind which children hear about from their grandparents.[9] The best known of these is the *Bhāgavata Purāṇa*, which deals with the early life of Kṛṣṇa, spent in the bucolic surroundings of the region around Mathurā.[10] The language of most if not all of this literature is Sanskrit.

History

It is customary to distinguish between the ancient (CE –1000), the medieval (1000–1800) and the modern period (1800–) in the history of Hinduism, but in order to present this history within a short compass, it might be useful to do so in terms of the major turning points in this history. Four such major turning points may be identified:

1. The Aryan invasion or immigration of 1500 BCE,
2. the rise of the Buddhist–Jaina heterodoxy in the sixth century BCE,
3. the Islamic incursions from around CE 1000, and
4. the Christian encounter from *c.* CE 1800.

The earliest information about Hinduism is derived from two radically different sources, the relationship between which is not entirely clear, though a working hypothesis has been evolved. These sources are the archaeological remains of the Haṛappan or Indus Valley culture of the third millennium BCE and the literary documents called the Vedas, especially the *Ṛg-Veda*, usually placed to the second millennium BCE. The general assumption is that the

---

9 See James A. Kirk, 1972, *Stories of the Hindus*, New York: The Macmillan Company.

10 Vasudha Narayanan, 1996, "The Hindu Tradition" in Willard G. Oxtoby ed. *World Religions: Eastern Traditions*, Toronto: Oxford University Press, p. 70.

Aryans, as the people of the *Ṛg-Veda* called themselves, either conquered or immigrated into the Indus Valley and in doing so absorbed many religious elements which are not directly traceable to the Vedas, but appear in Hinduism later. It appears that the people of the Indus Valley venerated a proto-Śiva depicted on seals, as also the mother-goddess, the *pīpal* tree and the *liṅgam*, the symbol of Śiva, perhaps phallic in significance. The ample provision for bathing is suggestive of concern with ritual pollution. These elements are to be found even in present-day Hinduism.[11]

The Aryans were once believed to have overrun the Indus Valley during the second millennium BCE with the help of their military innovation — the horse-drawn war chariot, and to have ushered in the Vedic age, but this scenario is now being challenged.[12] The main phases of the religious development from 1500 BCE to 600 BCE have already been outlined. What needs to be emphasized here is that it is the Vedānta, which was destined to play a major intellectual role in the history of Hinduism. Right from the eighth century CE onwards, if not earlier, it was to give rise to forms of intellectual Hinduism whose influence persisted through the centuries, in the shape of various systems of Vedāntic thought such as the Advaita (non-Dualism) of Śaṅkarācarya (CE 882–920), the Viśiṣṭādvaita (Qualified Monism) of Rāmānuja (CE 1017-37) and the Dvaita (Dualism) of Madhva (1199–1278 CE), to refer only to the major schools. In modern times, it is again to Vedānta that modern Hindus have, by and large, turned for spiritual sustenance.[13]

The next great moment in the history of Hinduism is represented by the challenge posed by the rise of the heterodox movements in the sixth century BCE, especially by Jainism and Buddhism. It was during this period of prolonged encounter and

---

11 Hopkins, op. cit., p. 1.

12 See Edwin Bryant, 2001, *The Quest for the Origins of Vedic Culture: The Indo-Aryan Migration Debate,* New York: Oxford University Press.

13 S. Radhakrishnan, ed., 1953, *The Principal Upaniṣads,* London: George Allen & Unwin, pp. 1, 4.

interaction that the various philosophical schools of Hinduism were systematized, and their basic texts composed in aphorisms. These schools, six in number, which accept the authority of the Vedas, are:

1. Nyāya: the school of logical realism;
2. Vaiśeṣika: the school of atomistic pluralism;
3. Sāṁkhya: the school of matter–spirit dualism;
4. Yoga: the school devoted to meditational techniques;
5. Pūrva-Mīmāṁsā: the school of Vedic ritualism; and
6. Uttara-Mīmāṁsā or Vedānta: the school based on Vedic philosophical speculation.[14]

At the social level, this was the period when the encompassing sociological doctrines of the four ends of man, the four classes, and the four stages of life, were formulated and synthesized through the various Dharmasūtras (aphoristic legal works), as distinguished from the philosophical texts mentioned earlier.[15] On account of the proliferation of such aphoristic works, this immediate post-Vedic phase is called the Sūtra (thread) period of Hinduism.[16] In the period following it, the sociological doctrines achieved their full formulation in the law books or Smṛtis. The Buddhists emphasized salvation or *nirvāṇa* (*mokṣa*); in Hinduism three other valid ends of life (*puruṣārthas*) were recognized:

1. the leading of a normative life in the context of the world (*dharma*),
2. the pursuit of wealth (*artha*), and
3. of the pleasures of the senses (*kāma*) consistently with morality.

---

14 M. Hiriyanna, 1978, *The Essentials of Indian Philosophy,* London: Allen & Unwin, pp. 4-8.

15 Ainslie T. Embree, ed., 1972, *The Hindu Tradition,* New York: Random House, p. 78.

16 Kenneth W. Morgan, ed., 1953, *The Religion of the Hindus,* New York: The Ronald Press Company, pp. 31-32.

The Buddhists emphasized monasticism; the Hindus developed the doctrine of the four stages of life (*āśramas*) — that of the celibate student (*brahmacārī*), the householder (*gṛhastha*), the hermit (*vānaprastha*) and the renunciant (*saṁnyāsī*). Each phase could be taken to cover a quarter of the ideal lifespan of 100 years, although there is evidence to suggest that they may have originally represented optional lifestyles. The Buddhists emphasised the absence of caste distinctions in the Saṅgha (the Buddhist order); the Hindus saw society as hierarchically organized into four *varṇas* (classes): those consisting of the priest and scholar (brāhmaṇa), the warrior and bureaucrat (kṣatriya), the merchant and cultivator (vaiśya) and labourers or servants (*śūdra*). Some sections of society, especially those engaged in polluting work, were accommodated at the bottom of the fourfold system, as untouchables. The Buddhists were atheistic or at best transtheistic; the Hindus incorporated theism into the life of the people with the rise of the Bhakti (devotional) movement. It arose in the south, where the devotional outpouring of twelve Vaiṣṇava Āḻvārs, and the sixty-three Śaiva Nāyanārs were compiled subsequently into the *Divyaprabandham* and the *Tirumurai* respectively. The Buddhists had used popular stories to spread their ideas. It was during this period that the popular epics, the *Rāmāyaṇa* and the *Mahābhārata*, and the eighteen Purāṇas, were composed. The Buddhists built *stūpas* and monasteries; the Hindus built temples during this period on a massive scale notwithstanding the aniconic nature of the Vedic tradition. It was supplemented by works of the Āgama (Tantra) tradition.[17] By around CE 1200 the Hindu response proved overwhelming and Buddhism as a separate religion gradually died out in India.

Hinduism next had to come to terms with Islam, when it acquired solid political ascendancy in India from CE 1200 onwards.

---

[17] Gavin Flood, 1996, *An Introduction to Hinduism,* Cambridge: Cambridge University Press, pp. 158ff.; Agehananda Bharati, 1965, *The Tantric Tradition*, London: Rider & Co.

The religious beliefs of the previous invaders of India had either been embroidered on the fabric of Hinduism or had been woven successfully into it, but this was not possible with Islam, with whose distinctiveness and missionary zeal the Hindus had to contend for several centuries. The Hindus presented a fourfold response: indifference, acceptance, rejection and synthesis. Islam was probably ignored so long as it was possible to do so, and in regions it did not penetrate into. But where its challenge had to be faced, many accepted it. By CE 1800 one out of every four Indians was a Muslim. But the mass of Hindus rejected it, presenting a kind of cellular defence by tightening the rules of caste. With the loss of political power, the leadership of the community passed into sacerdotal hands, encouraging the casteist line of defence.[18] There was also increased emphasis on Bhakti,[19] as represented by the flowering of devotional literature in the regional languages, which included the rendering of the *Rāmāyaṇa* into them.[20] Of these the best known is the *Rāmacaritamānasa* of Tulsīdās (d. CE 1623), which became the religious text par excellence in Hindu homes in northern India during this period. The Marāṭhā saints such as Jñāneśvar (*c.* 1275-96), Nāmdev (1270–1350), Ekanāth (1533-99), Tukārām (1598–1650) and Rāmdās (1608-82) also belong to this period, as do many other poet-saints from various regions of India, too numerous to mention.

Some innovators, however, attempted synthesis, the convergence between Bhakti and Sufism providing the necessary background.[21] Prominent among them was Kabīr (1440–1518) who

---

[18] Aziz Ahmad, 1964, *Studies in Islamic Culture in the Indian Environment*, Oxford: Clarendon Press, pp. 99-100.

[19] K.M. Panikkar, 1947, *A Survey of Indian History*, London: Meridian Books, p. 2.

[20] A.K. Majumdar, 1965, *Bhakti Renaissance*, Bombay: Bharatiya Vidya Bhavan, pp. 4-5.

[21] S.A.A. Rizvi, 1978, *History of Sufism in India*, New Delhi: Munshiram Manoharlal, vol. I.

rejected the formalism of both Hinduism and Islam, and Nānak (1469–1538) whose followers, combining the Hindu world-view with an Islamic rejection of image worship and emphasis on the revealed book, ultimately tended to evolve into a group distinct from the Hindus and the Muslims alike.[22]

The establishment of British Raj in India exposed India to Western and Christian influences, particularly through Christian missionary activity and the introduction of English as virtually the official language of India. The Hindu response to this encounter is represented by a wide spectrum of individuals and the organizations associated with them. Raja Rammohun Roy (1772/74–1833) founded the Brahmo Samaj in Bengal, in whose evolution Debendranath Tagore (1817–1905) and Keshub Chunder Sen (1838-84) were important influences, as was M.G. Ranade (1842–1901) in relation to the Prarthana Samaj in the Bombay region. Swami Dayananda Sarasvati (1824-83) founded the Arya Samaj in 1875, the same year in which the Theosophical Society was founded and which exercised considerable influence through Annie Besant (1847–1933). Swami Vivekananda (1863–1902) founded a Mission named after his *guru*, Ramakrishna (1836-86), perhaps one of the greatest mystics of all times. A number of remarkable individuals of all-India status such as Rabindranath Tagore (1861–1941); Sri Aurobindo (1872–1950); Ramana Maharshi (1879–1950); S. Radhakrishnan (1888–1975) but, above all, Mahatma Gandhi (1869–1948) were also consequential in initiating or sustaining trends.[23] In terms of the fourfold pattern of response: indifference, acceptance, rejection and synthesis, those parts of India least touched by British rule may be said to have remained indifferent. Acceptance was represented by conversion

---

22 See Khushwant Singh, 1966, *A History of the Sikhs*, Princeton: Princeton University Press, 2 vols.

23 D.S. Sarma, 1944, *Studies in the Renaissance of Hinduism in the Nineteenth and the Twentieth Centuries*, Banaras: Banaras Hindu University; Stephen Hay, ed., 1988, *Sources of Indian Tradition* (2nd edn), New York: Columbia University Press, vol. 2.

to Christianity by about 2 per cent of Indians. Rejection of the West, and especially of Christianity was represented by the Arya Samaj, though one wing within it reconciled itself to Western education but not to Christianity. The Śuddhi movement, sponsored by the Arya Samaj, aimed at the reconversion of those who had become Muslims or Christians, to the Hindufold.

But acceptance and rejection were two extreme reactions — the more typical Hindu response was one of synthesis and assimilation. This was represented, for instance, by the Brahmo Sabha, a society formed in 1828 by Raja Rammohun Roy for non-idolatrous monotheistic worship, whose name was later changed to Brahmo Samaj. Roy was active in social reform, agitating for the abolition of suttee (*satī*), the introduction of English education and so on. The Brahmo Samaj, after a checkered history, is now a spent force but partly because its agenda for social reform is now accepted without question. Another major reform movement centres around the figure of Swami Vivekananda who founded the Ramakrishna Mission. Ramakrishna, Vivekananda's *guru*, was a mystic but Vivekananda exhibited considerable dynamism and literally burnt himself out, dying before he turned forty. Some of his dynamism he was able to infuse into Hinduism. The trail of saffron-robed *swāmīs* travelling around the globe goes back to his presence at the Parliament of Religions in Chicago in 1893, where he made a considerable impression. Early Christian propaganda had put the Hindus on the defensive but Vivekananda, and the Mission he founded defended Hinduism with vigour, while at the same time emulating missionary techniques and applying them on behalf of Hinduism.[24] The Theosophical Society also produced similar results.

Broadly speaking, the Hindus accepted the Christian critique of Hindu society but not of Hindu theology or philosophy. Most of the major influential figures of modern Hinduism, such as Mahatma Gandhi, showed a concern for the masses, the abuses of casteism,

---

24 R.C. Zaehner, ed., 1962, *Hinduism*, London: Oxford University Press, pp. 212-23.

the position of women, and so on, to a great degree and in this they must have been influenced, at least to some extent, by the Christian critique of Hinduism. However, the attacks on idolatry seemed misguided to most Hindus, and the attempts to convert people to Christianity wicked, as neo-Hinduism evolved the view that all religions are equally valid. Among other leading figures, Sri Aurobindo tried to integrate obviously Western concepts, such as that of evolution, with Hindu thought,[25] while Rabindranath Tagore emphasized humanism, and Sri Ramana, Advaitic mysticism.

Trends in the Scholarly Study of Hinduism

Fundamental to an understanding, and even a description, of trends in the study of Hinduism is the fact that this study originated as a Western intellectual enterprise.[26] The main phases and assumptions of the scholarly study of Hinduism thus correspond to those in the study of religion in general in the West.[27] The first of these may be described as the missionary phase, a phase in which Hinduism was studied from a Christian perspective, as, for instance, in the works of the Serampore missionaries in the eighteenth century: William Carey, Joshua Marshman and William Ward. This statement applies not only to missionaries who were scholars but to those scholars as well who, like Monier-Williams, were not missionaries as such, but who shared the missionary perspective. The growth of textual criticism in biblical studies, which came next, stimulated critical studies of Hindu texts, as illustrated by Richard Garbe's and Rudolf Otto's attempts to determine the *ur-Gītā*. The tradition of critical textual studies of Hindu scriptures thus represented the next stage

25 John R. Hinnells and Eric J. Sharpe, 1972, *Hinduism*, Newcastle-upon-Tyne: Oriel Press, p. 93.

26 P.J. Marshall, ed., 1970, *The British Discovery of Hinduism in the Eighteenth Century*, Cambridge: Cambridge University Press; also see Arvind Sharma, ed., 2003, *The Study of Hinduism*, Columbia, South Carolina: University of South Carolina Press.

27 Milton Singer, 1972, *When a Great Tradition Modernizes*, London: Pall Mall Press.

in the scholarly study of Hinduism. It has had a distinguished history and is alive and well to this day.

With the growth of *religionswissenschaft* in Europe towards the end of the nineteenth century, the scholarly study of Hinduism became both an ancilla and a testing ground for the hypotheses being developed in this field, with the recognition that Hinduism was a religion with Indo-European connections if not roots. The discovery of the linguistic connection between the languages of India, specially those of north India, and Europe, was now followed up by an investigation of religious connections, specially in the field of mythology in which Hindu, specially Vedic, material was used to illustrate more general theories, as for example by Max Müller, and later by Georges Dumézil. With the rise of anthropology and sociology of religion as distinct fields in the academic study of religion, this trend was reflected, in the study of Hinduism, in the studies carried out by G.S. Ghurye, I. Karve, Louis Dumont, M.N. Srinivas and others.[28] With the general acceptance of the Great and Little Tradition hypothesis, textual studies remained the hallmark of the study of the Great Tradition in Hinduism, with anthropologists investigating the Little Tradition.[29] More recent trends in the study of Hinduism bear witness to the application of the phenomenological method to its study, as in the works of Mircea Eliade. Western Indology, however, is now increasingly been perceived as excessively Eurocentric, specially after the publication of Edward Said's *Orientalism* (1978).[30]

---

28 "Review Symposium on Louis Dumont's Homo Hierarchicus", *Contributions to Indian Sociology*, 1971 , V: 1-135.

29 C. Parvathamma, 1978, "The Remembered Village: A Brahmanical Odyssey"; Krishna Kumar Gupta, "Religion in Rampura: The Anthropological Approach Revisited", in *Contributions to Indian Sociology*, New Series 12(1): 91-107.

30 See Sharada Sugirtharajah, 2003, *Imagining Hinduism: A Post-Colonial Perspective,* London and New York: Routledge; Krishnan Ramaswamy, Antonio de Nicolas and Aditi Banerjee, eds., 2007, *Invading the Sacred: An Analysis of Hinduism Studies in America,* New Delhi: Rupa & Co.

2

Hinduism, The Great Tradition

Basic Teachings

THE basic teachings of Hinduism, as of most religions, centre around the nature of the ultimate reality, of the universe, the place of human beings in the universe, and the interrelationship between God, the universe and human beings.

The ultimate reality in Hinduism is designated by the term *Brahman*, a word of neuter gender derived from a root which means "to expand". In other words, the reality is spread all over around us — and beyond. This reality underlies the universe but is not exhausted by it. It is both immanent and transcendent, the universe is part of it yet it stands "ten digits beyond it" (*ṚV* X.90.1). Such a view of the ultimate reality has been called panentheistic as distinguished from the pantheistic, in which the reality is identified with the universe, and the theistic, in which the reality is placed outside the universe. This is the first point to bear clearly in mind about the nature of the ultimate reality as visualized in Hinduism — it is both immanent and transcendent. It is contained in the universe, as oil is contained in the seed; it contains the universe within it, as our mind contains a thought or dream. The second important point to bear in mind about *Brahman* is that it is, paradoxically, regarded as both devoid of and possessing attributes or qualities, as both without and with distinguishing features; as both without and with form. In its former aspect it is described as *Nirguṇa-Brahman* (*Brahman* without distinguishing qualities), and in its latter aspect it is described as *Saguṇa-Brahman* (with distinguishing qualities). It is a matter of considerable philosophical debate in Hinduism whether *Brahman* is, in the ultimate analysis, to be regarded fundamentally as *nirguṇa* or *saguṇa*; the absolutistic strand in Hindu thought emphasizes the former aspect, the theistic strand the latter. But that it possesses both these aspects is rarely denied. The featureless (*Nirguṇa-Brahman*) may be compared to water per se and *Brahman* with features (*Saguṇa-Brahman*) to the same water acquiring distinctiveness in the form of cubes of ice. Or, to use a more lavish comparison, *Nirguṇa-Brahman* is like the ocean in the warm water regions, and *Saguṇa-Brahman* like the ocean closer to the polar regions, frozen into blocks of different distinguishable shapes or icebergs. The effort to distinguish between God and Godhead in Christian theology reminds the Hindu of the distinction between *saguṇa* and *Nirguṇa Brahman*.[1] *Brahman* in either form is described as Saccidānanda — as *sat* (the truly real), as *cit* (pure awareness) and as *ānanda* (utter bliss). This description converts the metaphysical ultimate into a value, something to be realized in ecstatic states called *samādhis*. For notwithstanding the metaphysical architectonics to which Hinduism is prone, there is an insistence within it that genuine spirituality must be anchored in an actual experience of the ultimate reality, which may lie beyond the range of our thoughts but does not lie beyond the range of our experience. Thus, in an inspired moment, one of India's great philosophers, Śaṅkara, asked for God's forgiveness for his three great sins.

> I came on a pilgrimage to Kāśī forgetting that you are omnipresent;
> in thinking about you I forget that you are beyond thought and
> in praying to you I forget that you are beyond words.[2]

Brahman without features is best described by negative statements, as formless, and so on. More can be said of *Saguṇa Brahman*. As

---

1 Morgan, op. cit., pp. 48-50.

2 S. Radhakrishnan, 1960, *The Brahma Sūtra*, London: George Allen & Unwin, pp. 37-38.

possessing form, the ultimate reality can be visualised as either male or female. In its female version, the ultimate reality can then be worshipped as Goddess or Devī.[3] This Hinduism possesses a full-fledged theology, as well as a full-fledged theology. In its male version, the *Saguṇa-Brahman* is called *Īśvara* (God). *Īśvara* can be looked upon optionally as (1) the originator or the creator; (2) the preserver or sustainer; or (3) the destroyer or culminator or terminator of the universe.[4] Its deification in each of these cosmic roles provides the Hindu pantheon with its three chief gods — Brahmā, Viṣṇu and Śiva — respectively. For various reasons, the worship of Brahmā is no longer a prominent feature of Hinduism. Viṣṇu and Śiva are the two gods to whom most Hindus pay their reverence.[5] Viṣṇu in his role as preserver intervenes from time to time to save the cosmos from untimely dissolution — by incarnating himself in the universe. He has done so on numerous occasions in the past, of which there is a standard list of ten (*daśāvatāra*), and will do so in the future. The Hindus, however, recall with special devotion two such incarnations: as Rāma and as Kṛṣṇa, and Viṣṇu is often worshipped in these two forms.

Śiva as the third member of the Hindu *trimūrti* (the threefold form of God), presides over the destruction of the universe and can be an awesome figure. But his destructive function can have a creative aspect to it: he can destroy illness, enemies, bad luck, even the very process of one's involvement in the universe or *saṁsāra* — a term soon to be explained. This functional trifurcation of God with form (*Saguṇa Brahman*) is the basis not only of Hindu theism but also Hindu sectarianism, and when the latter developments became divisive attempts were made to synthesize the two chief gods, Viṣṇu and Śiva, into one. Similarly, the feminine theology in

---

3 Klaus K. Klostermaier, 1994, *A Survey of Hinduism* (2nd edn), Albany, NY: State University of New York Press, chap. 18.

4 Morgan, op. cit., pp. 53-65.

5 J. Gonda, 1970, *Viṣṇuism and Śivaism: A Comparison*, London: The Athlone Press.

Hinduism does not always possess a totally independent status, for the Goddess Śakti is often shown as the spouse of Śiva — though as the dominant partner in the divine pair. Sometimes Hindu syncretism combines these two — the male and female aspects — as in the famous depiction of Śiva in the androgynous *ardhanārīśvara* (half-female) form. The chief Hindu gods have their families, even certain animals as vehicles, and so on; these are also regarded as objects of worship and all of these constitute the subject of Hindu myths.[6]

The universe or *brahmāṇḍa* (the egg of Brahmā), as it is frequently described, cannot exist apart from *Brahman*, though again the exact nature of its relationship to *Brahman* is a matter of considerable philosophical debate, some schools regarding it as a mere appearance (*māyā*) grounded in *Brahman*, some as a transformation thereof, with other schools adding their own wrinkles. The universe is without beginning or end — it is eternal, but though beginningless and endless it undergoes phases of manifestation and dissolution; the universal process may have many commas but it never comes to a full stop. In such an infinite and eternal universe, the duration of whose cyclical phases of manifestation and dissolution is calculated in figures of mind-boggling magnitude,[7] the itinerant individual soul, called the *jīva*, moves along from one life to another. This process of the individual soul's involvement in the cosmos is called *saṁsāra*. Thus along with the ultimate reality of *Brahman*, and the pulsating eternality of the universe, one has the companion doctrine of the interminable involvement of the soul in *saṁsāra*, through a process of rebirth (unless the soul secures its release from this process). The guiding principle which governs the movement of the soul in the universe and determines the form it assumes in various rebirths, including

---

6 Wendy Doniger O'Flaherty, 1975, *Hindu Myths*, Harmondsworth: Penguin Books.

7 A.K. Basham, 1999 (1967), *The Wonder that Was India*, New Delhi: Rupa & Co., pp. 320-21.

those as animals or celestial beings, is called *karma*. The word means both action and the results of those actions, whether good or bad, results which seek out its subject as unerringly as a calf seeks out its own particular mother in a herd of cows.[8] The world of matter, in which this cosmic drama is played out, is sometimes referred to as *prakṛti*, which consists of three constitutive strands called *guṇas*: *sattva, rajas* and *tamas*. The constitution of a human being, as involved in this drama, is explained in terms of the view that the human personality can be dissected into three bodies (*śarīras*) or five sheaths (*kośas*), which are all to be distinguished from the *ātman*, his or her true self.

The interrelationship between the *Brahman* and the *jīva* situated in the *brahmāṇḍa* or, in less technical language, between the reality, living beings and the universe, is much discussed and debated in Hindu philosophy. The basic feature of the situation for a human being in the universe is constituted by the fact that the universe is impermanent and this "impermanence of any existence, however pleasant, makes existence itself a thing of misery", i.e. existence as we know it, as that of a creature caught in the toils of *saṁsāra*. Perfect and permanent happiness can never be obtained in the shifting sands of *saṁsāra* but must be sought outside it. Hinduism believes that it is indeed possible for the individual soul to extricate itself from the process of *saṁsāra*, wherein on balance its experiences are usually less than happy, and to achieve perfect and permanent happiness by experiencing *Brahman*. This is salvation (*mokṣa*). It consists of being freed from the process of rebirth. The word *mokṣa* literally means liberation, i.e. liberation from *saṁsāra*. This liberation follows from union or communion with *Brahman*; the process by which this is achieved is called *yoga*.[9]

The word *yoga* is etymologically related to the English word yoke which means both (1) union — as when "oxen are yoked to the

---

8 Morgan, op. cit., pp. 125-30.

9 Mahadevan, op. cit., chap. VI.

plough", and (2) discipline — as when "India came under the British yoke". The word *yoga* fuses these two senses; it stands for a system of discipline which leads to union. Numerous *yogas* are recognized within Hinduism but three are emphasized. *Jñāna-yoga* (the *yoga* of knowledge) emphasizes experiential realization of *Nirguṇa-Brahman* as the means of release from *saṁsāra*. *Bhakti-yoga* (the *yoga* of devotion) emphasizes loving devotion to any of the various gods of Hinduism, but especially to Viṣṇu or Śiva, as the means of salvation and thus emphasizes the experience of *Saguṇa-Brahman*. *Karma-yoga* (the *yoga* of works) is the third major *yoga*. The word *karma* in this context can mean both ritual action, or action in general, specially in relation to one's allotted station in life, when it is referred to as one's *dharma*. According to this view, *karma* in either sense can lead to salvation if performed in the right spirit, and thus human beings can literally work their way to salvation. Implicit in the doctrine of *yogas* is the belief that different beings possess different temperaments, that *jñāna*, *bhakti* or *karma-yoga* may be more suited for those whose intellectual, emotional or executive components of personality are respectively more developed. Nor are the *yogas* to be viewed as mutually exclusive. They may be blended in accordance with temperament and altered circumstances. One well-known Indian mystic of the nineteenth century, Ramakrishna, vouched for the effectiveness of all major and minor *yogas* as valid means of achieving salvation. His religious experiences, which have deeply affected modern Hindu consciousness, are unprecedented in their comprehensiveness. He not only tried out virtually every path of *yoga* within Hinduism but also claimed to experience the same reality through Islamic and Christian practices, thus providing neo-Hinduism with its most popular platform: that all religions are valid, a stance anticipated in the Vedas (*ṚV* I.164.46).

3

Hinduism, The Great Tradition

Characteristic Practices

Although the Hindu generally subscribes to the fundamental beliefs outlined above, he or she is, in general, more concerned with living out this life in a way which may be conducive to a better life in a future incarnation, than with attaining *mokṣa* forthwith. In order to achieve this end, and in general express the religious dimension of one's personality, he or she engages in certain characteristic practices.

Hinduism is very much a religion of the household.[1] In most Hindu homes there is a shrine (*pūjā* room) for the performance of ritual or prayer, a place of communion with God. Most Hindus follow the path of devotion (*bhakti*), which is popular even among those who follow other *yogas*. The household deity is worshipped with offerings of flowers, rice and so on, with hymns of praise and gestures of supplication. The deity worshipped may vary from household to household, in accordance with the Hindu view that one worships the god one feels the greatest affinity to. The Hindus are not a chosen but a choosing people — they choose their own god. If one's religious enthusiasm cannot be contained in a prayer room, one visits one of the temples dedicated usually to Viṣṇu or one of his incarnations, or to Śiva, or to the Goddess. The ritual followed at these temples basically conforms to or combines two models: paying respect to royalty or offering hospitality.[2]

---

1 Pandhari-Nath Prabhu, 1954, *Hindu Social Organization,* Bombay: Popular Book Depot, p. 6.

2 Mahadevan, op. cit., pp. 49-50.

According to the royalty model, the enshrined deity of the temple is treated like a king and is served by the priests as his servants while all creation, and specially those who come to worship, constitute his subjects. The deity is awakened in the morning with hymns befitting a king; is bathed and fed and holds court, and in the evening is fed again and put to sleep with due ceremony. The morning hymn, with which the deity at the famous temple of Tirupati in Andhra Pradesh is awakened, is very well known. Although describing that hymn as a form of saying "Good-morning to God" may be too familiar a way of describing it, this is in essence what it is. It is broadcast and many Hindus play its tape in the morning.

According to the hospitality ritual, the deity is treated as a welcome guest. His presence is requested, hymns are sung in his praise, he is offered sweetmeats. Camphor is burnt and an arc of light waved around him. The two models can, of course, be combined, the deity being treated as a royal guest. Although these models of worship can be traced back to Vedic times, the main form of worship current in Vedic times, namely, sacrifices offered in fire, is now the preserve of only a few ritualistic brāhmaṇa families, and animal sacrifices, which were a prominent feature of Vedic religion, have virtually disappeared.

Apart from worship in the household and the temples, objects of nature are also often worshipped, such as sacred trees, or sacred stones symbolic of Śiva or Viṣṇu. Among the objects of worship in nature, the sun is of some interest as representing the divine in its effulgent aspect. The most sacred verse of the Vedas — the Gāyatrī (*ṚV* III.62.10) — the verse of initiation into Vedic studies, is one addressed to the sun and may even have been regarded by the eager student as a prayer for the achievement of spiritual and intellectual brilliance, symbolized by the solar orb.

The greater importance attached to individual communion with God in Hinduism has led some to believe that congregational worship plays little role in Hinduism. This does not seem to be true. It is not merely recognized but even emphasized in the idea of *satsaṅga* or the getting-together of devotees. This can take place in a home or at a temple and consists of religious discourse and/or the singing of hymns called *bhajanas*. There are societies which meet regularly for the singing of *bhajanas*.[3] An associated institution is that of the *kathā* (reading from the great epics), usually the *Rāmāyaṇa*, accompanied by musical recitation and homiletic exegesis. This can also take place either in a temple or in a home. It is considered an act of religious merit to fund or organize one. A very popular *kathā* is that of Satyanārāyaṇa, which really forms a section of the *Skanda Purāṇa* but is read in its own right.

Individual or congregational worship can of course be performed at any time, but is often associated with the observance of festivals or holy days. These are connected with stories relating to Viṣṇu or his incarnations, to Śiva, or to Śakti. The spring festival of Holī is connected with the devotion of the demon-prince Prahlāda to Viṣṇu, in opposition to this father's wishes. Various efforts to destroy him or his devotion to Viṣṇu having failed, it was arranged that he be incinerated, while seated on the lap of the demoness Holikā, who herself possessed an asbestine immunity against fire. By Viṣṇu's grace Prahlāda survived but Holikā was reduced to ashes. This festival has a strong folk element in it as well[4] and is celebrated by the lighting of bonfires.

There is a cluster of festivals in winter involving several divinities of Hinduism. During the October–November period, days of worship of Śakti culminate in the celebration of Diwālī (from Dīpāvalī — a row of lights). This festival, sometimes accompanied by pyrotechnic displays but always by the lighting of lamps, is said to convert the darkest night of the year into the brightest. By one

---

3 Milton Singer, ed., 1966, *Krishna: Myths, Rites and Attitudes*, Honolulu: East-West Center, pp. 5-6.

4 See McKim Marriott, 2006, "Holi: The Feast of Love", in John Stratton Hawley and Vasudha Narayanan eds. *The Life of Hinduism*, Berkeley: University of California Press, pp. 99-112.

account, it commemorates the return of Rāma, the incarnation of Viṣṇu, to his capital after years of exile. Goddess Lakṣmī, the spouse of Viṣṇu, is also worshipped. It also marks the new year according to the commercial calendar. Two other festivals which fall around Diwālī include Navarātri and Dussehra some of the other festivals associated with Viṣṇu are Janmāṣṭamī (August–September) commemorating the birth of his incarnation as Kṛṣṇa; Rāmanavamī (March–April) commemorating the birth of his incarnation as Rāma, and Vaikuṇṭha-Ekādaśī (December–January) sacred to Viṣṇu. The main holy day associated with Śiva is Mahāśivarātri (January–February) when devotees keep a night-long vigil. One of Śiva's sons, Gaṇeśa, is honoured by a festival called Gaṇeśa-Caturthī (August–September), while young women desirous of husbands worship Śiva's wife, Pārvatī, at the time of Gaurī-Pūjā.

One rather charming domestic festival, called Rakṣābandhana in north India, falls in July–August. Sisters tie coloured threads on the wrists of male relatives, who offer them gifts. This custom is said to have originated with the wife of Indra tying a protective thread to the wrist of Indra — the chief Vedic God, when he set out to battle the demons. In south India the sacred thread, with which the twice-borns are invested in a ceremony described later, is changed on this day.

On these occasions many Hindus discard the Western dress in favour of the traditional. Hindu women are usually clad in colourful *sāṛīs* while celebrating the festivals, but are more soberly dressed when observing fasts or vigils. It is customary to serve vegetarian food at these feasts and festivals in most parts of India. In general, the dietic habits of the Hindus tend to be vegetarian, though the class one belongs to could make a difference. The brāhmaṇas are expected to be more rigorous in the observance of this rule than others. Often the onset of enthusiasm for the spiritual life finds its first expression, in the life of an average Hindu, in the form of abstention from eating meat and drinking alcohol, both of which are looked upon as spiritually deleterious. Most, if not all, Hindus avoid eating beef, even when they eat other forms of meat, especially in India. When abroad some Hindus do eat beef, sometimes offering the ingenious argument that only Indian cows are sacred!

Just as the passage of the year has certain points marked out for special attention, so is the individual's passage through life. The formal list of these rites of passage (*saṁskāras*) runs to sixteen, sometimes even exceeding it.[5] The two universal rites of passage are those associated with marriage and death. These find a place in the Vedas and are believed by historians to reach back to the time before the Indo-Europeans moved out of their original homeland. The rite of marriage essentially consists of the bride and the bridegroom circumambulating the sacred fire seven times. At the completion of the seventh round the couple becomes husband and wife. The fire serves as the witness to the exchange of the marriage vows, along with the other participants in the ceremony. There was a tendency in the history of Hinduism to treat marriage as indissoluble; it is no longer so considered. The obsequies consist of the cremation of the corpse (unless it be that of a renunciant, in which case it is buried). The last rites are ideally performed by one's son, preferably the eldest, and this has often been cited as a motive for securing male progeny on the part of the Hindus. But it is possible for other relatives to act as substitutes, according to Hindu law, and daughters are also now performing the rite. After due interval, follow the *śrāddha* rites. These consist of offerings of food and drink to the dead, actually consumed by invited brāhmaṇas. The ceremony is performed annually, sometimes at places considered particularly auspicious for its performance.

A very important ceremony for the three higher castes, by virtue of which they are called twice-born, is the investiture ceremony, during the course of which the grown child (at various ages specified for various *varṇas*) receives his initiation into Vedic

---

5 P.V. Kane, 1941, *History of Dharmaśāstra,* Poona: Bhandarkar Oriental Research Institute, vol. II, part I, p. 5.

studies.[6] It is usually called *upanayana* and implies the idea of being taken to a teacher. The rite is gradually falling into disuse and is confined to high-caste males. Mahatma Gandhi discarded his own thread in protest against the fact that it was denied to the lower castes.

A full-fledged Hindu householder of the three upper castes, duly invested with the thread and then with a spouse, was expected to perform daily the five sacrifices (*pañca-mahāyajñas*).[7] These consisted of studying the Vedas, making offerings to the gods, offering libations to the ancestors, feeding animals and birds, and extending hospitality and charity to human beings every day. These rites are rarely observed to the letter but are indicative of the spirit underlying common Hindu domestic rites and attitudes.

No account of Hindu practices can be complete without reference to the role that astrology plays in Hindu life.[8] In many Hindu households, horoscopes are cast at the time of a birth in the family and astrologers are often consulted, seriously in times of crisis and out of curiosity at other times. Though many Hindus would fight shy of saying they believe in astrology, most will admit to being interested in it. It seems that horoscopes also play an extra-astrological role as well. One standard way of initiating a marriage proposal is to ask for the horoscope of the bridegroom and it has been suggested that when a party is told that "the horoscopes did not match", it is merely a culturally stylized way of saying no.

Image worship is such a distinguishing feature of Hindu religious practices that it deserves some comment. The general Semitic aversion to image worship is rare in India. Perhaps the Hindu sentiment here is best captured by the Vaiṣṇava theologian, Pillai Lokācārya. He discusses the various forms of God as transcendental,

---

6 Sinclair Stevenson, 1971, *The Rites of the Twice-Born,* New Delhi: Oriental Books Reprint Corporation, p. 2.

7 Morgan, op. cit., pp. 179-84.

8 Ibid., pp. 97-101; Hopkins, op. cit., pp. 79-81.

as grouped in a set (*vyūha*), as manifest in an incarnation, or even within oneself (the last concept betraying, according to some, the influence of Hindu absolutism on its theism). But he finally points out the merit of the presence of God in the image form as follows:

> The attempt to comprehend the transcendent form is like getting water from the other world for quenching thirst; the *vyūha* form is like the legendary ocean of milk which also is not easy of access; the immanent form is like subterranean water which is not readily available to a thirsty man although it is right underneath his feet; the incarnated forms are like the floods that inundate the country for a while but do not last long; but the image is like the [still] pool from which anyone anytime could slake his thirst.[9]

The images at certain temples in India are said to quench one's spiritual thirst with particular efficacy. These places of pilgrimages, called *tīrtha*s or a passage, as it were, to the "other shore" are enthusiastically visited by most Hindus, seven of these being particularly productive of spiritual merit: Ayodhyā, Mathurā, Gayā, Banaras, Kāñcī, Ujjain, Purī and Dvārakā. Bathing in the sacred rivers, especially the Gaṅgā, is also spiritually salubrious, particularly under a special astronomical configuration when the Kumbha Melās are held.

---

[9] Mahadevan, op. cit., p. 94.

4

Hinduism, The Little Tradition

THE canvas of the *weltbild* of the Little Tradition of Hinduism is, as one would expect, smaller than that of the Great Tradition of Hinduism. The average Hindu in the villages is often less concerned with seeking release from the endless cycle of rebirths; or even with achieving metempsychotic upward mobility; he or she is more concerned with avoiding diseases, offsetting disasters (natural or supernatural) and with seeking material comfort and family happiness. Two pitfalls in the study of the Little Tradition may be pointed out here. The first is to see the Great/Little division as corresponding to the urban/rural dichotomy. At least in the case of Hinduism, one may find evidence of the Little Tradition in the heart of a metropolis. The second is to regard the Great/Little division as implying a discontinuity in the overall structure of the tradition — as separate compartments with no relation to or at odds with each other. There may be differences, both from the Great Tradition[1] and within the Little Tradition,[2] but it would be wrong to assume that the Little Tradition is not related to the Great Tradition.[3] Several studies have shown that it functions within the framework of an overarching Great Tradition. One way of demonstrating this point, and partly demarcating the functional area of the Little Tradition, would be to point out that Hinduism generally classifies

1 M. Marriott, ed., 1995, *Village India*, Chicago: University of Chicago Press, p. 224.

2 K. Nair, 1966, *Blossoms in the Dust*, New York: F.A. Praeger, pp. 191-94.

3 Oscar Lewis, 1965, *Village Life in Northern India*, New York: Random House, p. 259.

pain (*duḥkha*) as arising from three sources, all of which are to be appeased by the triple enunciation of the word *śānti* (peace) at the end of many a religious function. The first is called *ādhyātmika*. This refers to suffering due to organic causes, such as bodily disorders and mental afflictions. The second is called *ādhibhautika*. It refers to suffering produced by extra-organic natural causes, such as assault by animals or other human beings, or the danger posed by natural forces. The third is called *ādhidaivika*. It refers to suffering caused by extra-organic supernatural causes, like spirit possession.[4] The beliefs and practices of Hinduism at the popular level, specially in the villages, centre around the relationship of the Hindus to these various forms of pain and their alleviation, particularly those caused by supernatural beings or causes.

Several grades of such supernatural beings have been identified by scholars on the basis of field researches. The lowest level consists of (a) malevolent ghosts (*preta*), usually male, and (b) malevolent female spirits (*cuḍaila)*. The former are said to be spirits who could not make a smooth passage to the next world usually as a result of untimely or violent death, and the latter are usually regarded as the spirits of women who died in childbirth, and have become disposed to evil. To be distinguished from these are evil spirits in general, often said to reside in certain trees, who are ready to pounce on the unwary and go by the generic name of *bhūta* (ghosts). The usual way in which these evil spirits, of either the general or the specific types, intrude into normal human life in a disruptive fashion, is by causing physical or mental illness, especially fever or possession. Such intrusion can be either spontaneous or induced; when induced it represents a form of black magic called *jādu-ṭonā*. Relief in either case is obtained by taking recourse to an *ojhā* (witch-doctor) who shakes off the spirit.[5]

---

4 S. Chatterjee and D. Datta, 1968, *An Introduction to Indian Philosophy*, Calcutta: University of Calcutta, p. 280.

5 Stanley A. Freed and Ruth S. Freed, 1964, "Spirit Possession as Illness in a North Indian Village", *Ethnology*, IV(1): 152-71.

The next level is provided by the local deities. These consist of gods and goddesses and, unlike the previous level wherein the supernatural beings are evil per se, the local deities are not evil per se (though some may be more inclined to do harm than good) but rather have a good and evil aspect to them. When angered they spell ruin but if appeased they can be controlled, and if pleased may even confer benefits, especially those possessed of a naturally more benign nature. Thus they can be of a virulent or benevolent type, in spite of each possessing a dual nature. An example of the former would be Śītalā Devī, or the deity of the small pox,[6] of the latter would be a *grāma-devatā*, or the presiding deity of the village. Śītalā Devī is virulent but can be appeased, while the *grāma-devatā*[7] is generally benevolent, but can bring harm if offended. While the spirits of the lowest levels make their attack, usually nocturnal, on individuals, the disposition of the local deities may have implications for the local community as a whole, though individuals could also be affected.

The next level is provided by the local appropriation of gods of the pan-Indian pantheon, and by the elevation of a local deity into the pan-Indian orbit by bringing it into relation, usually familial or devotional, to the major gods of the Hindu pantheon. An example of the local appropriation of a pan-Indian figure would be the popular worship of Hanumān in some villages. Such appropriation may have a functional aspect to it. Thus Hanumān, representing celibacy (and through it restraint) and developed musculature, is often the deity adopted by wrestlers in a particular region. A more notorious example would be the adoption of Kālī as a patron-goddess by the thugs. An example of the elevation of a local deity to a pan-Indic claim would be the rise of the Ayappan cult in Kerala, through the belief that he is the son of Śiva and Viṣṇu in the form of Mohinī.

---

6 B.G. Bang, 1973, "Current Concepts of the Smallpox Goddess Sitala in Parts of West Bengal", *Man in India*, 53(1): 79-104.

7 Henry Whitehead, 1921, *The Village Gods of South India*, London: Oxford University Press, p. 1.

At this level, the local deity may begin to take on a regional aspect, perhaps even en route to taking on a national role. The Viṭhobā cult of Paṇḍharpur could well represent such a development.

Thus there is an ascending hierarchy, based on geographical correspondences, from the local up to the regional, the provincial (e.g. Murugaṉ in Tamil-Nadu) and the national level. With the general pattern thus established, one may now revert to a further discussion of folk religion.

The question naturally arises as to the manner in which one deals with the spirits and deities at the local level. Here a cardinal principle operates — the higher level of the hierarchy offers protection against the lower. Thus taking the name of Rāma, for instance, is supposed to be effective as a pre-emptive strike against attacks by evil spirits. Mahatma Gandhi mentions in his autobiography how he was introduced to this technique by his nurse. However, if one has already been attacked or the defence fails for some reason, other ways of dealing with the situation have to be considered. Here the basic model seems to be a psychological one as expressed in physical terms. The anger of the deity is associated with heat, and its appeasement with the coolness, in terms of what has been called "thermal Manichaeism". The offering of water on the objects of worship of the local deity is seen as making sense in this way. Such characterization of items as "hot" or "cold" is not limited to India; Marshall McLuhan famously characterized radio as a "hot" and television as a "cool" medium.

Some observers have pointed out that as one moves upwards through the levels of supernatural beings in a village, the level of voluntary accessibility on the part of the person increases. Thus evil spirits seek contact with human beings of their own accord, while they avoid them; the local deities are ritually accessible; the regional deities can be worshipped, and the pan-Indian gods like Viṣṇu and Śiva may appear remote, but are devotionally accessible. Thus basically the initiative seems to lie more with the worshipper in precipitating the encounter as one climbs up the hierarchy.

The range of folk religion, however, is not limited to dealings with spirits and local deities. It extends to the worship of plants, trees and animals — some of which may either have found their way into the Great Tradition, as instances of upward mobility, or may have filtered downwards into the local tradition.[8] The former possibility is more likely. The veneration of the *tulasī* plant and the *pīpal* tree, with offerings of water, is an example of sacredness attached to plants and trees in folk religion. Certain animals are also held sacred. Stones with images of cobras are often worshipped, and in some regions a snake-goddess, Manasā, is venerated. The origin of the sanctity associated with bovines in popular Hinduism remains a mystery but the sacred respect with which monkeys are treated in some temples, or even rodents in parts of Maharashtra, may be accounted for in terms of their association with Hanumān and Gaṇeśa respectively. It has been suggested that the vehicles of the gods of Hinduism represent the Hinduization of totemism.[9]

So far as the religious calendar is concerned, while the Little Tradition in general follows the religious calendar of the Great Tradition, certain sub-cycles within it are as important — as for instance the weekly and the monthly cycles. Particular days of the week, associated with the planets, can be important. Thus people afflicted by Mars may fast on Tuesdays and those by Saturn on Saturdays. The Hindu monthly calendar is lunar and operates in terms of the light and dark fortnight. In terms of the month, the days of the new moon (*amāvasyā*) and the full moon (*pūrṇimā*) are important, especially the latter for purposes of fasting. Certain days of the fortnight are associated with the gods, the fourth with Gaṇeśa, for instance, and the eleventh with Viṣṇu. These observances are carried out by women rather than men. To that

---

8 Ursula M. Sharma, 1970, "The Problem of Village Hinduism: 'Fragmentation' and Integration", *Contributions to Indian Sociology,* IV: 1-21.

9 Lawrence A. Babb, 1975, *The Divine Hierarchy,* New York: Columbia University Press, p. 7.

extent the statement by a Hindu professor that he represented the Great Tradition and his wife the Little, though facetious, and perhaps even chauvinistic, is to some extent illuminating.

Thus five terms hold the key to understanding the Little Tradition in Hinduism: hierarchy (of the pantheon), geography (as connected with the hierarchy), polarity (of supernatural beings or within their own nature on the basis of the auspicious or the inauspicious, heat or cold, male or female, etc.), accessibility (do they call us or we call them) and temporality (as related to the calendar).[10]

---

10 Babb, op. cit., p. 7.

5

Modern Developments

THE developments, which have occurred in Hinduism since 1800, briefly reviewed earlier, are nothing short of remarkable.[1] At the most general level, Hinduism's encounter with modernity has virtually converted it from an ethnic into a universal religion. The fact that a Hindu could become an outcaste for going abroad in 1800 may be contrasted with the ease with which Hindus, and spokespersons or spokesmen of Hinduism, now roam around the world with impunity. Another contrast highlights the same point: Hinduism, which was and even now is regarded as a non-missionary religion, is making converts all over the world through its spokespersons referred to above. What is more, these Hindu spokespersons have assumed a role of leadership in adopting a universalistic attitude toward religions in general, and have reformulated Hinduism in such a way as to make it invitingly universal. Thus it is said that having no dogma is the dogma of Hinduism; the idea of heresy is the only heresy in Hinduism; a Hindu is most a Hindu when least a Hindu, or that the only thing Hinduism is intolerant of is intolerance. These statements doubtless contain an element of exaggeration but the point to note is the liberal direction of the exaggeration. The neo-Hindu emphasis on the equality of all religions has filled it with a missionary zeal to broadcast this message. Thus whereas, in the early decades of the nineteenth century, Hinduism was on the defensive against propagandist attacks, it has now reversed the situation and

---

1 See Arvind Sharma, ed., 2002, *Modern Hindu Thought: The Essential Texts*, New Delhi: Oxford University Press.

assumed a position of virtual leadership in the interreligious encounter of our own times, by pleading for mutual tolerance and accommodation, in accordance with the view that even a broken watch gives the correct time at least twice a day.[2]

Hinduism has also undergone a sea change in the social sphere in modern times. In the nineteenth century, Hindu social life included such dubious practices as *suttee*, polygamy, child-marriage, infanticide, temple prostitution and untouchability. The list can be lengthened into a catalogue of what are now regarded as benighted forms of religious enthusiasm. Today most of these excesses stand abolished. There can be little doubt that the lot of the lower classes and women in Hinduism today is much better than it was 200 years ago. The full emancipation for these members of the Hindu body-politic still remains to be achieved and change is more apparent in urban than in rural areas[3] — but even if the destination has not been reached (if it indeed can be in matters as elusive as egalitarianism) the movement in that direction is clear.[4]

Hinduism stands not only socially but also politically transformed today by comparison with earlier times. And no account of the political dimension of modern Hinduism can ignore its relation to the rise of Indian nationalism. It may be useful here to distinguish between political nationalism and religious nationalism. These two streams of nationalism, though never entirely separated from each other, are distinguishable from each other and provide warp and woof out of which the destiny of modern India was woven. To begin with, they seem to have been relatively independent. The major spokesmen of the Hindu renaissance in the nineteenth century, people like Swami Dayananda Sarasvati and Swami

---

2 A.L. Basham, 1967, "Hinduism", in R.C. Zaehner ed. *The Concise Encyclopedia of Living Faiths*, Boston: Beacon Press, p. 260.

3 William H. Wise and Charlotte V. Wiser, 1971, *Behind Mud Walls 1930-1960*, Berkeley: University of California Press, pp. 155-59, 256-59.

4 D.S. Sarma, 1967, *Hinduism through the Ages*, Bombay: Bharatiya Vidya Bhavan, p. 265.

Vivekananda, by and large, stayed away from "politics". This was not to be the case later, at least to the same extent, as when Mahatma Gandhi was to write:

> Those who say that religion has nothing to do with politics do not know what religion means.[5]

Within this overall context, the relationship between Hinduism and nationalism[6] seems to have passed through two broad phases.

> The trend in the nineteenth century toward the combination of religious and national emotion culminated, in the first decades of the twentieth century in open forms of violent religious nationalism.

However,

> religious chauvinism lost its preeminence in the second decade of the present century, with the emergence into leadership, in their various spheres, of Aurobindo, Gandhi, Tagore and Radhakrishnan, each representing a faith in universal human values.[7]

It is thus ironic that the partition of the Indian subcontinent, into a Muslim Pakistan and a secular but predominantly Hindu India, should have occurred in the liberal phase of the relationship between Hinduism and nationalism. With the creation of Pakistan, Hindu liberalism on the subcontinent seems to have suffered a setback — a fact which is reflected in the emergence and occasional success of political parties tinged with a Hindu ideology. It is easy to overlook the fact in this context that the Hindus had been politically

---

5 Mahadev Desai, ed., 1972, *M.K. Gandhi: An Autobiography,* London: Jonathan Cape, p. 420.

6 L.S.S. O'Malley, ed., 1941, *Modern India and the West,* London: Oxford University Press, pp. 90-100; Christophe Jaffrelot, ed., 2007, *Hindu Nationalism: A Reader,* Princeton and Oxford: Princeton University Press.

7 Charles J. Adams, ed., 1977, *A Readers Guide to the Great Religions,* 2nd edn, New York: The Free Press, pp. 146-47.

under the more or less continuous domination of non-Hindus from *c.* CE 1200 to 1947, so that although numerically in a majority they have developed the psychology of a minority. The end of the political domination of the Hindus by the non-Hindus is bound to be consequential for Hinduism, though the exact consequences are as yet difficult to foresee.

From what has been said it is clear that, of the three main *yogas* — those of *jñāna*, *bhakti* and *karma*, special emphasis has come to be placed on *karma yoga* (the *yoga* of action) in modern times. Indeed, on a yogic view of the history of Hinduism, one might say that, broadly speaking, the classical, the medieval and modern periods in Hinduism have been distinguished by a relatively greater emphasis on *jñāna-yoga*, *bhakti-yoga* and *karma-yoga* respectively. This Karma-yogic activism is reflected not merely in greater social and political concern within Hinduism but also in increased missionary activity on its part in the West, as represented by the activity of the Ramakrishna Mission, the Vedānta societies, the Self-Realization Fellowship, the Transcendental Meditation movement and so on. Buddhism has been described by some scholars, with an obvious fondness for the commercial idiom, as the export product of Hindu culture in ancient times. In modern times, Hinduism seems to be exporting itself, with considerable sophistication in product differentiation.[8]

It is difficult to prophesy the future of Hinduism. It confounded its critics, who confidently foresaw its demise in the nineteenth century, by surviving into the twentieth. But as a tolerant religion opposed to only one "ism", namely, fanaticism, it may prove unexpectedly vulnerable to the modern surrogates of religion such as scientific materialism, communism or humanism, though the Western conflict between science and religion has not been felt as keenly in India as in the West, even in the form of a clash between

---

[8] Robert S. Ellwood, Jr., 1973, *Religious and Spiritual Groups in Modern America*, New Jersey: Prentice-Hall, p. 7.

tradition and modernity.[9] On the one hand, Hinduism has displayed remarkable powers of resilience in the past, but, on the other, longevity does not guarantee immortality, and the Hindus will do well to remember that no religious tradition, including their own, is more than a generation away from oblivion.

9 Lloyd I. Rudolph and Susanne Hoeber Rudolph, 1967, *The Modernity of Tradition*, Chicago: University of Chicago Press, Introduction.

II
Alphabetical Entries

1. Abhaya-Mudrā

The gesture which banishes fear, also known as the *abhayahasta*; it consists of an upraised hand with an open palm.

2. Abhāva

One of the seven categories identified in the Vaiśeṣika school of Hindu philosophy, which was subsequently added to its original list of six. It is usually translated as non-existence. It refers to negative facts. In this school it is always particularized and does not refer to general nothingness. Moreover, if it is said that something is not green, it does not also necessarily imply that it has some other colour. That which is absent, the colour green in this case, is said to be the correlate (*pratiyogin*) of non-existence. Non-existence can be cognized through perception, inference, or verbal testimony, and is of four kinds:

1. prior non-existence (*prāg-abhāva*): as that of a pot before it is produced; it is without a beginning but comes to an end, as when the pot is made;
2. destructive non-existence (*pradhvaṁsābhāva*): when the pot is destroyed; its non-existence has a beginning but no end;
3. absolute non-existence (*atyantābhāva*): as the non-existence of colour in the air. It is said to be external; and
4. mutual or reciprocal non-existence (*anyonyā bhāva*: also called *bheda*) as when we say a pot is not a jar. This type of non-existence is also eternal in nature.

(Also see Vaiśeṣika School of Philosophy).

3. Abhicāra

Black magic; its practice is recognized as a minor sin. These malefic rites are performed anti-clock-wise, as distinguished from the benefic rites, which are performed from left to right. (Also see Pradakṣiṇā.)

4. Abhimanyu

A young handsome hero of the Mahābhārata war. He was the son of Arjuna and Subhadrā, hence his other name, Saubhadra. He was called Abhimanyu because he was endowed with heroic features from his very birth. During the war, the Kauravas arrayed their forces in a formation called *cakra-vyūha* (wheel formation), hoping to overcome the Pāṇḍavas because Arjuna, who alone was capable of neutralizing the formation, was engaged elsewhere. This lad of sixteen, however, took the Kauravas on and was able to pierce the formation, proving more than a match for many veterans in doing so, but could not hold out and was ultimately trapped and killed. Legend has it that he had imbibed the knowledge to pierce the *cakra-vyūha* while in the womb, when Arjuna was satisfying his pregnant wife's martial curiosity. Unfortunately she dozed off by the time he began to explain how one extricates oneself from it.

One of his two wives, Uttarā, was pregnant when he was slain and her son, Parīkṣit, succeeded to the throne at Hastināpur, after the Pāṇḍava brothers abdicated. (Also see *Mahābhārata.*)

5. Abhinavagupta (975–1025)

A prolific polymath from Kashmir, the author of over forty works, whose ancestors had immigrated there from the Gangetic plains in the eighth century. In his commentaries on Bharata's *Nāṭyaśāstra* and Ānandavardhana's *Dhvanyāloka*, he synthesized the theory of *rasa* (aesthetic experience) with that of *dhvani* (suggestion) to produce the regnant theory of aesthetics in Hindu culture. He considered aesthetic experience as providing a foretaste of the ultimate mystical experience and therefore comparable to it, though not identical with it (*sahodara*). He also marked the culmination of the school of Kashmir Śaivism, which synthesizes all the six orthodox systems, as well as Buddhism and Tantra. This school considers the universe like an idea in the mind of God rather than a dream, and is simultaneously monotheistic and monistic. Abhinavagupta also commented copiously on the Śaivāgamas but is best known for his independent work *Tantrāloka* (*The Light of Tantra*), which attaches equal importance to revelation, instruction and intuition. He also wrote a commentary on the *Bhagavad-Gītā*. (Also see Tantra and Tantra: Left-Handed).

6. Abhiṣeka

The act of sprinkling with water, central to many a ritual in Hinduism. It is a particularly important component of royal sacrifices, such as the Rājasūya *yajña*, wherein the king is anointed with water.

7. Ācārya

A teacher or preceptor in general, as when Mahatma Gandhi is described as the *ācārya* of non-violence; or, more specially, a teacher who invests one with the sacred thread and thus initiates one into Vedic studies. At the more elevated level, it points to one who instructs by practice (*ācāra*), by example rather than words. The *Manu-Smṛti* (II.140-42) distinguishes between an *ācārya*, who initiates one into Vedic studies; an *upādhyāya*, who teaches a portion of the Vedas for a living; and a *guru*, who performs the natal rites for the child. The exact meanings of these terms and their respective understandings have fluctuated in the history of Hinduism.

Whether one needs an *ācārya* (or *guru*) or whether one can achieve salvation on one's own has been a debated point in the tradition; majority opinion insisting on the requirement of one.

8. Acintya-Bhedābheda

"Inexplicable difference and non-difference." A school of Vedānta founded by Caitanya (1485/6–1533), also known as Kṛṣṇacaitanya and Gauraṅga Mahāprabhu. Although Caitanya is the founder of this school, his own contribution is essentially inspirational; the work attributed to him, known as *Daśamūla-Śloka*, consists of ten verses. The system was elaborated by his successors, Jīva Gosvāmī prominent among them as the author of *Ṣaṭ-Sandarbha*, with his own commentary on it called *Sarvasaṁvādinī*. The ultimate reality in the system is *Parama Brahman*, identified with Rādhā-Kṛṣṇa. The word *Brahman* is here interpreted etymologically to mean both "one who is great" and "one who makes great" and it is the combination of these senses which makes *Parama Brahman*, or the Supreme Reality. Thus not only is *Brahman sat* (absolute existence), *cit* (absolute intelligence) and *ānanda* (absolute bliss), it also possesses *śakti*s (powers), the three main ones being *svarūpa-śakti*, *māyā-śakti* and *jīva-śakti*; the first one is also called *cit-śakti* on account of being eternally sentient, and *antaraṅga-śakti* on account of being internal to it. The other two are external (*bahiraṅga*). God is what God is through *svarūpa-śakti* and indulges in various sports (*līlā*s); through *jīva-śakti* the various *jīva*s appear and through *māyā-śakti* the insentient universe is created. The *śakti*s are graded in the order mentioned: *svarūpa-śakti* is supreme and called *parā-śakti* on that account. *Brahman* is thus obviously *saguṇa* as possessing these *śakti*s. God is, however, not only Saccidānanda in this system but also *rasa* (relish) and *rasika* (relisher) specially in his role as Śrī Kṛṣṇa, which gives to this system a unique devotional flavour. The supreme enjoyment of *rasa* is said to consist of it not merely as an object but also a subject, which accounts for Rādhā's high status in the system, as enjoying the love of Kṛṣṇa, but creates the paradox of Śrī Kṛṣṇa not being able to relish his own sweetness the way Rādhā does. This divine longing is fulfilled in his incarnation as Śrī Caitanya. The universe is created by God through *māyā-śakti*, in its twofold aspects of *guṇa-māyā*, through which the material world is created, and *jīva-māyā*, through which the *jīva*s get trapped in it. *Brahman* spreads Itself in the universe like threads in a piece of cloth; which is thus a transformation (*pariṇāma*) of *Brahman*, and God is both its material and efficient cause, but God's *svarūpa-śakti* remains untouched by the process. The *jīva*s are a part (*aṁśa*) of *Brahman*, just as *śakti* is part the one who possesses it. The *jīva*s entitatively differ from God and continue to do so even after salvation is achieved. The royal road to salvation is *bhakti*, in the form of unconditional surrender to God. This system is notable for pushing the limits of liberation, inasmuch as it regards pure love (*śuddha-bhakti*) as an end in itself — as the fifth *puruṣārtha*, transcending *mokṣa*, and finds true happiness in the post-salvific state in serving God (*sevānanda*).

The various schools of Vedānta tend to develop their own views to account for the relationship between *Brahman* on the one hand, and the world and the souls on the other. According to this school the relationship between cause and effect, part and whole, power and its possessor, cannot be explained in a logically satisfactory way. Take the example of musk and perfume. We cannot think of musk without odour, hence non-difference between the two may be posited; but one can smell the odour at a distance, hence difference is indicated. An attempt to explain the relationship between fire and heat creates the same bind. To simultaneously posit both non-difference and difference seems logically untenable, but the facts speak for themselves and cannot be denied, hence the relationship should be considered as not falling in the category of either absolute difference or absolute non-difference (*bhinnābhinntvādi-vikalpaiśca cintayityam aśakyaḥ*). (Also see Caitanya.)

9. Adhvaryu

As the Vedic ritual became more systematized, priests began to be associated with the distinct Vedas on the basis of their expertise. Thus the *hotṛ* (pourer) became linked to the *Ṛg-Veda*; the *udgātṛ* (singer) with the *Sāma-Veda*; the *adhvaryu* with the *Yajur-Veda* and the brāhmaṇa (priest) with the *Atharva-Veda*, who supervised their work. *Adhvaryu* thus performs the manual part of the sacrifice, just as the *hotṛ* pours, the *udgātṛ* sings and the brāhmaṇa supervises. Originally the same priest recited the hymns and made the offerings, but then the roles got separated and specialized. (Also see Veda.)

10. Aditi

The word literally means unbounded or boundless and represents a goddess by that name in the *Ṛg-Veda*. She possesses simultaneously an abstract and a concrete dimension, which has puzzled scholars. Her name suggests freedom and infinity, but she is also described as the mother of seven (*ṚV* VIII.72.8) and then eight *ādityas* (*ṚV* IX.114.3). The pattern persists at other levels: in one passage she is identified with the cosmic cow, in another she comprises time and all the gods (*ṚV* I.89.10). Later depictions are more concrete than abstract. In the epics, she is the wife of Kaśyapa, the two being depicted as the primeval couple. She is sometimes described as the mother of Viṣṇu, and sometimes the mother in his incarnation as Vāmana. Similarly, her relationship with Dakṣa displays shifting patterns. The *Ṛg-Veda* states mystically that Dakṣa arose from Aditi and Aditi from Dakṣa but, in the *Viṣṇu Purāṇa*, she is Dakṣa's daughter and Kaśyapa's wife.

This variability at the concrete levels has been explained as representing changing relationships in different births — a favoured Hindu technique of reconciling differences; or sometimes, more philosophically, as attempts to capture the enigmatic nature of existence, specially if characterized by boundlessness. A more direct explanation of some dimensions of Aditi's role may be neither metempsychotic or philosophical but theological, in the sense of the roles of a god or goddess undergoing gradual expansion. This is clear in the Purāṇic role of Aditi. She is the mother of Indra, then of a set of another twenty-one *ādityas* and, finally, she becomes the mother of all the gods (*devamātṛ*). (Also see Mahādevī.)

11. Āditya

Literally son of Aditi, whose number rose to twelve in the *Śatapatha Brāhmaṇa*, representing the twelve months of the solar year, and the sun itself when used in the singular. The myth of the seven *ādityas* (explained as the sun, moon, and five planets by some) is also said to be found in the *Avesta* as Amesha Spentas.

12. Ādivāsīs

Tribal people whose religion is usually considered included within Hinduism, but not always. Their population is estimated at over 50 million. The word literally means "original inhabitants".

13. Adṛṣṭa

"Unseen", an important concept in the schools of Nyāya and Vaiśeṣika philosophy. In the former school, its main implication is moral (without excluding the metaphysical) where it is used to explain the differences in conditions of the *jīvas* in the world, as representing the unseen power of *karma*. In the context of the atomic theory of matter, as propounded by the Vaiśeṣikas, the question arises: what brings the atoms together, the building blocks of the world, to build the world? The Vaiśeṣikas ascribe this action to what is called *adṛṣṭa*, the stock of *puṇya* and *pāpa* (merit and demerit), acquired by the *jīvas* in previous lives which needs to work itself out. These unseen forces of moral desserts in the eternal individual souls lead to creation under the will of God. (Also see Nyāya, Vaiśeṣika School of Philosophy.)

14. Advaita Vedānta

An influential school of Hindu philosophy, which offers a distinct interpretation of the Upaniṣads, as well as the *Brahma-Sūtra* and the *Bhagavad-Gītā*. Hinduism has a long tradition of debating the final message contained in the final portions of the Vedas, called Upaniṣads or Vedānta, as well as in the allied texts mentioned above. The school of Advaita Vedānta claims that this final message is one of non-dualism or not-two (*a-dvaita*). At issue is the question of the number and nature of ultimate reality or realities, and this school, in its classical formulation by Śaṅkara around the eighth century, maintains that according to the Upaniṣads, this ultimate reality is not-two; the word one is avoided lest it convey the sense of "one among many", or of "two things becoming one", positions which are refuted within the school. It is best to understand non-two as referring to an undivided single ultimate reality, called *Nirguṇa-Brahman*, thus rendering any perception of duality, such as of this world or even of God, ultimately unreal. Then how did this variety all around us come about? Advaita explains it as the work of *māyā*, the finitizing principle which makes the infinite appear finite, or the one appear as many. If all difference is unreal, then the perception of one's own difference from the *Brahman* also becomes unreal, thereby making one, in one's true form, identical with *Brahman*. Thus we obtain the three basic postulates of the system:

1. that *Brahman* alone is real;
2. that the world is ultimately unreal or *māyā,* and
3. the *jīva* is identical with *Brahman*.

(Also see Bhrama, Śaṅkara, Māyā, Mahāvākyas, Nirguṇa-Brahman, Jñana-Yoga.)

15. Āgamas

The doctrinal and liturgal texts of the various *sampradāyas* (sects as they are often translated) in Hinduism. The Vaiṣṇava Sampradāya considers the Pāñcarātra Āgamas as authoritative, so called because they are said to have been revealed by Nārāyaṇa himself over a period of five nights. According to the *Nārada Pāñcarātra*, "Everything is Kṛṣṇa from Brahmā to a blade of grass". The Śaiva Āgamas number twenty-eight, the best known being the *Kāmikāgama*, used, for instance, in many temples in Tamil Nadu. The form of Śaivism represented mainly in Tamil Nadu and Kashmir regards the Āgamas, along with the Vedas, as its basic texts. Different Āgamas are sometimes connected with different parts of India. The Śākta Sampradāya lists seventy-seven Āgamas, the word sometimes being used to refer to this sect, and sometimes to include all the Āgamas. There is another traditional list of 108 Pāñcarātra or Vaiṣṇava Āgamas (also called Saṁhitās), 28 Śaiva Āgamas and 77 Śākta Āgamas. (Also see Tantras.)

16. Agastya

Agastya is a major figure in Hindu lore, and it might be useful to distinguish his Vedic portrayal from later ones. The circumstance of his birth, recounted in the *Ṛg-Veda* (I.166-91), is unusual. He is therein depicted as the offspring of Mitra and Varuṇa (hence his name Maitrāvaruṇi), whose seeds were released at a sacrificial session by the sight of the celestial nymph Urvaśī, part falling into a jar (*kumbha*) and part outside; from the former was born Agastya (hence also called Kumbhaja) and from the latter Vasiṣṭha. In the *Ṛg-Veda* he reconciles Indra and Maruts (*ṚV* I.165, 170) and is depicted with Lopāmudrā as his wife, in a way suggestive of the incompatibility of marriage and philosophy. The circumstances of his marriage are elaborated in later literature. He discovers his dead ancestors hanging on to life by a thread in the other world, because he had not begotten a son to perform the necessary ancestral rituals to sustain them. He thereupon creates a girl child with the most appealing parts of the objects and beings found in the forest, hands it over to a king for upkeep, and reclaims her when she turns nubile. His wife epitomizes the virtue of conjugal devotion to the husband in Hindu lore. In later lore, Agastya is depicted as crossing the Vindhya mountains, which started rising out of spirit of rivalry with the Himalayas, until it blocked out the sun. This development caused great alarm. The Vindhya mountain, however, was a disciple of Agastya, and, at his approach, prostrated himself before him, whereupon the sage asked him to remain in that position until he returned, and he never did. This story is generally accepted as symbolizing the spread of Aryan culture beyond the Vindhyas. It wasn't an entirely smooth affair. Vātāpi and Iḷvaḷa were not pleased by his arrival and devised a bizarre plan to kill him but he turned the tables on them. Another class of demons, called Kāleyas, hid themselves in the ocean and kept oppressing the world, whereupon he drank up the whole ocean to expose their hideout. He later released his excessive intake of water in the usual way, which is supposed to explain the briny taste of the ocean. This earned him the name of one who drank the ocean: Samudra-culuka. Some scholars see in this story the suggestion of the spread of Aryan influence not only into the south but beyond the landmass of India, across the seas. Agastya appears in the *Rāmāyaṇa* as the host of Rāma and Sītā during their exile, while living south of the Vindhyas. His association with the south is so strong that he is curiously depicted in some Purāṇas as the son of Pulastya, the same line to which Rāvaṇa belonged. Agastya is as much celebrated in Tamil lore. He is credited with composing the first Tamil grammar, called *Agastyam* (*Akattiyam*) after him, in 12,000 *sūtras* (aphorisms). It is not extant although this fragment has survived:

> There is no language without literature, even as there is no oil without seed; but as oil is extracted from seed, so is language (grammar) evolved from literature.

His disciple, Tolkāppiar, is said to be author of another ancient Tamil work called *Tolkāppiyam*. Beyond Tamil Nadu, Agastya receives the highest honours in the local divine hierarchies in Java, Cambodia, and even Borneo.

17. Agni

After Indra, who is called his twin brother, the largest number of hymns in the *Ṛg-Veda* are devoted to Agni (fire god). The very first hymn, with which the traditional recitation of the Veda commences, is dedicated to him, and begins with the word *agni* itself. Its importance could well reflect human memory of the pivotal role played by fire in the emergence of human culture. There is a tendency in the *Ṛg-Veda* to anthropomorphize deities but given the nature of fire, this tendency in the case of fire is slight and obvious. The point can be traced as far back as the *Nirukta*. Its author, *Yāska* (fifth century BCE), distinguishes between gods who may (*puruṣavidhāḥ*) or may not (*apuruṣavidhāḥ*) be described in anthropomorphic terms. He is flame-haired, he eats with his tongue, is nourished thrice during the day and is smoke-bannered (*ṚV* I.45.6d). The polygenetic origin of Agni is variously explained (1) from the kindling-sticks (*araṇīs*) which are his parents; moreover, because he is born anew with each kindling he is considered immortal; (2) from the aerial waters – suggested by lightning (*ṚV* II.9.2 and 4). Thus he was brought down from heaven to earth by Mātariśvan, the Indian Prometheus. The third origin is celestial. The three origins establish Agni's tripartite character; Agni has even been called the earliest representation of the Indian trinity. Agni manifests himself triply in heaven (as the Sun, *ṚV* VII.2.1), in the atmosphere (as lightning), and on the earth (as fire). Another threefold manifestation is represented by the three sacrificial fires: *gārhapatya*, *āhavanīya* and *dakṣiṇa* (*ŚatBrā* I.1.1.) which respectively represent earth, heaven and atmosphere. Bṛhaspati (also Brahmaṇaspati), or lord of prayer, is both distinguished from and identified with Agni and this ambivalence may rest in the fact that Agni is sometimes considered the "divine counterpart of earthly priesthood" (*BṛUp* I.4.15). Thus Agni, in this aspect, may be considered the prototype of Brahmā, the first member of the *trimūrti* (Hindu trinity of classical Hinduism), as well as well as of *Brahman* which came to denote the ultimate reality in classical Hinduism, for already in the *Ṛg-Veda*, Agni "is inherent in every god; he is the priest of the gods as well as the god of the priests". Many Vedic gods receded in significance as new forms of Hinduism arose, which holds true for both Indra and Agni. Agni is thus provided with a new genealogy in the Purāṇas. At the celestial level he is described as the proud (*abhimānī*) son of Brahmā, or alternatively as emerging from the cosmic person (*virāṭ-puruṣa*). At the atmospheric level, he is depicted as a guardian of space (*aṣṭadikpālas*), while on the terrestrial level he is the fiery child of Vasubhāryā and Dharma and is due course himself married to Svāhā. These allow for iconographic descriptions of the god, as possessing a specific number of heads, horns, feet and arms, and subsequently their scriptural depiction. Thus while Agni receded from sacrificial prominence, invoked in offerings requiring oblations, its use in the domestic ritual and rites in Hindu life remains uninterrupted from very ancient times. Although Hindus may no longer perform the fire ritual everyday, they still get married by a rite in which Agni bears witness to the union. When they die they are usually cremated. Fire as funeral pyre, however, given its very character, arouses ambivalent feelings. Already in the funeral hymn (*ṚV* X.145) the offering-conveying (*havya-vāhana*) role of the fire is distinguished from his role as the flesh-consuming (*kravyāda*) fire. In the early hymns he leads the dead to the higher realms, but his mortuary role was later taken over by Yama.

The popular Holī festival has links with both Holikā and Agni. The Holikā part points to the story of Prahlāda but the Agni part points to another story. The brāhmaṇa Bhṛgu worshipped Agni daily, leaving his beautiful wife Pulomā in its care as he took his morning bath. The demons however one day carried her away, by feeding Agni *ghī* to the point of inducing drowsiness. The sage cursed Agni to die. Viṣṇu mollified the sage so that on Holī, Agni would receive his due when bonfires would be raised of discarded items during the festival. Some unusual concepts associated with fire are those of *vaḍvāgni* and *jaṭharāgni*. *Vaḍvāgni* refers to a submarine and subterranean fire, which burns up the excess water in the ocean and thus prevents it from overflowing. It is supposed to emerge from the mare's mouth (*vaḍvāmukha*) and come time will destroy the world. Some scholars see in this image of fire inside the water a unique, even ultimate union of opposites, without either side compromising its integrity. *Jaṭharāgni* (fire in the belly) (which here does not quite possess the meaning the expression does in English) is a description of the digestive process with a fiery flourish, even alluded to in the *Bhagavad-Gītā* (XV.14). (Also see Vedic Religion, Vedic Ritual and Ahalyā.)

18. Ahalyā

Ahalyā represents perhaps the best-known case of adultery in ancient Hindu lore. She was the wife of Ṛṣi Gautama, and was seduced by Indra while the husband was away performing the morning rites (*ŚatBrā* III.3.4). When this became known, she was expelled from the hermitage and cursed into invisible oblivion, while Indra was cursed with displaying marks of the pudenda all over his body, with some measure of poetic justice. These were changed later into eyes to lessen his mortification. According to another myth, Indra's punishment involved penile cosmetic surgery, with his genitals being replaced by that of a goat.

Later traditions offer other details. She is also described in some accounts as being tricked by Indra, who in one case assumes the form of Gautama, and in another gets the moon-god to change himself into a rooster and crow before the proper time to get the sage to leave so that he can take his place. Some accounts are less forgiving of Ahalyā, who is depicted as welcoming the advances. In the *Rāmāyaṇa*, we find her literally petrified by the sage's curse, from which she is released when touched by Rāma, who restores her to the husband. Kumārila Bhaṭṭa explains the whole episode metaphorically. Indra connotes the sun, and Ahalyā night, whose shades are carried away by the rising sun. Despite this background, she is one of the five maidens (*pañca-kanyās*), who destroy all sins upon being remembered in the morning, the others being Draupadī, Sītā, Tārā and Mandodarī.

19. Ahiṁsā

Ahiṁsā, first mentioned in *Chāndogya Upaniṣad* (III.17.4), literally means non-violence and gradually became accepted as a fundamental virtue in the three classical religions of India: Hinduism, Buddhism and Jainism, although not without some struggle. Its specific place in a spiritual regimen had already been assured in systems such as *yoga*, wherein it is among the five cardinal restraints called Yama (*YS* II.30). According to *Manu-Smṛti* (IV.148) it helps acquire knowledge of previous lives, and its practice leads the hermit to *mokṣa* (*MS* VI.39-40). It gradually found expression, in normal living, in vegetarianism so that the Chinese Buddhist pilgrim, Fahian, who visited India in the fourth century states, perhaps with some exaggeration, that not only killing animals, but drinking wine and eating onions and garlic were unknown to Madhyadeśa (Middle Country).

The importance attached to *ahiṁsā* in modern times can be traced to Mahatma Gandhi (1869–1948), who made non-violence resistance to British Raj his weapon of choice in the struggle for Indian Independence. It doubtless gave a moral tone to the struggle, although some have argued that India had been disarmed so effectively by the British that Indians had no real choice in the matter. (Also see Yoga.)

20. Aihoḷe

Aihoḷe, near Bādāmī, was the regional capital of the Cāḷukya dynasty and is an important location for several reasons. It is the site of the famous Aihole inscription of Pulakeśin II of the seventh century, which records how King Harṣa's attempts to march westward were thwarted. This famous panegyric contains the first epigraphic mention of the name of Kālidāsa, as well as the first epigraphic reference which places the battle of Mahābhārata in the third millennium BCE. It is also the site of several temples of the Cāḷukya period from fourth to sixth centuries, particularly of the Durgigudi Temple.

21. Airāvata

The celestial elephant, who is the vehicle of Indra. In some accounts his lineage is traced to sage Kaśyapa. We might talk at how an elephant could emerge from a sagely lineage, but such metamorphoses are not unknown to Hindu lore, variously explained, if pressed, as sages assuming animal forms during lovemaking, or simply changing their forms to those of animals. The more popular account identifies him as one of the items to emerge from the churning of the oceans. In this account he has four tusks. How this account is reconciled with the previous one offers a good insight into how discrepancies are resolved in the

Hindu imaginary: that the story of the Airāvata, as emerging from the churning of the ocean is said to belong to the sixth *manvantara*, and the previous account pertains to the seventh, as each age has its own Indra and its own Airāvata.

22. Akṣaya-Tṛtīyā

A festival which falls in spring, so called because it falls on the third day of the bright half of the Hindu month of Vaiśākha (also considered the first day of Satya-Yuga). All meritorious acts performed on that day are considered "inexhaustible" (*akṣaya*), making it particularly auspicious for the performance of rites dedicated to the dead (*śrāddha*), because it ensures them a permanent place in the other world. (Also see Vrata and Women's Rituals.)

23. Akṣaya Vaṭa

A banyan tree in Allahabad, now located within the Allahabad Fort, believed to have been in existence from day one, under which Rāma, Lakṣmaṇa and Sītā sought shelter in an earlier age. The Chinese Buddhist pilgrim Xuanzang notes its presence in the seventh century, as a place from where pilgrims flung themselves to death in the hope of attaining liberation. Attempts to chop it down in the sixteenth century are alluded to. The fact that it is still standing reinforces its mythical perception as indestructible until the end of time.

24. Al-Bīrūnī (973–1048)

Muslim scholar who wrote a famous book on India referred to as *Al-Bīrūnī's India* and widely regarded as a masterly account of Indic civilization. Al-Bīrūnī anticipates the phenomenological method in the study of religion by trying to present Hinduism on its own terms. He also frequently distinguishes between the views of the Hindu philosophers from those of the people at large, anticipating the anthropological distinction between the Great Tradition and the Little Tradition. He notes some convergences between the views of the Hindus and the Greeks, and the monotheistic world-view to which he was accustomed.

25. Āl̠vārs

From around the seventh to ninth century, Tamil Nadu witnessed an upsurge in devotion to Viṣṇu and Śiva, which found expression in beautiful poetry sung by a number of saints. In the subsequent period these were collected and compiled, and form the basis of Tamil devotional literature. Those saints who worshipped Viṣṇu were known as Āl̠vārs, while those who worshipped Śiva were known as Nāyanārs or Nāyanmārs.

The Āl̠vārs were twelve in number, and came from all walks of life and strata of society. Tradition places them in three groups in terms of legendary chronology, going back to *c.* 4200 BCE. To the first group belong: (1) Poykai Āl̠vār, (2) Bhutattar, (3) Peyāl̠vār, and (4) Tirumaḷiṣai Āl̠vār; to the second group belong (5) Nammāḷvār, (6) Madhurakavi Āl̠vār, (7) Kulaśekhara Āl̠vār, (8) Periāl̠vār, and (9) Āṇḍāl. To the third group belong, (10) Toṇḍaraḍiproḍi Āl̠vār, (11) Tiruppān Āl̠vār, and (12) Tirumaṅgai Āl̠vār. Although the dates assigned to them are hardly acceptable, the traditional order has generally been accepted. Their poems were compiled by Nāthamuni (824–924) into what is known as *Nālāyira-Prabandham* or *Divya-Prabandham*. Its best known part is the *Tiruvāyamol̠i*, attributed to Nammāl̠vār (*c.* 800), who is said to have been lost in trance for sixteen years and then woke from it to compose four hymns, which contain the essence of the four Vedas. Another famous Āl̠vār is Āṇḍāl, who worshipped God as a husband and is reputed to have merged into his image. Her *Tiruppāvāi* is particularly esteemed. The Āl̠vārs are revered in the Śri-Vaiṣṇava community with great enthusiasm; they are honoured as devout individuals and their hymns are sung in temples and households. (Also see Ubhaya-Vedānta.)

26. Amara-Citra-Kathā

The name of an immensely popular series of religious comic books in India appearing in English and other languages, broadly portraying Hindu themes in a non-sectarian way, and as tolerant of other religions. The series has published over 200 titles and sold more than 280 million copies under the editorship of Anant Pai, simultaneously popularizing and standardizing Hindu narratives. (Also see Hindu Polytheism.)

27. Amarakośa

A famous Sanskrit dictionary, also known as *Nāmalingānuśāsanam*. It is more like a thesaurus written in verse, named after its author, a Buddhist, usually assigned to a period between CE 400 to 600. It formed part of the traditional curriculum of Sanskrit education in India, along with the *Aṣṭādhyāyī* of Pāṇini, with the student ideally committing both texts to memory.

28. Ambedkar, Bhimrao (1891–1956)

Dr B.R. Ambedkar, as he is often referred to, was born as the fourteenth child into a untouchable Mahār family. Son of a school headmaster, somewhat fittingly education was the key to his rise to prominence. As a child he suffered the many disabilities the untouchables were subject to, but a brāhmaṇa teacher at school used to help him out and so he adopted the teacher's surname, Ambedkar (for his own, Ambegoanker). He earned a BA from Elphinstone College, Bombay in 1912, and with financial support from the Mahārājā of Baroda, was able to travel overseas for higher studies, obtaining an MA and Ph.D. from Columbia University, making him one of the few figures in Indian national life at the time with an American academic background. He went on to obtain a D.Sc. from London University and also passed the bar exam from Grey's Inn, London. He began working for the amelioration of the lot of untouchables in the 1920s, agitating for having temples opened to them and symbolically burning discriminatory verses in the *Manu-Smṛti* at Mahad, in Maharashtra, on 25 December 1927. He rose to national eminence with his selection, by the British, to represent the untouchables as a delegate to the London Round Table Conference (1931). Gandhi's fast to death in opposition to the separate electorates, granted by the British to the untouchables in 1932, and welcomed by him, resulted in the so-called Poona Pact, under which the number of reserved seats for untouchables were increased but in a joint electorate. He was a member of the Viceroy's executive council during the war years and joined the "national" Cabinet as Law Minister, after the arrival of Indian Independence in 1947, Ambedkar chaired the drafting committee of the Indian Constitution. He parted company with the Indian National Congress in 1951. In 1956, six months before his death, he converted to Buddhism, fulfilling his proclamation in 1935: "I was born a Hindu, but will not die a Hindu". His brāhmaṇa wife continued his legacy. A brilliant mind, he held some remarkable views. He favoured the formation of Pakistan, provided it involved transfer of population, wanted Sanskrit to be the official language of India, and argued against the extra-Indian origin of the Aryans on academic grounds. (Also see Untouchability.)

29. Amṛta

The word *amṛta*, cognate with Greek ambrosia, denotes the elixir of immortality, or anything which could be so called. It is often referred to in the *Ṛg-Veda* (I.23.19-20, etc.) and *Atharva-Veda* (I.4.4, etc.), wherein it is sometimes likened to *soma*, milk, and water. A major episode in the Purāṇas it is linked with the churning of the ocean, by the gods and the demons, to obtain various coveted goods, but they fall out when it comes to the distribution of these goods, specially nectar (*amṛta*) (*ViṣṇuP*, chap. 22). The gods get hold of it but the demons steal it. Viṣṇu in the form of the bewitching beauty, Mohinī, helps recover it, and becomes immortal by partaking it. In the to and fro, however, according to the legend associated with the Kumbha Melā, drops of it fell on four sites on earth: at Haridwar, Nasik, Ujjain and Prayāga, thus providing the legendary basis for the festival rotating among them at the interval of three years. The word occurs in such words as *amṛta-bandhu* (for the horse Ucchaiḥśravas, because it also appeared in the churning); *amṛta-ghaṭaka*, the vase or vessel containing nectar with which the gods (and sometimes the physician Dhanvantari) are depicted, and *amṛta-kalaśa*, the finial of the temple symbolizing immortality.

30. Ānanda

The word denotes bliss, to be distinguished philosophically from *sukha* and *duḥkha* (quotidian joys and sorrows), representing the enjoyment of a state which transcends them. The word often appears in the names assumed by the renunciants upon *saṁnyāsa*. (Also see Samādhi.)

31. Ananda Marg

The name of a new Hindu religious movement, short for Ananda Marg Pracharaka Sangha (Association for Propagation of the Path of Bliss), which was founded in Jamālpur, Bihar in 1955, by Anandamurti P.R. Sarkar (1921-90), a functionary in the Indian Railways who slowly developed a following, which ultimately came to include a monastic order and many social service and educational institutions. It also evolved an international outreach but fell foul of the government and was banned during the Emergency imposed by Indira Gandhi during 1975-77. Earlier, in 1971, its founder was tried for allegedly trying to murder former members of the organization, but was exonerated of all charges in 1978; some members even immolated themselves in the 1970s in protest against his imprisonment. The movement also contained a Tantric element, unlike most new Hindu movements.

32. Anandamayi Ma (1896–1981)

A famous woman mystic of modern India, born in what is now known as Bangladesh. Her parents were religiously disposed and given to Hindu hymn-singing. She was married at thirteen to Ramani Mohan Cakravarti, otherwise known as Bholānāth, and went to live with him when she was eighteen. It was around this time that an acquaintance, much impressed by her mystical qualities, first addressed her as the (divine) "Ma" or Mother and it stuck, giving her the name by which she became known. Her marriage to Bholānāth was never consummated and although his relatives urged him to remarry, in the end he accepted her as his *guru*, taking initiation from her. She was extremely sensitive to spiritual stimuli and would go into trances, or start displaying yogic *āsanas* or making symbolic gestures when in the state of *bhāva* (a state of rapturous transport). She was suspected of being mad until her behaviour was recognized as a form of divine madness. Her spiritual sensitivity was not restricted to Hinduism and once, when visiting her natal home which lay in a Muslim majority area, she spontaneously started reciting what seemed like passages from the Qur'ān. She set up *āśrama*'s and schools and gained a wide following, which included India's former prime minister, Indira Gandhi. Numerous incidents of telepathy, clairvoyance and other *siddhis* are associated with her and her teachings, although delivered in a homely style, are reminiscent of Advaita Vedānta. (Also see Advaita Vedānta.)

33. Angkor Wāt

The word literally means "temple of the city". It was built by the Khmer king, Sūryavarman II (1112-52) in Kampuchea as a depiction of the Purāṇic cosmos, with the Mt. Meru at the centre, with walls standing for the circumambient ranges, and a moat representing the legendary oceans. Its architectural structure is characterized by pyramids and galleries; the main temple contains a series of concentric courts, each surrounded by a gallery, rising one above the other to the shrine with a *śikhara*. The shrine was crowned by a golden lotus over 200 ft above the ground. The central tower contained the image of the Devarāja (or divine king). Thus while in cosmology it replicates Indic ideas, in political thought it surpasses them, for the king was never divinized in India the way it was in the cult of Devarāja in Cambodia.

34. Antyeṣṭi

The last rites. The body is to be cremated as soon as possible, preferably before sundown according to some traditions. The body is washed and then raised on a bier and carried to the cremation ground (*śmaśāna*), usually located by the bank of a river. The eldest son is supposed to light the pyre for the father and the youngest for the mother. An important point in the cremation is the bursting of the skull (*kapāla-kriyā*), which is supposed to signify the exit of the soul. The remains of the body, specially the bones, are collected for immersion ideally in the Ganges, or in some other river. Traditionally women did not go to the cremation ground but nowadays daughters have also begun performing the last rites for their parents. (Also see Saṁskāras.)

35. Anugītā

There are four texts in Hinduism in which Kṛṣṇa instructs Arjuna. He does so famously in the *Bhagavad-Gītā*, but also once again in the *Anugītā* in the *Mahābhārata* itself; then in another text called the *Uttaragītā* also associated with the *Mahābhārata*, and finally in the *Arjunopākhyāna*, found in the *Yoga-Vāsiṣṭha*. The context of the *Anugītā* is provided by the visit of Arjuna to his friend Kṛṣṇa in Dvārakā, long after the war is over. As they reminisce Arjuna tells Kṛṣṇa that he would like to once again hear the inspiring sermon he delivered on the eve of the war. Kṛṣṇa chides Arjuna for forgetting it because he was inspired (*yoga-yukta*) at the time, but so as not to let Arjuna down, recounts whatever he can. The *Anugītā* is remarkable for omitting the cosmic theophany (*viśva-rūpa-darśana*), which some consider the high point of the *Bhagavad-Gītā*. (Also see *Bhagavad-Gītā*.)

36. Anumāna

One may conclude a fire is burning not because one can see it, but because one sees the smoke produced by it. One may thus have an inferred knowledge of fire as opposed to direct knowledge.

Anumāna, which literally means after-knowledge, is knowledge acquired after some other knowledge, as that of smoke in the above illustration. One may use this form of knowledge to infer things for oneself (*svārthānumāna*), or to convince another (*parārthānumāna*). The latter case usually involves a syllogism, of which the following is a classical example:

1. There is fire on the hill (*pratijñā*);
2. because there is smoke (*hetu*);
3. whatever has smoke has fire, e.g. the kitchen (*udāharaṇa*);
4. The hill has some smoke which is always accompanied by fire (i.e. the two are characterized by invariable concomitance) (*upanaya*); and
5. therefore there is fire on the hill (*nigamana*).

This five-membered (*pañcāvayava*) syllogism begins with a statement, and then offers it as a conclusion to convince the other party. All inference, whether for oneself or others, involves three elements:

1. the subject where a character is to be established called *pakṣa*, which in this is the hill;
2. the character or fact which is to be established called *sādhya*, here fire; and
3. the mark, sign, or means it is to be established called *liṅga*, *sādhana* or *hetu*, here smoke.

The corresponding terms in Aristotelian logic are minor term (*pakṣa*, hill), middle term (*liṅga*, smoke) and major term (*sādhya*, fire). By comparison with the Aristotelian syllogism, this one is both inductive (in adducing an observation) and deductive (in invoking universal concomitance) but the basic principle of inference, which consists of attributing character to a subject on the ground of another character, with which it is universally connected, is the same. This makes the ground cited the crucial source of error if it is misplaced (*duṣṭa hetu*). This expression of inference in verbal form is however considered a courtesy (*upacāra*), for the working of logic is a matter of thought, not language.

Two important classifications are developed in Nyāya school of Hindu philosophy, which turn on *vyāpti*, the universal concomitance between *liṅga* and *sādhya*. According to one such classification, inferences can be of three types:

1. *pūrvavat*,
2. *śeṣavat*, and
3. *sāmānyatodṛṣṭa*.

In the first case, one infers an unperceived effect from a perceived cause (as rain from clouds); in the other, one infers an unperceived cause from a perceived effect (as rain from slush); in the third case, the concomitance does not depend on causality (one might infer that an animal has horns from only seeing its cloven hoofs). The other set of classification also involves three types: *kevalānvaya*, *kevala-vyatirekī* and *anvaya-vyetirekī*, depending on whether the middle and major terms are only positively related, only negatively related, or related both positively and negatively. (Also see Nyāya and Pramāṇa-Śāstra.)

37. Ānupūrvī

The term used in Mīmāṁsā school of Hindu philosophy to denote the particular order in which the words occur in the Vedas, setting the Vedas apart from other literary works. According to Mīmāṁsā language theory, a letter, which is called *varṇa*, is eternal (as distinguished from the various ways in which it may be pronounced, called *dhvani*). The words formed by these letters and the relation of the word to the meaning is eternal, but all literary works are not eternal, like the Vedas, because the order of words available in literary works is traceable to a person, but the Vedas are not the work of any person, human or divine. (Also see Mīmāṁsā-Darśana.)

38. Apauruṣeya

"Not of a person, human or divine", that this to say, without an ascribed author. The Vedas are such according to both Mīmāṁsā and Vedānta, because they are eternal (*nitya*) and therefore do not require an author, being repromulgated at the beginning of each cosmic cycle in accordance with the previous, hence the usual pairing of the terms *apauruṣeya* and *nitya*. Modern scholars interpret the word to mean "impersonal", thereby implying the spiritual truths, like scientific truths, are independent of the discoverer of it, just as the law of gravity is independent of Newton. In the same spirit, the word *nitya* is interpreted as indicating that such truths are also eternal, again on the analogy of science. (Also see Mīmāṁsā-Darśana.)

39. Apūrva

The Mīmāṁsā school of Hindu philosophy emphasizes the centrality of ritual in the interpretation of the Vedas. One such category of ritual consists of *kāmya-karma* (optional rites), such as the rite of Jyotiṣṭoma, by performing which one goes to heaven (*svarga*) after death. The question arises: the rite is performed and done and over with in the present, so how could it conceivably produce an effect in the future? The answer is provided by the concept of *apūrva*, which involves the notion of an invisible potency. It comes to reside in the sacrificer as a result of performing the rite and bears fruit in due course. This principle applies to *pratiṣiddha karma*s (forbidden acts) like murder as well, which similarly produce a negative effect in the future. (Also see Vedic Religion and Vedic Ritual.)

40. Ari

The word *ari* in classical Sanskrit means an enemy, but in the *Ṛg-Veda* it seems to refer to one of two competing groups of the Aris and the Sūris. According to Enric Aguilar I Matas (and Mahinda Palihawadan), these two elites vied for dominance in the Aryan camp, with the Sūris supporting the Indra cult, and the Aris that of Varuṇa. The dominance of Indra in the *Ṛg-Veda*, and the lesser role accorded to Varuṇa in it, is said to represent the triumph of the Sūri faction.

41. Aryan Culture

To the extent that the Vedas are the foundational texts of Hinduism, and that the people who upheld the Vedic way of life considered themselves Aryans (as also in the *Avesta*), Hinduism can be considered as a product of Aryan culture. This was earlier contrasted with a Dravidian culture, which either preceded or coexisted with it, sometimes identified with Indus Valley culture. New developments however have cast the thesis of a necessarily antithetical relation between the two in doubt:

1. It is no longer certain whether an Aryan invasion, on which the thesis rests, occurred;
2. Dravidian influences are already traceable in the language of the *Ṛg-Veda*, so what is considered Aryan already contains Dravidian elements;
3. Hinduism claims to be Vedic rather than Aryan in origin and it is possible to point to elements within it, which are non-Aryan but not non-Vedic, as has been argued in relation to some elements of Vaiṣṇavism.

The more crucial issue is that of the origin of Aryan culture. There are three major hypotheses in competition at the moment:

1. The Aryan invasion theory, according to which the Aryan people, speaking an Indo-European language, swept through the mountain passes of north-western India such as Khyber (*c.* 1500 BCE), overran and overcame the existing Indus Valley civilization, and introduced a system of apartheid in the form of the caste system to keep the surviving elements in subjugation.
2. The Aryan migration theory, according to which the Aryans still entered from outside but not in a cataclysmic event but

rather gradually, and may have coexisted with the Indus Valley culture for a while, which was ultimately absorbed.

3. The indigenous Aryan theory, according to which the Aryans are indigenous to India, whose culture and language developed in interaction with Dravidian culture, into the later culture of India.

The first two scenarios share the view that the Aryans entered India from outside India, and the third rejects it. Linguistic evidence in general tends to back the first view, archaeological the second. (Also see Aryan–Dravidian Hypothesis and Asko Parpola.)

42. Aryan–Dravidian Hypothesis

It was the cornerstone, until very recently, of Western Indology. According to this view a light-skinned people, speaking an Indo-European language, invaded India through the north-west in the middle of the second millennium BCE, defeated the dark-skinned original inhabitants, who spoke Dravidian languages and then drove them away into the south. Thus India could be seen as consisting of two separate zones of north and south, divided by language and race. The hypothesis clearly accepted the racial and cultural superiority of the Aryans. As the language of the Vedas was related to that of the Europeans, the people in India who spoke languages derived from Vedic Sanskrit could also flatter themselves at being related to their white rulers. Thus the fact that the hypothesis served the emotional needs of both the conquered and the conquerors might explain its longevity. With even greater irony, it served the emotional needs of both higher-caste or elite groups by connecting them with the conquerors, and of the lower caste or subaltern groups, who could now take up cudgels against the higher-caste people as they were racially distinct. In a further twist, these low-caste groups, who held these views, rallied against the higher castes now perceived as racially different, on the one hand, but on the other, also looked upon the white Britons in India with favour as custodians of their interests, although both the higher castes and the whites belonged to the same racial group.

43. Asceticism

Both Ṛg-Vedic culture and Haṛappan culture prefigure asceticism, the *Ṛg-Veda* through the mention of *muni*s who fly through air, wear ochre, and live on the outskirts of society, and Haṛappan culture, through its links with *yoga* as indicated by depictions of *āsanas*. Asceticism was destined to become a lasting strand within the Indic religious tradition, even though Buddhism was critical of its extreme forms. This strand may also have played a role in the emergence of the Upaniṣads, specially if we also accept esotericism as a dimension of asceticism.

44. Asko Parpola

Finnish archaeologist, whose work has been very influential in the context of Indus Valley or Haṛappan civilization. He has been a strong proponent of its Dravidian connection, identifying the Indus script, although not yet deciphered, as Dravidian. He has explained the steatite seal, interpreted as proto-Śiva by John Marshall, as a seated bull on the strength of similar depictions of Elamite seals of the same period; argued for the depiction of the God Murukaṉ, mainly associated with south India (specially Tamil Nadu) in the Indus Valley script; and reinterpreted another seal, usually interpreted as reflecting a Mesopotamian motif, as a contest between Durgā and the Buffalo-Demon and thus related to her as Mahiṣāsuramardinī. He also argues against the identification of Haṛappan civilization with the Aryan on the grounds that the latter civilization was strongly characterized by the presence of horses and chariots, conspicuous by their absence in Haṛappan civilization. According to him, the area of the distribution of the kind of pottery known as painted grey ware, found in the Gangetic plain and carbon-dated between 1100 and 300 BCE, coincides with that of Vedic culture. (Also see Aryan–Dravidian Hypothesis and Dāsas.)

45. Āstika

Literally yes-sayer; the word is widely used in Hinduism in three distinct senses:

1. for one who believes in life after death;
2. for one who believes in God; and
3. for a school of Indian philosophy which accepts Vedic authority.

It is most commonly used in the second sense, and philosophically in the third. (Also see Darśana Literature.)

46. Astrology

The priest was always, to a certain extent, an adviser of the family, and with the growth of astrology he became even more closely involved. Priests had long been consulted for auspicious and inauspicious times but there is evidence from the *Manu-Smṛti* that priests had begun to move beyond such elementary calculation. By the time of the classical work, *Bṛhajjātaka* (The Great Jātaka) of Varāhamihira, placed around CE 500, horoscopes were clearly being cast. The idea took hold that one's karmic balance across lives could be transmitted celestially, just as nowadays accounts are transmitted electronically. The chart at the moment of birth thus provided a map of one's karmic disposition. Although there is a tradition of placating planetary influences, it should be noted that the stars only conveyed the karmic information and did not produce karmic consequences by their own actions. The fact that one's horoscope is unique to oneself thus enabled an individual to interact with and engage cosmic forces at an individual level, impersonal as they might appear.

Astrology however connects one with not only one's past (*prārabdha*) but also one's present (*āgāmī, kriyamāṇa*) *karma*. If one's *karma* in daily life, in a practical way, is in fact unknown, then this ambiguity itself opened up life to astrology. (Also see Karma.)

47. Atomic Theory

Hindu thought, like Greek, developed theories about the atomic structure of matter, of which the Vaiśeṣika school is the chief representative, as it subscribed to the view that matter could be ultimately reduced to entities which were irreducibly indivisible. The universe is composed of composite entities. Any composite entity is divisible but obviously such a division could not be carried out indefinitely. The entity, which can no longer be further subdivided, is the atom (*aṇu*), which could also be called the minutest part of matter. The Vaiśeṣika school thus reduces the whole material universe to four kinds of atoms; those of earth, water, fire and air. It accepts ether as an element but does not regard it as atomic in structure: the four kinds of atoms are classified on the basis of the qualities they possess: air possesses one quality, touch; fire two: touch and colour; water three: touch, colour and taste; and earth four, these three plus smell. Thus each of the four elements had individual features and belonged to a class different from non-atomic substances (*dravyas*) — time, space, mind, and self. The variety of objects in the universe is to be explained in terms of the number of atoms involved, and in terms of the qualitative difference among them explained earlier. This process visualizes two atoms of water, for instance, coming together to constitute *dvyaṇuka* (binary compound); three such binaries then constitute a *tryaṇuka* (triad). This is identified with the mote in the sun-beam, and the triads, grouped further, lead to other finite things. If such is the process of "creation", "destruction" follows the opposite course, when the atoms dissolve into their original eternal form, to be reconstituted again into the universe by God, when the next round of creation became due. (Also see Vaiśeṣika.)

48. Basavanna (1106-68)

Basavanna or Basava is said to have been a minister of in the court of King Bijjala Kaḷcūri in the Kannaḍa-speaking region, who usurped the throne of the Cāḷukyas of Kalyāṇī in 1156. He is the founder of the Vīraśaiva or Liṅgāyata religious community, noted for its single-mind devotion to Śiva, whose symbol the devout wear upon their person. Although its philosophical position is close to traditional "qualified monism", Basava challenged many Hindu beliefs and practices such as Vedic authority, rebirth, cremation, child marriage, rejection of widow remarriage and acceptance of brāhmaṇa priesthood, instituting instead his own priesthood called Jangama. Basava famously arranged a marriage between a brāhmaṇa boy and an untouchable girl which caused much commotion. The sect has now moved closer to main line Hinduism but continues to exist as a distinct caste-cum-community, constituting 20 per cent of the population of the state of Karnataka. (Also see Vīraśaivism.)

49. Bhagavad-Gītā

The word, which translates in English as "the Lord's song", is the name of the most popular scriptural text in Hinduism. The entire text, in fairly simple Sanskrit, consists of 700 verses and can be read in two hours. It is in the form of a dialogue between the warrior, Arjuna, and his charioteer, Kṛṣṇa, which takes place on the eve of the battle of Mahābhārata. Arjuna suddenly becomes reluctant to engage in combat upon seeing his kinsmen in the armies arrayed for battle, and this leads to a question and answer session at the end of which Arjuna sheds his reservations and proceeds to fight and win. Kṛṣṇa came to be regarded as an incarnation of God within the Hindu tradition, and this fact lends divine potency to his words uttered on this occasion. This is one reason why the text is considered sacred — it is the word of God to man, or human beings, in the form of Arjuna. Another factor which adds to the value of the text is the fact that Arjuna covers a lot of moral and metaphysical ground in the questions he asks, so that the text ends up as offering a summary statement of the Hindu world-view. A third factor which enhances the value of the text is the fact that a number of commentaries have been written on it and continue to be written. One reason underlying this could be that every major thinker felt compelled to demonstrate that his views were consistent with the text, given its immense popularity, although in doing so they often make the text agree with them rather than necessarily making themselves agree with the text. Finally, the text is important for modern Hinduism because its teachings can be interpreted as quite consistent with modernity and indeed have been so interpreted.

The best known classical commentaries on it are by Śaṅkara, Rāmānuja and Madhva; the best known modern commentators on it are B.G. Tilak, Mahatma Gandhi and Sri Aurobindo. An exegetical feature of the text deserves special recognition. In trying to rouse Arjuna to his feet, Kṛṣṇa discusses soteriological possibilities which have typically been reduced to the trichotomy of the path (*yoga*) of knowledge (called *jñāna*); the path (*yoga*) of devotion (called *bhakti*); and the path (*yoga*) of action (called *karma*). Commentators have long debated the message of the *Bhagavad-Gītā*, as it the case with the scriptures of many religions, and all of these three *yoga*s have been identified as its ultimate message. It is possible to argue that in the hermeneutical tradition associated with the *Bhagavad-Gītā*, perhaps the exegetical tradition associated with it on the whole tended to favour the orientation towards *jñāna* during ancient India, towards *bhakti* during medieval India and towards *karma* in modern India — although a credible case can be made out for all three, and even for combining them, on the basis of the text.

50. Bhakta

(See Bhakti movement.)

51. Bhakti

The word used to denote loving devotion to God in Hinduism, signs of which are already present in the *Ṛg-Veda* although the word as such occurs for the first time in the *Śvetāśvatara Upaniṣad* (6.23). It has always been the most popular and visible form of religiosity in India, although one among the several *yoga*s or paths within Hinduism, along with knowledge (*jñāna*) and action (*karma*), with which it is often combined.

52. Bhakti Movement

The name given to the movement characterized by an ecstatic devotion to God, often bursting out in poetry, which arose in the Tamil Nadu from around seventh century and then gradually spread over the rest of India, to become the chief characteristic of Hindu religiosity during medieval times. It tended to transcend the limits of caste and even religion and employed the various regional languages of India rather than Sanskrit as its linguistic medium. A central figure in its movement from the south to north India is Rāmānanda (fourteenth/fifteenth century). Its eminent figures are often referred to as *santas* (saints) or *bhaktas* (devotees).

53. Bhāmatī School of Advaita Vedānta

Bhāmatī is the name of a commentary, on Śaṅkara's commentary on the *Brahma-Sūtra* by Vācaspati Miśra (ninth century), so called, according to tradition, to honour his wife who bore that name. Another important scholar in this sub-tradition of Advaita Vedānta is Amalānanda (thirteenth century), whose *Vedānta-Kalpataru* is a commentary on the *Bhāmatī*. There are two commentaries on Amalānanda's commentary in turn: *Kaplataru-Parimala* by Appaya Dīkṣita (1550) and *Ābhoga* by Lakṣmī-Nṛsiṁha (seventeenth century), who has a gift for offering felicitous illustrations: the Vedas, though part of *māyā*, could still point to *Brahman*, as a snake drawn on a board, while illusory, can still convey an impression of the real snake.

Bhāmatī is one of the two major schools of post-Śaṅkara Advaita; the other is known as *Vivaraṇa*, whose origin is traced, through the *Pañcapādikā-Vivaraṇa* of Prakāśātmā, to Padmapāda, as it is a commentary on the *Pañcapādikā* of Padmapāda (*c.* 800), which is itself a commentary on Śaṅkara'a commentary on the *Brahma-sūtra*.

The concise nature of Śaṅkara's commentary on the *Brahma-Sūtra* led to this bifurcation of the Advaita tradition into these two schools, as his successors tried to develop his ideas further and differences of opinion emerged on such issues as:

1. What is the locus of *avidyā* (nescience)?: Is it the *jīva* (empirical self) or *Brahman*? *Bhāmatī* tended to favour the former option, *Vivaraṇa* the latter.
2. How is the nature of the relationship of *Brahman* to the *jīva* to be explained? Is it best explained on the model of Avacchedavāda — or the doctrine that the unlimited appears as the limited, just as one might consider space limited to a pot, (as pot-space), instead of considering it infinite; or is it best explained on the model of Pratibimbavāda — or the doctrine that the *jīva* is a reflection of *Brahman*, just as the one sun might appear as many when reflected in many water pots?
3. Is merely *śravaṇa* (audition) of the truth enough to trigger realization or must *Śravaṇa* be supplemented by *manana* (cogitation) and *nididhyāsana* (meditation). These and similar issues became matters of continuous debate in post-Śaṅkara Advaita. (Also see Vivaraṇa School of Advaita Vedānta.)

54. Bhedābheda

The doctrine that both identity and difference may coexist in the ultimate reality (*Brahman*), which in the state of the manifestation of the universe, is characterized by difference (*bheda*) but, which, when the universe is resolved back into it, is characterized by identity (*abheda*). This was an important strand in Hindu thought prior to the emergence of Advaita Vedānta. The rise of Advaita Vedānta had the effect of orienting Hindu thought more towards identity in general (see Identity). Treated as a general concept, rather than as a specific position, the expression is useful on account of its versatility, as it captures the gamut of possible relationships between identity and difference, a negotiation which lies as at the heart of Hinduism. One could thus place both on the same footing, or prioritize *bheda* (difference) over *abheda* (identity) or vice versa, or read various shades of degrees of difference-in-identity or identity-in-difference. The expression *bhedābheda* can semantically embrace all these possibilities.

The term could thus be used to encapsulate the various relationships posited between the individual self (*jīva*) and the ultimate reality (or *Brahman*). For instance, Śaṅkara believes in the absolute identity of the two (Advaita); Madhva in their absolute difference (Dvaita), and according to Rāmānuja the two are related as part and whole (Viśiṣṭādvaita). These, and various other views on the nature of the relationship, could be presented in terms of *bhedābheda*. Śaṅkara, for example, emphasizes one kind of identity (*abheda*); Madhva one kind of difference (*bheda*) and Rāmānuja one kind of identity-in-difference (*bhedābheda*). (Also see Advaita Vedānta; Viśiṣṭādvaita Vedānta and Dvaita Vedānta.)

55. Bhīmbeṭkā

The name of a site known for its pre-historic cave paintings in central India, 45 km south of Bhopal, dated *c*. 30,000 BCE.

56. Bhrama

Advaita Vedānta differentiates between two kinds of *bhramas* (illusions): *nirupādhika* (or without adjuncts) and *sopādhika* (or with adjuncts). When, in an illusion, something is taken as given which is not given at all, then it is called *nirupādhika bhrama*. The stock example here is the mistaking of a rope for a snake. A hallmark of this form of illusion is that when a rope is recognized as a rope, the illusory snake vanishes completely. When, however, someone takes as given only a feature of something which is not given, then the illusion is called *sopādhika bhrama*. The stock example here is a person with jaundice looking at a white shell, which appears yellow to him. When the illusion is removed, the shell remains as it is, but it ceases to appear yellow. The importance of the distinction between these two forms of illusion lies in the fact that Advaita Vedānta explains the world as an illusory appearance of *Brahman* along the lines of the first, and the appearance of the *jīva*, as an illusory manifestation of *Brahman*, along the lines of the second. (Also see Advaita Vedānta.)

57. Birthdays

The birthdays of the two primary incarnations of Viṣṇu — Rāma and Kṛṣṇa — are celebrated with much of enthusiasm. Similarly each *sampradāya* may celebrate the birthday of its founder *ācārya* and other famous *ācāryas*. There is some evidence to suggest that the birthdays of children were also celebrated in ancient India.

58. Body–Mind Relationship

It is a matter of common observation that body and mind are empirically implicated; when the mind is disturbed the body becomes restless; and when the body is relaxed the mind also feels at ease. The equation works both ways. Three "limbs" of *yoga* — *āsana*, *prāṇāyāma* and *pratyāhāra* — utilize this connection, using the body to produce a particular effect on the mind. *Āsana* uses posture for this purpose; when the body is relaxed the mind becomes calm. *Prāṇāyāma* uses breath for this purpose; the slowing down of breathing stills the mind. *Pratyāhāra* withdraws the mind from the field of sensory inputs, to induce meditative states. When the mind is absorbed, it becomes indifferent to physical sensory inputs. One could also use the mind as the point of intervention to affect physical consciousness. Thus controlling the mind puts the body in a set position, steadies breathing and induces detachment from the senses. (Also see Yoga.)

59. Brahma Kumaris

This sect traces itself to their Guru Lekhraj (1876–1969), a jeweller in the city of Hyderabad now in Pakistan. He developed an apocalyptic vision of the world from which one could be saved through purification, which involved vegetarianism, abstention from tobacco and alcohol, the practice of *yoga*, and the observance of celibacy. He established the Brahma Kumari sect in 1936 around these teachings, but had to relocate to Karachi because of the tensions caused by his teaching that even married couples should observe celibacy, which is reserved in main line Hinduism for monks. After Partition in 1947, he relocated to Mount Abu, which remains the international headquarters of the movement. The movement is build around *rāja-yoga* centres, where one is taught to mediate with eyes open, and is led largely by women, as its name would suggest. It thus invokes that dimension of Hinduism which is associated with the power of Śakti. Although drawing on many Hindu concepts and divinities, it disowns the label "Hindu", although considered so by others. It is international in character, and collaborates with the UN. In 1997 it had 4,000 centres (most of them in India), run by 8,000 priests, and a membership of 500,000.

60. Brahmabandhav Upadhyay (1861–1907)

Hindu convert to Christianity in the nineteenth century, who remained culturally a Hindu and favoured the use of Hindu rites in Christian worship.

61. Brahman: Nirguṇa and Saguṇa

If there is an ultimate reality, is it more like a principle, something impersonal, for which philosophers might use the word Absolute, or more like a person, for which theologians often use the word god? This is the point at stake in the description of *Brahman*, the ultimate reality as *nirguṇa* (without distinguishing attributes) in keeping with orientation represented by the word Absolute or as *saguṇa* (with distinguishing attributes) in keeping with the orientation represented by the word god. This distinction is formalized in Advaita Vedānta in the two ways in which the ultimate reality may be defined: as it is by itself (*svarūpa-lakṣaṇa*) or as it is in relation to the world (*taṭastha-lakṣaṇa*). According to the system of Advaita Vedānta, the ultimate reality by itself is more like an Absolute but assumes the form of God in relation to the world. In doing so, however, it loses its absolute character. It then becomes less than ultimately real, and turns into the penultimate real, a view not shared by other schools of Vedānta.

62. Brāhmaṇas

Also spelled brahmins, the brāhmaṇas constitute the priestly class in Hinduism and serve as a legitimizing authority specially in ritual matters but yield to saints as the generating-centres of Hinduism, especially where spirituality is involved. They are the self-conscious custodians of the tradition and therefore bear the blame or share the credit for its failures and successes. The *brāhmaṇas* represented the religious elite of India. Estimates of their proportion in the population vary from 4 to 8 per cent, the ratio being lower in the south than in the north, and lower in the north than in the north-west and hilly regions. They have a long history of going into secular pursuits, thereby raising the question of whether secular *brāhmaṇas* were entitled to privileges accorded to practising *brāhmaṇas*, a point of issue already by the time of the *Manu-Smṛti*. They also began to participate in politics directly; one hears of *brāhmaṇa* armies already in the fourth century BCE and *brāhmaṇa* dynasties by the second century BCE, such as the Śuṅga. The rise of the Peśwās in Marāṭhā history is a modern example of this trend. On account of being professionally literate, thorough in religious literature and ritual, they made a quicker transition to English education than many other groups and consequently occupied a disproportionately large number of jobs in the colonial administration, by one estimate holding 50 per cent of all elite jobs at one time. This probably accounts as much for the sentiment against them in some parts of the country, such as Maharashtra and Tamil Nadu, as the hyperbolically exalted status accorded to them in many texts, which needs to be reconciled with the fact that two grand narratives of the tradition, as embodied in the Vedas and the *Rāmāyaṇa* involve the slaying of a *brāhmaṇa* (of Vṛtra by Indra and Rāvaṇa by Rāma). (Also see Caste, Varṇa.)

63. Bṛndāban Holī

Holī is a popular spring festival in the north, celebrated in the month of Phālguna (February–March) but Holī in Bṛndāban (or Bṛndāvan of Vṛndāvana) has a special quality, where it is associated with Kṛṣṇa as the child-trickster. For about three days, the prevailing hierarchies of caste and gender are suspended, and even reversed, and people spend time in making merry, by dousing each other with coloured liquids or just spraying each other with colour. In keeping with this mood, the festival is characterized by the consumption of hashish (*bhāṅga*), which further adds to the consciousness-altering character of the event.

64. Caitanya (1486–1533)

Caitanya or Caitanya is a major figure of medieval Hinduism, whose legacy is carried forward in modern times by groups such as the International Society for Krishna Consciousness (ISKON). Caitanya was born in a traditional Bengali Brāhmaṇa family and had a conventional education. His visit to Gayā in 1508 to perform the *śrāddha* (memorial service) for his father proved consequential. There he underwent what is best described in modern terms as a "conversion experience", as a result of encountering a renunciant from south India, after which he began worshipping Kṛṣṇa vigorously in the open. He took *saṁnyāsa* in 1510 and began living at Purī, famous for the Jagannātha Temple where the wooden icons of Kṛṣṇa and his siblings are worshipped. He had a confrontation with the Qāẓī in Navadvīpa, when he objected to Caitanya's passion for public chanting and it has been suggested that political reasons may be a factor behind his moving to Orissa from Bengal. He is said to have died by drowning in the sea during one of his ecstasies. He popularized singing in public as an act of devotion and his followers believe that Kṛṣṇa incarnated himself as Caitanya to experience Rādhā's devotion. (Also see Acintya-Bhedābheda.)

65. Caste

A term originally used by the Portuguese (*casta*) to describe the various distinct social groups they found in India, which was subsequently used to describe the social reality of India. The term is used to cover two distinct but related concepts of *varṇa* (class) and *jāti* (caste proper). Early texts refer to the four classes of:

1. Brāhmaṇas: priests and the intellectuals;
2. Kṣatriyas: rulers, warriors and bureaucrats;
3. Vaiśyas: merchants and cultivators; and
4. Śūdras: workers, including menial workers.

Post-Vedic texts, called the Dharmaśāstras, speak of *jātis*, or social groups inter-dining and marrying among themselves, often associated with a particular craft. The number of *jātis* varies across history, but the four *varṇas* constitute a stable category. The so-called caste system combines these two features, by notionally allotting each *jāti* to a *varṇa*, and by tying the birth in one's *jāti* to the doctrine of *karma*, with birth in a natal group serving an index of the quality of one's past *karma*. (Also see Jāti and Varṇa.)

66. Cat Logic and Monkey Logic

These terms, *mārjāra-nyāya* or *markaṭa-nyāya* in the original, have to do with the role of God's grace in the economy of salvation, and particularly with the role of human effort in facilitating the reception of grace. Two schools emerged on this point in Śrīvaiṣṇavism — one which emphasized total surrender to God, without any reliance whatever on human effort, and another which, while relying on surrender to God, admitted of some human role in the process. The former school adopts the position called Cat Logic: When the cat moves her kitten, she does so by lifting them entirely by herself, the kitten helplessly going along with her. This corresponds to the theological position in which the devotee relies wholly and solely on God. The latter school adopts the position called Monkey Logic: When the mother monkey leaps from branch to branch she carries the young one along with her, but the young one has to cling to her underside. The correspondence of these doctrines to the Augustinian and Pelagian positions on grace in Christianity have often been noted. (Also see Viśiṣṭādvaita Vedānta.)

67. Classical Hinduism

The form Vedic Hinduism assumed, after interacting with the non-orthodox traditions of Buddhism and Jainism, a process which produced a vast synthesis which ultimately found a place for much of Buddhism and Jainism within Hinduism, as also for the various regional and popular manifestations of religiosity on the continent. This synthesis had come to embrace the whole of India by *c.* 1200. (Also see Hinduism: Chronology.)

68. Dakṣiṇā

A word ranging in meaning from fees to donation, with the underlying sense of renumeration in some form for services rendered, these services being religious or spiritual in nature.

69. Darśana

The word has several connotations in Hinduism. It could mean a school of philosophy, as representing an insight into reality, or a world-view. See *Ṣaḍdarśana* for more on this. In popular, as distinguished from philosophical usage, it is used to denote visual interaction of a religious nature with an image or a person. Thus one has the *darśana* of an image in a temple, of one's *guru* or of a holy figure. Perhaps this sense harks back to the use of the phenomenon of sight to indicate a profounder grasp of reality as in "I see" or "the scales fell from my eyes", with the further implication that there may be more to an encounter with a holy person or object than meets the eye.

70. Darśana Literature

The various schools of Indian philosophy are called *darśana*s and are usually listed as:

1. Cārvāka or Lokāyata;
2. Jaina;
3. Bauddha;
4. Nyāya;

5. Vaiśeṣika;
6. Sāṁkhya;
7. Yoga;
8. Mīmāṁsā; and
9. Vedānta.

No systematic work on materialism exists and information about it has be culled from secondary sources. The Jaina school contains several texts in Prākṛta, but the one text which both the Digambara and Śvetāmbara schools of Jaina accept is the *Tattvārtha-Sūtra* (also known as *Tattvārthādhigama-Sūtra*) of Umāsvāti, also known as Umāsvāmī. The Buddhist schools in general go back to the Tripiṭakas (Three Baskets) consisting of the Vinaya, the Sutta and the Abhidhamma, the latter two being particularly relevant, specially the last. The various different Buddhist philosophical schools, as distinguished from Buddhism in general, have their own individual foundational texts. As the schools of philosophy developed, their teachings came to be formulated in aphorisms called *sūtras* (literally threads), with their authors being referred to as *sūtrakāras*. This is particularly true of the *āstika* schools of Indian philosophy (also referred to as the Hindu schools), although we noticed above that the Jaina tradition did produce one. The teachings of Nyāya were formulated by Gautama in the *Nyāya-Sūtra*; of Vaiśeṣika by Kaṇāda in the *Vaiśeṣika-Sūtra*; of Sāṁkhya by Īśvarakṛṣṇa in the *Sāṁkhya-Kārikā* (in an exception to the general rule, although a later *Sāṁkhyapravacana-Sūtra* does exist); of *yoga* by Patañjali in the *Yoga-Sūtra*; of Mīmāṁsā by Jaimini in the *Mīmāṁsā-Sūtra* and of Vedānta by Bādarāyaṇa in the *Vedānta-Sūtra* (also known as the *Brahma-Sūtra*). This *sūtra* stage in the evolution of philosophical literature in Hinduism was followed by the *bhāṣya* (commentary) stage. The aphorisms tended to be terse to the point of being opaque, so scholars and savants wrote commentaries on them to unfold their meaning. These works were also supplemented by various manuals on the systems, such as the

Aṇṇambhaṭṭa's *Tarka-Saṁgraha*, a seventeenth-century text which deals with Nyāya, or Āpadeva's *Mīmāṁsā-Nyāya-Prakāśa* also known as Āpadevī (seventeenth century). These may be said to represent a third stage, after the *sūtra* and the *bhāṣya*, in the sense that although such manuals may date from a time when the *bhāṣya* was the main style of philosophical writing, there was a gradual shift in this direction, which may be referred to as the *grantha* (book) stage, when the system is either treated comprehensively, or one aspect of it is explored in book form. Those books which deal with a part of the main topic were called *prakaraṇa granthas* and those which dealt with the system, *ākara granthas*. (Also see Darśanas.)

71. Darśanas: The Schools of Indian Philosophy

From around fourth century BCE onwards, the philosophical tradition of India began to crystallize into distinct schools, each with its own text and philosophical viewpoint, which came to be called *darśanas*. By the eighth century, these had been formalized into the "Six Schools", as illustrated by the *Ṣaḍdarśana-Samuccaya* (a Compendium of Six Schools) of the Jaina scholar, Haribhadra. The figure of "six" however is accounted for in different ways in the doxographies. The entire range of Indian philosophical schools is represented by:

1. Lokāyata;
2. Jaina;
3. Buddha;
4. Nyāya;
5. Vaiśeṣika;
6. Sāṁkhya;
7. Yoga;
8. Mīmāṁsā; and
9. Vedānta.

These are then classified into *nāstika* (non-orthodox) and

āstika (orthodox) schools, depending on whether they do not acknowledge, or acknowledge, Vedic authority. By this criterion, the first three schools are considered *nāstika* and the last six *āstika* (orthodox). These nine schools represent the philosophical spectrum of India but number is sometimes compressed to six by enumerating the *nāstika* schools as such, but hyphenating the *āstika* schools, as follows:

1. Lokāyata (or Cārvāka);
2. Jaina;
3. Buddha;
4. Nyāya-Vaiśeṣika;
5. Sāṁkhya-Yoga;
6. Mīmāṁsā-Vedānta.

Texts also speak of a set of six *nāstika* schools, as follows:

1. Lokāyata;
2. Jaina;
3. Vaibhāṣika;
4. Sautrāntika;
5. Mādhyamika; and
6. Yogācāra.

The last four in the above list are distinct schools of Buddhist philosophy. The foil to these is then provided by a list of six *āstika* schools:

1. Nyāya;
2. Vaiśeṣika;
3. Sāṁkhya;
4. Yoga;
5. Mīmāṁsā; and
6. Vedānta.

This latter list has now become standard in the field as representing the six schools of Hindu philosophy. (Also see Darśana Literature.)

72. Dāsa

People mentioned in the *Ṛg-Veda* as the opponents of the Aryans, along with the *dasyus*, although the Aryans seem to be less hostile towards the *dāsas* compared to the *dasyus*. According to Asko Parpola, they represent a group of Indo-European speakers who preceded the appearance of the Aryans in India, which may help explain this friendlier attitude. (Also see Asko Parpola.)

73. Dayananda Sarasvati (1824-83)

A major Hindu reformer of the nineteenth century. Dayananda Sarasvati was active in western India, just as Raja Rammohun Roy was in Bengal. Unlike Roy, Dayananda Sarasvati did not know English but arrived at a comparable theological and social agenda through indigenous inspiration, based on the acceptance of Vedic authority. He however did not assign so much privilege to the last portions of the Vedas (as is done in Vedānta), but rather to the earlier Mantra or Saṁhitā portion. According to him, the Vedas preached monotheism, which had been compromised by an idolatry and the polytheism he associated with Purāṇic Hinduism, and which he rejected. Hence his call to harken back to the Vedas, which were free of any reference to child marriage, untouchability and mistreatment of women — practices he vigorously denounced. Even as he promoted the reform of Hinduism, he defended it against attacks by Islamic and Christian missions and also criticized these religions in his magnum opus, the *Satyārtha-Prakāśa*. He also simplified Hindu liturgy, and was more innovative than many other reform movements in making room for converts to Hinduism through the process of *śuddhi* (purification). He was also politically more opposed to British rule than either Roy or Vivekananda and was trying to build support for this position among the princely rulers of Rajasthan, when he was poisoned by a mistress, whose association with a ruler he had denounced. The Arya Samaj, which he founded, has therefore been politically more influential than the many other contemporary reform movements. Dayananda Sarasvati has been called the Luther of modern India, if Roy has been called its father. Arya Samaj also spread beyond the borders of India.

74. Devadāsī

The word literally means "woman who is the servant or slave of God" and actually referred to the women who traditionally danced in the temples in honour of the deity. Modern reformers tended to view it as a form of temple prostitution and ensured its abolition, but modern scholarship encourages a more nuanced view of the institution. That some aspects of it were considered morally ambiguous as early as the eleventh century, and that its introduction was resisted is clear from Al-Bīrūnī's testimony.

75. Devas

The word literally means "the shining ones" and refers to the various gods of the Hindu pantheon, especially of the Ṛg-Vedic pantheon.

76. Dharma

The closest etymological equivalent of this word in English is the word "form" (best understood perhaps as in Emile Durkheim's *Elementary Forms of Religious Life*), although the closest modern semantic equivalent to it is the word "religion", and the conceptual equivalent "a way of life". Thus it exceeds the word religion in its semantic range, a whole world being lost in its translation as religion. It is derived from the word *dhṛ*, which means "to uphold", and thus pertains to what makes a thing what it is, and points to the law of its being. It is variously classified into *varṇa-dharma* (duties of class); *āśrama-dharma* (duties of stages of life); *varṇāśrama-dharma* (combined duties of both, an expression sometimes used to stand for Hinduism itself, as characterized by these two institutions); *sādhāraṇa-dharma* (or duties common to all classes in all stages of life); *naimittika-dharma* (such as rites of atonement or *prāyaścitta*) and *guṇa-dharma* (bounden duty, whether formally assigned to one or not, as the duty of a king to protect, whether kṣatriya or not).

77. Dharma and Mokṣa

The tension between these two values has been much debated by outsiders but is perhaps not felt that keenly by the Hindus themselves. The Western scholars contrast the social orientation of the former with the soteriological orientation of the latter, but this may reflect a Western dichotomization. They emphasize this contrast through the category of *saṁnyāsa*, which represents the abandonment of the social for the sake of the soteriological. The two orientations differ but their divergence can be overemphasized, if the role of *dharma* as a mediating category between *varṇāśrama-dharma* and *saṁnyāsa* is overlooked. *Dharma* regulates *artha* and *kāma*, the primary orientations of worldly life as represented by the life of the householder, and, in the form of *sādhāraṇa-dharma*, lays the moral foundation for the pursuit of *mokṣa*. Thus it mediates these two realms. Similarly, the very definition of *dharma* recognizes both *abhyudaya* (well-being in the world) and *niḥśreyasa* (the achievement of *mokṣa*) as its goals. The confusion seems to have arisen by mixing the categories of the *puruṣārthas* with that of the *āśramas*.

78. Dharmabhūta-Jñāna

"Attributive knowledge", a concept associated with Viśiṣṭādvaita Vedānta. Usually the soul (*jīva*) in Hindu thought is described as possessing consciousness or knowledge; here the idea is refined into describing it as an entity which both "is and has knowledge". As knowledge it is invariable, but the knowledge it has is variable. Knowledge could thus be considered both as its essence and as its attribute, and attributive knowledge can change. Such knowledge is possessed by both souls and God and is inseparable from them. It is all-pervading in the case of God, which explains his omniscience; in the case of the *jīvas* it is contracted and requires external aids, like the organs of sense, for its operation, but expands to the full when the *jīva* is liberated. (Also see Viśiṣṭādvaita Vedānta.)

79. Dharmaśāstra

The general name for the body of Hindu literature devoted to the study of *dharma* or the normative lifestyle. It comprises three genres of literature — the Dharmasūtras, the Smṛtis and the Nibandhas. Sometimes the word *dharmaśāstra* is used in a narrower sense, as referring to the Smṛtis alone.

80. Diwālī

The Hindu calendar has two new years, one starting with the vernal equinox and other with the autumnal equinox. In terms of this description, the Hindu calendar year commences with the vernal equinox and the financial year with the autumnal equinox, in the sense that shopkeepers do their annual accounting and stocktaking around this time of Diwālī, and worship Goddess Lakṣmī for prosperity in the coming year. The kind of lighting associated with Christmas in the West is a special feature of the festival which is also called Deepāvalī. Families visit each other, hotels celebrate Diwālī nights, and even Diwālī cards have made their appearance. (Also see Hindu Calendar.)

81. Doordarshan

This neologism for the English word television, by which the official TV broadcasting system in India is known. Its relevance to modern Hinduism lies in the fact that in 1987 it began televising the epic *Rāmāyaṇa*, as presented by Ramananda Sagar. It was a sensational success. It has even been suggested that it contributed to the rise of the Ramjanmabhumi movement. This weekly one-hour Sunday morning serial was watched by an estimated 80 million people, on approximately 94 per cent of all TV sets in India. Meetings, even train schedules, were adjusted to facilitate its viewing and in some homes and parts of India watching it became tantamount to religious viewing (*darśana*), with people sometimes even bathing in preparation of the show and turning the set into a shrine. The epic, in being broadcast through a new medium, produced unexpected consequences. The original series was intended to end with the triumphal return of Rāma to Ayodhyā after vanquishing Rāvaṇa (which ushers Rāma-Rājya or the golden rule of Rāma) but it had to be extended when the sweepers in Delhi, whose patron saint is Vālmīki, went on strike in protest against the exclusion of that part of the epic which deals with Vālmīki and his rescue of the pregnant Sītā, after she had been abandoned by a scandalized Rāma. The *Mahābhārata*, the second national epic, so to say, was also subsequently televised with comparable success. (Also see *Mahābhārata*, *Rāmāyaṇa*.)

82. Dṛṣṭi: Pāramārthika and Vyāvahārika

Śaṅkara illustrates the difference between the two viewpoints (*dṛṣṭi*) — the ultimate or absolutistic (*pāramārthika*) and the empirical or relative (*vyāvahārika*) with the help of the example of an actor (*naṭa*). If a shepherd plays the role of a king in a play, then from the (relative) standpoint of the play he is a king who marches and conquers but from (absolutistic) standpoint of who he is by himself, he is a shepherd. Moreover, the two standpoints do not mean that there are two *Brahmans*, the absolutistic (*nirguṇa*) and the theistic (*saguṇa*) constitute different realities, no more than the actor on the stage and off the stage are two different people. This doctrine of two standpoints is not as much removed from the real world as one might initially imagine, because we live it everyday: a currency note from one standpoint is merely paper, from another worth the amount printed on it. Similarly, from an absolute point of view the earth goes round the sun, but from a relative point of view the sun goes round the earth. (Also see Advaita Vedānta.)

83. Durgā

Durgā is one form of Śakti, specially celebrated in the *Devī-Māhātmya* section of the *Mārkaṇḍeya Purāṇa* (*c.* fifth century), also known as *Durgā-Saptaśatī* (seven hundred verses of Durgā). This also happens to be the number of verses in the *Bhagavad-Gītā* and the two texts are quite popular in Hinduism.

The *Durgā-Saptaśatī* contains four important cycles of myths. The most important of these is the slaying of the buffalo-demon, on account of which Goddess is known as Mahiṣāsuramardinī. The buffalo-demon earned from Brahmā the boon that no male would be able to kill him; a female was not mentioned probably because the demon did not expect any danger from this quarter. Armed with this boon, the demon went on such a rampage that even Indra had to seek refuge with the gods of the Hindu trinity — Brahmā, Viṣṇu and Śiva. Finally, the combined energies of the gods assumed the form of a beautiful woman, whom the gods supplied with arms and other accoutrements. The buffalo-demon, on hearing the commotion caused by this event in heaven, send his armsmen to inquire into the matter, and upon hearing of her great beauty from them the demon send a marriage proposal to her, which she spurned. A second proposal, made in person, met with the same fate. The Goddess revealed that her role was to protect the righteous. In the ensuing battle, the buffalo-demon, a shape-shifter, assumed many forms but was finally beheaded as he was emerging in a human form from the buffalo. The gods hailed the victory, and the Goddess promised her help whenever necessary.

The other three cycles of myths are shorter:

1. In Vaiṣṇava accounts, Viṣṇu is often depicted asleep on the cosmic ocean, with Brahmā sitting on a lotus emerging from his navel. Two demons attack Brahmā but he is saved in these accounts by an awakened Viṣṇu. In the *Devī-Māhātmya* version, Viṣṇu's sleep is depicted as *yoganidrā* (meditative sleep), which is an embodiment of the power of the Goddess, whose intercession is required to secure a favourable outcome.

2. In another myth, two other demons, Śumbha and Niśumbha attack the goddess on another occasion but Kālī emerges from Durgā's forehead and makes short work of them.

3. In another cycle, seven little mothers, called Saptamātṛkās, emerge from the Goddess but a demon by the name of Raktabīja (blood seed) attacks them. He clones himself, as drops of his blood fall on the earth, so the Goddess Cāmuṇḍā appears from the furrowed brow of Durgā, and slurps up all the blood before it can hit the ground. These myths also explains how the Goddess acquired the names of Durgā, Kālī and Cāmuṇḍā. (Also see Mahādevī.)

84. Durgā-Pūjā

A rite of Daśahar, which involves making animal sacrifices made to the Goddess. It coincides with the rice harvests and elements of ecological balance may be involved, for this is time for culling, as otherwise the rice paddies may not be safe from wanton animal depredation. (Also see Durgā.)

85. Dvaita Vedānta

This system of Vedānta, formulated by Madhva (1199–1278), may be described as theistic, dualistic and pluralistic. It is theistic because it accepts Viṣṇu-Nārāyaṇa as the ultimate reality, it is dualistic because it is not monistic either in its absolute or qualified versions and it is pluralistic because the concept of difference (*bheda*) is central to its formulations, as recognized in the popular statement: "the things in the world are diverse and possess diverse properties" (*bhinnāśca bhinnadharmāśca padārtha nikhilā amī*). Śaṅkara's Advaita transcends difference and Rāmānuja's speaks of three ultimate entities, but Madhva posits a set of five crucial differences:

1. between God and soul;
2. between soul and soul;
3. between God and matter;
4. between soul and matter; and
5. between one material thing and another.

As in Rāmānuja's system, while God, the souls and the world are all eternal, God alone is totally independent. The souls and matter are entirely dependent on God and would collapse if his grace were withdrawn, so that the sovereignty of God is asserted with almost Islamic severity. Again, like Rāmānuja, God possesses various forms (*vyūha*), incarnates himself periodically (*avatāras*) and is present in the image (*arcā*). There is however one important difference between the systems of Rāmānuja and Madhva. According to the former, God is both the material (*upādāna*) and the efficient (*nimitta*) cause of the universe, but according to Madhva he is the efficient but not the material cause of the universe. The universe is neither an apparent manifestation of *Brahman* (*vivarta*), nor is it an actual transformation (*pariṇāma*). While ruling out these two versions of Satkāryavāda, Madhva propounds his own doctrine of Sadasatkārya-vāda, or the doctrine that the effect is both existent and non-existent in the cause. Before production, it exists as the cause but not the effect, and after production it exists as effect, and no longer as cause, so it is "both existent and non-existent". *Prakṛti* or matter is the material cause of the world. As for the *jīvas* they are many, atomic and eternal, and are classified into:

1. *nitya* (or eternal): those eternally free, like Lakṣmī;
2. *mukta* (or liberated): those now free; and
3. *baddha* (or bound).

This last category consists of:

1. those who are eligible for liberation (*mukti-yogya*); and
2. those who are not.

Those who are not eligible may wander forever in *saṁsāra* (*nitya-saṁsārīs*) or may be destined for "blinding darkness" (*tama-yogya*). Thus the Dvaita, unlike many other systems of Hindu thought, believes in eternal damnation. One is saved by the knowledge on one's dependence on God, the Supreme Being who alone is the doer (*ekaḥ sarvottamo jñeyaḥ eka eva karoti yat*). This knowledge generates love of God, by which one is saved. Even in heaven, however, the difference between the *jīvas* persists. A statement attributed to

Vyāsatīrtha but not found in any of his existing works, summarizes the system of Madhva as follows:

> In Śrī Madhva's system, Hari is the Supreme Being, the world is real, difference is true, the host of *jīvas* are dependent on Hari, there are grades of superiority and inferiority among them, *mokṣa* consists of the soul's enjoyment of its innate bliss, faultless *bhakti* is the means thereto, perception, inference and verbal testimony are the three ways of knowing (*pramāṇas*), and Hari is knowable only through the Vedas.

(Also see Madhva.)

86. Dvaitādvaita Vedānta

"Dualistic-cum-non-dualistic", a school of Vedānta associated with Nimbārka, who is generally believed to have flourished after Rāmānuja and has been placed in the twelfth century. Although this form of Vedānta may be said to have been formulated by Nimbārka, the Nīmavats, as his followers are called, claim that their *sampradāya* was founded by Viṣṇu himself in his incarnation as the *haṁsa avatāra*. Its centres are found in the region of Mathurā, and in Bengal and Rajasthan. Nimbārka wrote a commentary on the *Brahma-Sūtra* called *Vedānta-Pārijāta-Saurabha* (The Redolence of the Divine Flower of Vedānta) but it is so condensed that it would have been virtually incomprehensible without the lucid commentary on it by his immediate disciple, Śrīnivāsa, called *Vedānta-Kaustubha*. He is also the author of a tract of ten verses called Daśa-Ślokī. In these texts he propounds his basic doctrine of the three eternal realities (*tri-tattva*): *Brahman*, *cit* (soul) and *acit* (matter). *Brahman* is identified here with *Saguṇa* and not *Nirguṇa-Brahman*. *Brahman* is *nirguṇa* because it is free of evil qualities. *Saguṇa-Brahman* is identified with Gopāla-Kṛṣṇa, accompanied by Rādhā. *Cit* and *acit* are powers (*śaktis*) of *Brahman*; the material *cit* proceeds from sentient *Brahman*, just as fire has the power to produce smoke without itself being smoke. *Acit* is composed of three categories:

1. *aprākṛta*: which is not derived from *prakṛti* (nature) and is

hence celestial, as in what celestial bodies are composed of;

2. *prākṛta*: or product of *prakṛti;* and
3. *kāla* (time), a fundamental principle of the cosmos like *prakṛti.*

The *cit* consists of *jīvas* who are infinite in number and of two kinds: bound (*baddha*) or free (*mukta*). They are atomic in size and essentially sentient, i.e. wholly non-material (*ajaḍa*). The *jīva* is conscious as well as has consciousness, a position similar to that of Rāmānuja's school. There are five means (*sādhanās*) by which the soul can attain liberation:

1. *karma* (performance) of actions selflessly which purifies the mind and thus leads to liberation but only indirectly as in Advaita Vedānta;
2. *jñāna* (knowledge) of the right relationship between the self and *Brahman*. This *jñāna* subsumes *bhakti*;
3. *upāsanā* (meditation), which in this system is not identical with *bhakti* as in the school of Rāmānuja but involves an even deeper love of God;
4. *prapatti* (complete self-surrender); and
5. *gurupasatti* (self-surrender to the *guru* rather than God).

All of these five *sādhanās* lead to salvation, either separately or jointly. The *dvijas* are entitled to the first three and everyone for the last two. Those who rely on others follow the first three, others the last two, reminding one of distinction between *tariki* and *jirki* in Zen Buddhism. This system also distinguishes between devotion to God based on his glory (*aiśvarya-pradhāna-bhakti*) or his sweetness (*mādhurya-pradhāna-bhakti*), reminding one of the distinction, in Ibn Arabi's Sufism, between the *jalāla* (majesty) and *jamāla* (beauty) aspects of the divine. The relationship between *Brahman*, *cit* and *acit* is a matter of philosophical reflection in this school as in others. It is emphasized that *Brahman* is the only independent ultimate reality, while the other two are dependent ultimate realities. One way of describing the relationship is to regard *Brahman* as the controller (*niyantā*), *cit* as the subject of experience (*bhoktā*) and *acit* as the object of experience (*bhogya*). But how is the relationship between *Brahman* on the one hand, and *cit* and *acit* on the other to be understood metaphysically? The term used in this school is to describe this relationship is *svābhāvika-bhedābheda* (natural difference and non-difference). The two, *cit* and *acit,* are different from *Brahman* inasmuch as *Brahman* is independent of them, they both have dependent relationship in relation to *Brahman*, and they are also distinct *Brahman* (*paratantrasattā bhāva*). That are not different, inasmuch as they are totally dependent on *Brahman* (*svatantrasattā bhāva*). They are thus both different and non-different from *Brahman* just as a pot is both different and non-different from clay.

87. Dvandva

The word denotes "polarities" whether philosophical or sociological, but even when philosophical their social implication is equally important. One such major polarity is represented by the lifestyles of the householder (*gṛhastha*) and the renunciant (*saṁnyāsī*), and the underlying ideologies. One major Hindu technique of resolving the tension involved in the polarities is by resorting to *krama* (sequence). Thus the tension between the householder and the renunciant lifestyles is diffused by having stage of the householder precede that of the renunciant, in the course of a life. Another such technique is *prādhānya-vyapadeśa* (prioritizing). The major polarities in Hinduism, at the sociological level, are between sacred and profane (*pavitra* and *apavitra*), pure and impure (*śuddha* and *aśuddha*), and auspicious and inauspicious (*maṅgala* and *amaṅgala*). These overlap but not completely. For instance, the inauspicious Ṛg-Vedic Rudra may be sacred. Traditionally a widow could be inauspicious, while leading a pure life; Ganges water around the cremation ground could be sacred and pure but inauspicious. (Also see Dharma and Mokṣa.)

88. Dvija

Dvija (twice born) indicating that one has been initiated into Vedic studies, which is likened to a second birth. The four *varṇas*, in classical and medieval Hinduism, were not on par so far as access to Vedic studies and ritual was concerned. This right was restricted to the male members of the first three *varṇas*: brāhmaṇa, kṣatriya, and vaiśya. The right to be invested with the sacred thread was a ritual manifestation of this right. This concept may be compared to that of the WASP in American society, an acronym coined significantly by a student of Hindu sociology. (Also see Varṇa.)

89. Esotericism

The Hindu religious traditions contain esoteric as well as universalistic elements. The formal restriction of Vedic studies to the male members of the first three *varṇas* in a sense makes the Vedic transmission esoteric, with the Gāyatrī *mantra* being whispered into the ear of the initiate. At the same time, it is important to recognize the distinction between sacred and soteriological knowledge. While the study of the Vedas was thus considered sacred in an esoteric sense, it did not mean that śūdras and women did not have access to liberation. They did not have the right to liberation through *Śruti*, but other texts were available to them. Similarly, while the Tantras did not restrict themselves in terms of class or gender, they also possessed an esoteric dimension, with the *guru* transmitting knowledge to the disciples, who could be drawn from any level of society. (Also see Tantra.)

90. Ezour Vedam

A text used by Voltaire as a source for Indic traditions, which turned out, with "delicious irony", to have been made up by Jesuits, his chief antagonists. (Also see Veda.)

91. Festivals

Festivals could be classified as either celebratory or purificatory. To the celebratory category would then belong the commemoration of the coming of *avatāras*, like Rāma and Kṛṣṇa, but also Narasiṁha. The day Buddha achieved enlightenment is commemorated in Buddhism. Events are similarly celebrated. One in particular is instructive as it explains the 16,000 plus wives of Kṛṣṇa. A demon, Naraka by name, went on a rampage and seized the daughters of gods, men, semi-divine beings and also corralled the celestial nymphs (*apsaras*es), thereby creating a harem of 16,000 plus women for himself. Kṛṣṇa finally killed him and rescued these women, accepting them as his wives to restore their dignity, just as women raped by Pakistani soldiers during the Bangladesh war were given the title of Birāṅganā (brave woman) by Sheik Mujib-ur-Rehman. Festival sanctify points in time, just as temples sanctify points in space, thus facilitating a spatio-temporal view of Hindu sacrality. (Also see Diwālī; Durgā-Pūjā; Nāgapañcamī; Kumbha Melā and Utsava.)

92. Gai Jātrā

This is a festival marked out for honouring the sacred cow, often referred to as "Go Māī" (mother cow). On this day, the cow is garlanded like a living deity and worshipped. Even children dress up as cows in some localities. The gift of a cow, called *godāna*, is considered particularly auspicious in Hinduism, given the sanctity attached to the cow. This is considered the most auspicious day for making the gift either to a brahmaṇa, or for a recently deceased's family member. A controversy arose in India whether the cow is a deity or not and opinions were divided. Those who argued that the cow, though venerated, was not a deity pointed to the fact that there is not a single temple dedicated to the cow. The opposite view was that all the gods are said to reside in various parts of the cow's body. (Also see Sacred Cow.)

93. Gaṇeśa

A popular Hindu God who is propitiated at the beginning of any performance or undertaking on account of his role as the remover of obstacles. He is one of the two sons of Śiva and Pārvatī, and also has a separate cult associated with him.

94. Gaṇeśa's Milk Miracle

On 21 September 1995 word spread across north India that images of Gaṇeśa had begun to drink milk offered to them, creating a major sensation. The phenomenon was also reported from the Hindu diaspora. Then the phenomenon disappeared as suddenly as it had appeared. Although a scientific explanation of the phenomenon was also offered, the believers saw in this event an example of another performation of the thin veil which separates the divine from the mundane world in the Hindu imagination. Many Hindus, however, also saw this as rank superstition and rationalist organizations were formed to expose such charlatanry, harking back to the long-standing strands within Hinduism espousing agnosticism and atheism, which can be traced back to Buddha's age and even earlier. (Also see Gaṇeśa.)

95. Gaṅgā

Along with mountains and temples, rivers often serve as focal points of pilgrimage, and Gaṅgā is one of them, as are its various tributaries in the upper reaches of the Himalayas, such as Alakanandā. The same holds true of the plains where the Yamunā, sacred in itself, merges with the Gaṅgā and also the subterranean Sarasvatī, thus involving a triple infusion of sanctity. This point of triple merger known as the Triveṇī (triple braiding) was important enough in classical Hinduism to be referred to in glowing similes by the famous Sanskrit poet, Kālidāsa. The Gaṅgā is considered divine and its waters have the capacity to sanctify places, wash way the sins, or bad *karmas*. There is also the view that Gaṅgā is in a sense the mother of all rivers, mythically connected with all of them and charging them with its saving power.

96. Gaṅgājala

Gaṅgājala (water of the Ganges) considered to be sacred and potent both salvifically and medicinally, often administered to a dying person.

97. Ganges, Pollution of

One of the issues facing the Hindu community and its leadership is the pollution of the Ganges (Gaṅgā). The Ganges occupies a lofty place in the Hindu imagination literally, figuratively, ritually and mythically. It descends from the high Himalayas, and enjoys the status of a goddess; its waters wash away the sins of the living and the dead, and its descent is supposed to have redeemed the 60,000 relations of Sagar. Nor it is a river of merely holy significance. As it runs like a ribbon through the north Indian plains, it serves as its lifeline, irrigating fields, carrying cargo and so on. Its waters are now in danger of being overwhelmed by waste with the introduction of sewage and factory systems. A major campaign to clean up its waters was announced in 1985 but not much progress has been made.

98. Gauḍapāda

An early exponent of Advaita Vedānta, whom Śaṅkara refers to as the *guru* of his *guru* (*paramaguru*), and placed in the seventh century. His *Māṇḍūkya-Kārikā*, which expounds the small but significant *Māṇḍūkya Upaniṣad*, is regarded as the earliest systematic treatise on Advaita Vedānta available. There is some controversy surrounding the extent to which he was influenced by Buddhism. His form of Advaita Vedānta has been identified as Ajātivāda or the view that nothing really comes into being in the form of the universe because *Brahman* alone really exists, just as on awakening from a dream one might say that nothing in the dream really happened. (Also see Advaita Vedānta; Śaṅkara; and Om.)

99. Gender Studies

Gender studies attempts to retrieve feminine elements in an intellectual discourse which has been dominated by males for ages. This also includes the study of religion, as well the religions themselves, which tend to be male dominated, with the possible exception of Taoism and Tantric Hinduism. The key question raised by feminists is whether religions are androcentric by nature or as a result of historical circumstance, giving another wrinkle to the "nature" vs. "history" debate. Although many forms of Hinduism are heavily patriarchal, it, almost alone among the world's religions, possesses a full-fledged theology alongside a theology, which makes it potentially an interesting tradition to explore in gender studies. There is also the implicit and unresolved debate within Hinduism as to who decides what Hinduism is: the male members of the three higher *varṇa*s, known as the *dvija*s, or all Hindus, including śūdras, the fourth class, and women. It is true that at least formally, the former view has had the upper hand in classical and medieval Hinduism; it is equally true that the debate has been a running one.

100. Ghāṭ

The river bank specially one used for ritual bathing, or for cremation. The *ghāṭ*s on the banks of the Ganges, specially when it flows through Banaras, are particularly well known and even have specific names like Daśāśvamedha or Maṇikarṇikā Ghāṭ. (Also see Gaṅgā.)

101. Gopīs

The term refers collectively to the milkmaids of Vṛndāvana, among whom Kṛṣṇa spent his childhood and adolescence, and with whom he performs the *rāsa-līlā* in which each *gopī* feels that Kṛṣṇa is dancing with her individually. How to interpret such bucolic pastimes of Kṛṣṇa is an issue in Hindu hermeneutics, as in one episode, when he was eight, he stole their clothes while they were bathing, which were returned to them only after they stopped feeling shy and asked for them with upraised hands. They are depicted as abandoning their domestic duties upon hearing Kṛṣṇa's flute in their yearning for him and thus disregarding social constraints. The *Bhāgavata Purāṇa* hints at one special *gopī* who is later identified as Rādhā. The amorous pastimes of Rādhā and Kṛṣṇa are the subject of poetic narration in the *Gīta-Govinda* of Jayadeva (twelfth century). Tradition has interpreted these accounts as an allegory for the soul's longing for God. The *gopīs* symbolize the soul, whose life revolves around God. The significance of the episode of stolen clothes then lies in having to stand stark naked before God, by spiritually baring oneself, and the extramaritality of the *gopīs* is said to represent a world-transgressing longing for God. The ideal devotee then is represented by the *parakīyā nāyikā*, by a wife's love for her paramour, of whom she constantly thinks even while engaged in domestic duties and serving her husband. The perfect devotee similarly performs all the worldly duties, but his or her heart is set on God in the midst of it all. Vallabhācārya treats the accounts of *gopīs* as both real and allegorical. When taken as real, however, it should not be understood as tinged with sensualism but representing extreme devotion. The *rāsa-līlā* is understood allegorically by him to represent Śrutis (Vedic passages) and thus the fact that the *gopīs* enjoy the company of Kṛṣṇa means that God is the purport of the Vedas. Vallabha did much to promote the worship of Kṛṣṇa as Gopījanavallabha (or beloved of the *gopīs*) but when renouncing the world this is what he said standing at the Hanumān Ghāṭ in Banaras.

> My dear fellows! You should always serve the lord to the best of your ability; you should not look upon Lord Kṛṣṇa as an ordinary worldly master; once you become His, He will always take care of you. But if, somehow or other, you forget the Lord — and think of worldly matters, you will fail.

(Also see Kṛṣṇa; and Śuddhādvaita Vedānta.)

102. Great and Little Traditions

A distinction drawn by the anthropologist Robert Redfield (1897–1958) between the textual, philosophical and classical account of a religious tradition and as it is actually practised by the people especially at the village level. This distinction was anticipated in Indian music, as the *mārgī* and *deśī* traditions, or classical and popular traditions. Outsiders tended to analyse Hinduism in terms of the great, pan-India, Brāhmanical tradition and ignored the local and popular until relatively modern times. Sanskritists usually take the global view and tend to see the local as a residue or reflection of global. They may even be prone to emphasizing the global at the expense of the local. Those who espouse the local view are usually anthropologists, who tend to recognize or even emphasize the local character, sometimes, some would claim, at the expense of the global. The Hindu tradition itself tends to be resource blind and so the focus is on how religious life is enriched by either or both, or by their interaction. It has resisted the temptation to assimilate one at the expense of the other and has encouraged the free exchange of these two flows. The Bhakti movement provides an interesting example of a regional movement which became global; the spread of Brāhmanical rituals all over India provides an example of an opposite movement. (Also see Sanskritization.)

103. Gṛhastha and Saṁnyāsa

The relative merits of these two stages of life are much debated within the tradition. The householder has to discharge the three debts owed to the (1) sages, (2) gods, and (3) manes — by Vedic study, tending the fires and begetting offspring respectively, while the renunciant performs one's own funeral ceremony, as a way of demonstrating that one is "dead" so far as normal social and civic life is concerned. The reconciliation between them has been attempted by recourse to two strategies: by recommending their successive pursuit or by providing a framework of their simultaneous pursuit. In accordance with the first, one is supposed to take *saṁnyāsa* after having lived the life of *gṛhastha*. According to the second, worked out in detail in the *Bhagavad-Gītā*, renunciation is of the mind and not of the body, so that it is possible to work for *mokṣa* even while leading the life of a householder. As the householder follows the duties of both *varṇa* and *āśrama*, it is interesting that the *Mahābhārata* reconciles *varṇa* duties with the pursuit of *mokṣa* in the case of Arjuna in the *Bhagavad-Gītā* at the beginning of the battle and reconciles *āśrama* duties with the pursuit of *mokṣa* in the case of Yudhiṣṭhira at the end of the battle, when he is assailed by misgivings similar to the ones Arjuna had at the start of the battle. (Also see Dvandva.)

104. Guru Nānak (1469–1539)

Founder of the Sikh Panth, Guru Nānak was born during the period of the Delhi Sultanate and was an eyewitness to the invasion by Babur, the founder of the Mogul dynasty, which lasted several centuries (1526–1858). Nānak was a householder with a wife and two children, when, at the age of thirty he disappeared for three days and was suspected to have drowned. He returned to proclaim, however, that he was raised to the company of God and commissioned to spread his name. He started his ministry with the startling claim that there is neither Hindu nor Muslim. When both objected to this statement, he explained:

> There is neither Hindu nor Muslim, so whose path should I follow?
> I shall follow God's path. God is neither Hindu nor Muslim and
> the path I shall follow is God's.

He spent the next twenty years travelling through the subcontinent, during the course of which he visited Sri Lanka, travelled to Mecca, and had numerous encounters with religious practitioners of various kinds. He finally returned home at fifty and founded a community at Kartārpur, which became the nucleus of the community which came to be known as Sikhs or disciples. His followers included both Hindus and Muslims, and won acclaim from both the communities, as a *guru* of the Hindus and as a *pīr* by the Muslims. The teachings of Guru Nānak combined elements shared by Islam and Hinduism. The emphasis on the creator God, the rejection of image-worship and doctrine of incarnation resonate with Islam, while the acceptance of the ideas of *saṁsāra*, *karma* and rebirth resonate with Hinduism. A historian has remarked that if the Hindus and Muslims "had agreed to negotiate their differences, they could hardly have reached a more reasonable theological compromise than the tenets of Sikhism afford". (Also see Sikhism.)

105. Guru-Pūrṇimā

The full-moon day in the month of Āṣāḍha (July–August). Ancient Indian educational system, although assisted by royal patronage, was based on voluntary donations made by the students as they graduated in the form of *dakṣiṇā*. This was the day selected for the largest donation, along with honouring the teacher. This was also the day for changing the sacred thread (*janeū*). Past teachers are also honoured and their pictures or images duly garlanded. (Also see Dakṣiṇā.)

106. Heresy

There are words for heretics in Hindu but it remained a relative term because heresy trials are such are virtually unknown to Hinduism. According to modern Hinduism, heresy itself may be the only heresy. Truth in India was continually debated both within and outside the court, and the proper maintenance of the so-called non-orthodox sects was part of the royal orthodoxy.

107. Himalayas

Hindus have considered the highest mountain chain in the world, probably for that reason, as the playground of the gods. These mountains have inspired countless Hindus and also perhaps the conceit of the Pāṇḍavas, that they could enter heaven by climbing it. According to a passage in the *Skanda Purāṇa*, seeing any of the Himalayan peaks is transformative of one's *karma*: "As the dew is dried up by the morning sun, so are the sins of mankind by the sight of the Himalayas".

108. Hindu

The word was first used by the Persians to refer to the people who lived around the region watered by the Indus (Sindhu in Sanskrit), and then extended to cover those who lived beyond it. It was then used to designate the religion of these people, as distinguished from those of the Muslims, as a catch-all term, although in Arabic the term continued to mean a resident of India (Al-Hind) until fairly recent times. The geographical meaning thus gradually gave way to the religious, with the Hindus beginning to use the word to describe themselves after the fourteenth century. In its journey outside India, it continued in its geographical semantic trajectory to Greece and ultimately accounts for the term India. After the Greek conquest of Persia, it entered their language without the "H" for which they had no alphabetic character, just as the "S" (in Sindhu) had turned into "H" at the hands of Persians who had difficulty pronouncing the sibilants. The Vedic Soma turning into Avestan Haoma is another example of this process.

109. Hindu Calendar

The Hindus use a luni-solar calendar called *pañcāṅga*, which is still used for determining the proper dates for various ceremonies and festivals. The months are calculated on the basis of the moon, but the year is based on the passage of the sun. The discrepancy between the lunar and the solar year, caused by the fact that the former falls short of the latter by eleven days, is adjusted through a process called intercalation, so that the months do not deviate from the seasons. This adjustment was already in place during Ṛg-Vedic times. The fact that the calendar is luni-solar symbolizes the importance attached to the sun and the moon, although other planets are also important; for instance, the movement of the planet Jupiter is crucial to calculating the dates of the famous Kumbha Melā. The waxing and waning of the moon an obvious phenomenon; the moonbeams nourish the beings and the gods, and when depleted are replenished by the sun. The full moon is thus seen as brimming with cosmic energy and hence the marker of many rituals. The rising and setting of the sun is an equally obvious phenomenon, including its reaching the meridian at midday. This therefore provides the occasion for the morning, noon and evening prayers (*trikāla-sandhyā*). The movements of the sun and the moon are viewed in the background of the various *nakṣatras* (constellations).

As they are twenty-six or twenty-seven in number and often bear feminine names, they are poetically described as brides of the moon. The Hindu calendar includes the following planets (*grahas*): Sun (Sūrya); Moon (Candra); Mars (Maṅgala); Mercury (Budha); Venus (Śukra); Jupiter (Bṛhaspati) and Saturn (*Śani*). To these seven are added the ascending and descending nodes of the moon called Rāhu and Ketu, which then constitute the *navagrahas* (nine planets) of Hindu astronomy and astrology.

110. Hindu Ethics

The best way to understand Hindu ethics is by contrasting its approach to ethical decision-making with two other approaches, which may be defined as fideist and rationalistic. Fideism, in this context, would stand for the view that if we only had enough faith, all moral dilemmas could be resolved. And rationalism would then stand for the view that, if we only had enough reason at our disposal, all moral dilemmas could be resolved. Hindu ethics is pervaded with the assumption that ethical issues are so complex that no amount of faith and no amount of reason could resolve these dilemmas, although they might both contribute to their resolution. The Hindu approach may, in this sense, be described as neither fideist nor rational, while containing these elements, but ultimately existential. It is perhaps for this reason that whenever ethical issues are discussed within Hinduism — in the form of issues which centre around *dharma* (right thing) to do in a situation — the discussion does not take the form of texts being cited one way or another, or arguments being urged one way or other, though this happens — but rather consists of a narrative concerning how someone else in the past dealt with the situation. Here we may also have an explanation of why Hindu ethics predominantly consists of narratives on ethical issues rather than their propositional formulation, the way one is likely to proceed in the West.

This also allows us to recognize in a fresh way the relationship between *karma* and *dharma* in Hindu ethics. The usual way in which this is understood is to say our *dharma* in the past — our moral conduct — determines our *karma* in the present, in the sense of the situation we find ourselves living in. But this way of looking at it, by placing the effect first and surmising its cause, makes the doctrines of *dharma* and *karma* past-oriented. *Karma*, however, means not just past action but also present action. And if we now reverse the perspective and move from cause to effect, then our present moment provides a moment of ethical decision-making. Most ethical decisions do not come in chromatic contrast of black and white but in shades of grey. What this means is that whatever moral decision we make will have an up and a down side to it. This fact cannot be rationalized away and the decision will have to be taken in full awareness of the pluses and minuses. What we decide as our *dharma* then will become our *karma*. In other words, we will have to live with the consequences of our decision. Example: a couple with young children decides to divorce as in everybody's best interest, but with the knowledge that they will be called upon by the children to explain themselves later on in life, and when that happens it will be their *karma*.

111. Hindu Polytheism

The fact that Hindus apparently worship many different gods, and often through many different idols in all shapes and sizes, has caused enormous problems for understanding the nature of Hindu worship. For many outsiders, this apparent convergence of polytheism and idolatry in Hinduism is a reminder of a unredeemed pagan religion. Both polytheism and idolatry however can be properly understood in the Hindu context by coining the word *polymorphism*. In Hinduism, the one ultimate reality can assume many forms such as those of Viṣṇu, Śiva and so on, and even this one form can assume multiple forms, as in the various incarnations of Viṣṇu. Although some have even argued that polytheism may constitute a more rational approach to the ultimate reality than monotheism, just as a point is easier to establish with a single equation but a curve may require multiple equations to explain it, Hinduism clearly subscribes to the idea of one ultimate reality, although that one ultimate reality may be perceived in innumerable forms as its manifestation. No Hindu is confused by this plentitude. The confusion rampant in this respect may be dispelled in some measure by the following remarks of a seasoned observer of the Hindu scene:

> Many Hindu homes are lavishly decorated with colour prints of a great many Hindu gods and goddesses, often joined by the gods and goddesses of other religions and the pictures of contemporary heroes. Thus side by side with Śiva and Viṣṇu and Devī one can see Jesus and Zoroaster, Gautama Buddha and Jina Mahāvīra, Mahatma Gandhi and Jawaharlal Nehru, and many others. But if questioned about the many gods even the illiterate villager will answer: *Bhagvān ek hai* — the Lord is One. He may not be able to figure out in theological terms how the many gods and the one God hang together and he may not be sure about the hierarchy obtaining among the many manifestations but he does know that ultimately there is only One and that the many somehow merge in the One.
>
> — Klaus K. Klostermaier, *A Survey of Hinduism*, 1994: 149

These various manifestations of the divine can be brought in relationship with either *Nirguṇa-Brahman* or *Saguṇa-Brahman*. As expressions of the Absolute, they point to it just as peaks may point to the sky. As manifestations of God, they point to the one transcendent God, who may be represented in various forms. The various forms of the divine may be compared to the various bulbs of different voltage which manifest electricity according to their capacity, a metaphor more in keeping with perhaps with the *Nirguṇa-Brahman* model. The case for *Saguṇa-Brahman* could probably be illustrated with the example of the various photographs of a person in an album. It is same person in various guises, or in various stages of growth, and the profusion of pictures never causes confusion of identity. God as seen in many, God as seeing is one.

112. Hindu Rāṣṭra

The idea that the India as a country belongs properly to the Hindus as a nation, because when people, otherwise of Indian origin, embrace a foreign religion like Islam or Christianity, this change of faith may also entail a change of political loyalty. (Also see Hindutva, Vishva Hindu Parishad.)

113. Hindu Ritual

Some scholars have highlighted the role of the ritual as a unifying factor in the otherwise such diverse tradition of Hinduism but it is possible to locate this unity in the conceptual framework of the tradition itself whose motto may be summed up in the statement: "Preference without exclusion".

114. Hindu Studies, Bias in

The problem of bias in Hindu studies has gained salience in over the past few decades in the form of the question: who speaks for Hinduism: the outsider or the insider? The outsider's claim is based on objectivity, the insider's on sensitivity and authenticity. The debate rages on and cannot be settled by merely distinguishing between willful representation and honest errors. Its roots are historical. (Also see Subaltern Studies.)

115. Hindu Terrorism

A recent development in Hinduism as a response to Islamic terrorism in India and the perceived failure of the Indian state to tackle it successfully. For long it was considered an oxymoron given the nature of Hinduism but its existence is now well-documented.

116. Hinduism

The term used to designate the religion of the people of South Asia, who do not declare themselves to be Christians, Muslims, Jews, or Zoroastrians. The Hindus tend to look upon followers of other Indic tradition — such as Buddhists, Jainas, and Sikhs — as co-religionists.

The sentiment may not always be reciprocated, hence allowing for a broader and narrower understanding of the term. This residual character of Hinduism is clear from the history of the word itself, which is derived from the word Sindhu (or Indus), referred to as Hindu by the Persians. It was used to designate the people who lived around or beyond the Indus, first by the Persians, and then by the Muslims when they arrived in India and later ruled over it. It thus came to designate the non-Muslim natives of India, the word shifting from a geographical orientation to a religious one. The process was complete by the time of Indian Independence. India now contains most of the more than 800 million followers of the religion, who constitute about 80 per cent of India's population. But Hindus are also found outside India, in Nepal, which is predominantly a Hindu country, and in Pakistan and Bangladesh, where they constitute 3 per cent and 16 per cent of the population respectively. About 15 per cent of Sri Lanka's population is also Hindu. Hinduism was carried into the Caribbean, Fiji Islands and parts of Africa by indentured labour in the nineteenth century; in the twentieth, Hindus constitute a worldwide diaspora of about 30 million.

117. Hinduism, an Eight-Point Definition

1. There are two types of religions, those in which the doctrines and practices come first, and then a community coalesces around them; and those in which the community comes first, and the doctrines and practices are an expression of the togetherness of the community. If the first type of religion is described as associational and the latter communitarian, then Hinduism is a communitarian religion. Implication for definition: One must define who is a Hindu (i.e. member of the community) before defining Hinduism.
2. There are two ways in which one may define a Hindu on account of Hinduism's close association with India: from the point of view of those inside it, and from the point of view of

those outside it. This dualism implies a double-definition of who is a Hindu. Implication for definition: A person who is an Indian citizen is presumably a Hindu unless one denies being one; a person who is not an Indian citizen is presumably a non-Hindu, unless one asserts being one, for while Hinduism may not seek converts, it tends not to reject them, either.

3. Since in its original location, one must deny being a Hindu in order not to be considered one, Hinduism is non-exclusive, others exclude themselves from it. Implication for definition: Others may exclude themselves from the Hindus but Hindus do not exclude the religious ideas of those people. This means that from the Hindu point of view, "Hinduism" is identical with the Indic religious tradition, although from the point of view of the followers of the other Indic religious traditions, such as those of Buddhism, Jainism and Sikhism this may not be so, should they choose to exclude themselves.
4. While in the case of Indic religions, Hindus identify with both the religious communities as well as their religious ideas, even if they exclude themselves; in the case of non-Indic religions they are unwilling to identify with such communities (Muslims, Christians, etc.) if these communities exclude themselves from the Hindus, but Hindus remain hospitable to the religious ideas of these communities. Implication for definition: The Hinduism will always be more than just the sum of religious ideas of the "Hindus".
5. Just as Hindus do not exclude others, others exclude themselves, Hindus do not exclude what has happened in their past, or the past of others, whatever it might be. Implication for definition: Hindus believe in a cumulative as well as an inclusive tradition of religion.
6. Hinduism may now be defined as the religion of the Hindus. Implication for definition:

   i. Hinduism is the sum total of beliefs and practices of those who identify themselves as Hindus, which is what they are because of this non-exclusive and cumulative attitude displayed by the Hindus.

ii. Because Hindus also welcome the religious ideas and experiences of others it will always be more than itself.

7. The sum total of these beliefs and practices held in mutual tolerance and acceptance need not have any common thread running through them, except this attitude of mutual acceptance. Implication for definition: Some broad similarities may be discernible but although these may be descriptive of Hinduism, they can never be definitional of Hinduism.
8. Thus Hindus can be identified but Hinduism cannot be defined, except as the religion of the Hindus. And being a Hindu requires no definition other than self-assertion, by implication if one is an Indian citizen and by articulation if one is not. Implication for definition: Hinduism is a threshold, not an enclosure. Hinduism will always be more than itself.

118. Hinduism and Science

A striking feature of modern Hinduism is its lack of antagonism towards modern science, specially in view of the history of conflict between religion and science, which has characterized Christianity in the modern age. This could be traced in part to Hindu pluralism, and Hinduism's emphasis on experience and conduct over doctrine. A willingness to accept many possible positions relieved it of the pressure generated by the need to defend dogmatic assertions, while the primacy of experience in it as a system may have predisposed it to appreciate the role of experimentation in science. Major schools of Hindu philosophy such as Sāṁkhya-Yoga and Advaita Vedānta, as well as Buddhism and Jainism accept the concept of *jīvan-mukti* or that of living or embodied liberation. This means that, at least, in principle, the fruits of the religious life could be realized in this very life. Such a view radically alters one's understanding of faith (*śraddhā*). Because salvation is a post-mortem state in the Abrahamic religions, faith must remain faith in things unseen. In Buddhism, Jainism and many forms of Hinduism, however, such faith is faith pending proof for oneself; it is the kind of faith one much have to conduct Cavendish's experiment, in order to discover that water is H_2O. Thereafter it ceases to be a matter of faith, because it becomes a fact. Those forms of religion which believe in living liberation similarly only ask for preliminary faith, required to undertake their regimen; the result of the pursuit is entirely independent of faith. Thus what is required in these systems is only "temporary faith". Moreover, to the extent that Hindu thought is not only theistic but also atheistic and transtheistic, it avoided the problems posed for theism by the rise of science. The theory of evolution also did not create the ripples it did in the theological circles in the West. One reason for this could have been the absence of as sharp a distinction between human beings and the animal world within it as found in the Abrahamic religions, for it was karmically possible for human beings to incarnate as animals, and for animals to incarnate as human beings. The fact that modern Hinduism contains a strong philosophical orientation towards Advaita Vedānta may also have played a role in its attitude towards modern science. Although Advaita Vedānta believes in God, its ultimate position is transthetic and described in terms of *Nirguṇa-Brahman*. Moreover, its doctrine of *māyā*, or the metaphysical deceptiveness of the world, leaves the door open for its unending investigation. This system also shares the cosmology of the rest of Hinduism, in which the creation and destruction of the universe is an unending process, more in keeping with modern scientific cosmology, although not identical with it. Moreover, the vast dimensions of time with which the Hindu imagination is familiar, in which *kalpa* is a major unit, is comparable to the concept of light-years in science. A whole constellation of factors may thus be responsible for the science-friendly attitude of Hinduism. (Also see Atomic Theory.)

119. Hinduism and Social Reform

Almost all modern Hindu religious movements, which arose after *c.* 1800, have possessed a strong social reform component, and it has sometimes been suggested that in this they were following the example set by missionary Christianity. There is an interesting facet to this if we accept this as true; that the Hindu reform movement accepted the reform agenda of Christianity but rejected its theological agenda. But one needs to examine the original premise more closely, namely, that the Hindu reform movements were reacting to Christianity. They were certainly reacting by way of challenging its missionary agenda but one needs to examine the idea that Christian missions were used as examples more closely. Christianity links religious conversion with social service; this does not seem to be the case with most of the reform movements. Moreover, when the East India Company took over an Indian principality, then the business of managing its temples also fell to its lot. There is evidence to suggest that, in order to maximize its profits as a trading company, it would cut out the social services provided by the temple, while continuing to honour the ritual functions. So the Hindu reform movements were as much resurrecting a Hindu past, as they might be emulating the missions. What is undeniable is that modern Hindu movements are consciously this-worldly in this sense, and find inspiration for it from several sources. One such source is the emphasis on *karma-yoga* which characterizes modern Hinduism; another is to set an example, specially to the lay people; yet another could be the modern realization of the close connection between education and democracy. (Also see Dayananda Sarasvati and Mahatma Gandhi.)

120. Hinduism as a Global Phenomenon

Hinduism has now gone global in more than one sense. The world-wide Indian diaspora is of course a demographic fact, and comprises almost 30 million Hindus. There are over a million Hindus in USA, with the highest per capita income among all ethnic groups.

Moreover, second and third generation diasporic Hindus have also emerged. Hindus in the diaspora have continued, in a most impressive way, the tradition of building temples, and that too in traditional style. Sometimes even artisans, and certainly priests, have been brought over from India. There are temples in Los Angeles, Texas, Houston and a number of other cities, which remarkably resemble those in India. Hindu sects also, like the Arya Samaj and the Swaminarayan, have also engaged in temple-building.

To the physical presence of Hindu overseas, one must also add the spread of ideas and institutions connected with Hinduism overseas. The *Yoga Journal* has over 350,000 subscribers and while one may question whether *yoga* must be called Hindu, few can deny that it is Indic. Similarly, the Hare Krishna movement demonstrates the spread of Hindu institutions as well. A monastic organization in Hawaii publishes the widely read journal *Hinduism Today*. Over 10,000 websites deal with Hinduism.

121. Hinduism as a Religion

Hinduism's word for itself is Dharma (Sanātana Dharma). When it is treated as a "religion" in English-language discourse both within and outside India, then the following points need to be borne in mind:

1. Religion in the West is closely associated with the idea of a creedal formulation and its acceptance, as suggested by the use of faith as a synonym for it. Hinduism does not fit this picture neatly, wherein practice is more important than doctrine.

2. There is a tendency in modern discourse to define religion itself in terms of the idea of family resemblances developed by Wittgenstein, on the analogy of a game, for which no single definition may suffice and various examples of which may bear family resemblance to each other. This idea may apply not only to the definition of religion but to Hinduism itself.

3. Sometimes it is urged, on the basis of prototype theory, that some elements in a category may be more prototypical of it than others. One can see the connection between this and the previous view of family resemblance but typically, when it comes to religion, the Abrahamic religion tend to be held up as prototypes, causing problems from the point of view of Hinduism.
4. It has been urged, by scholars like Wilfred Cantwell Smith, that the evolution of the term religion is in the sense of bounderied entities is an example of post-Enlightenment intellectual reification and that therefore there are Hindus but no "Hinduism". Such an understanding of religion is in keeping with the Hindu self-understanding.
5. Some Western definitions of religion, a specially those developed by sociologists like Emile Durkheim and Peter Berger, emphasize the role of the "sacred" in understanding a religion, specially in the context of it acting as a cementing force in society. This raises the question: does society come first or religion come first? To the extent that religion is viewed as the expression of the togetherness of the group, rather than the group forming around a religion, such an understanding is in keeping with Hindu self-understanding.

122. Hinduism, Chronology

The history of Hinduism is closely linked with the history of India. Periodization is a time-honoured method of evolving order out of archival chaos. James Mill established such an order by dividing Indian history into three periods — a Hindu period, a Muslim period, a British period, renamed by modern scholars, along more secular lines, into the ancient, medieval, and modern periods of Indian history. The broad outlines of this chronological framework divide the history of Hinduism into four periods.

I. VEDIC AND PRE-VEDIC HINDUISM (*c.* 7000 – *c.* 400 BCE)

Hinduism has no historical founder so it is difficult to date its beginning with any precision. However, archaeological finds in the region of the Indus Valley, from the 1920s onwards, have led to the identification of what is known as Haṛappan culture, which reached its mature phase around the middle of the third millennium BCE. This culture contains elements which can be traced in what we now know as Hinduism and its earliest phase has been traced back to Mehrgaṛh in *c.* 7000 BCE. One may therefore tentatively date Hinduism from that period. Haṛappan culture is usually considered pre-Vedic, the Vedas being generally regarded as the work of a people who called themselves Aryans and entered India around the middle of the second millennium BCE. The Vedas are the foundational scriptures of Hinduism but the relationship of Haṛappan to the Vedic, and their priority, has now become a subject of vigorous and even vituperative debate. The Vedic corpus evolved over centuries and this Vedic tradition then had to face the challenge of two religions which arose subsequently, namely, Buddhism and Jainism. Their emergence is traditionally placed in the sixth century BCE (a revised dating of fifth century has also been proposed). The Vedic tradition interacted with these new movements.

II. CLASSICAL HINDUISM (*c.* 400 BCE – CE 1000)

The Vedic tradition, shaped by this encounter with Buddhism and Jainism, gave rise to Classical Hinduism. It is during this period that the standard sacred texts of the tradition arose, as successors to the Vedas, the revealed texts. These include the *itihāsas* of the *Rāmāyaṇa* and the *Mahābhārata*, the Purāṇas, and so on. Hinduism kept interacting with Buddhism and Jainism throughout this period; by the end of the period they had found a place within its overall architecture.

III. MEDIEVAL HINDUISM (*c.* 1000 – *c.* 1800)

The main feature of this period is the arrival and spread of Islam in India, and the establishment of Muslim rule around 1200 in

Delhi, and then gradually over most of India. This period is thus characterized by Hinduism's encounter with Islam and the rise of the Bhakti movement, whose roots go back to the Classical period but which now spread to cover the entire country.

IV. MODERN HINDUISM (*c.* 1800 –)

Muslim rule was then replaced by British rule. During this period, Hinduism has to face the challenge posed by the West in the form of the British Raj, Christianity, and modernity.

The complexity of the issues involved in studying Hinduism and its history may be demonstrated by the fact that at least four different points of origin can be assigned to Hinduism, after one gets beyond the point that it is without a beginning (*anādi*), in the sense that it is a continuous tradition, whose beginning point cannot be discerned because no founder or founding event is attached to it, except perhaps creation, which then takes us beyond the realm of the empirical into the cosmological. Upon a less rarefied view, one could assign the origin to around *c.* 7000 BCE on the basis of the fact that such markedly Hindu cultural features as *namaste*, women filling the hair-parting in red, sanctity of the *pīpal*-tree, obsession with ablutions to mention only some of them, can be traced back to Haṛappan culture which thus makes it identifiably Hindu, and the origins of this culture can be traced to the site of Mehrgaṛh, dated *c.* 7000 BCE. One may also date the origin of Hinduism not on the basis of archaeological but literary evidence. No such evidence is so far forthcoming from the Haṛappan period because the Indus script, which belongs to this period, has not yet been deciphered; some have even questioned whether it is one. The earliest literary evidence of the existence of Hinduism at the moment is provided by the Vedas, among which the *Ṛg-Veda* is the earliest by common consent. The dating of this text is itself highly contested but scholarly consensus still assigns it to *c.* 1500 BCE, which then enables us to assign the origin of Hinduism to that time. It has however been argued that Hinduism, as we know it, is sufficiently different from Vedism, or the religion of the Vedas. What we call Hinduism, according to this view, is the product of the interaction of Vedism with the Buddhism and Jainism. According to this view the origin of Hinduism should be dated from *c.* 400 BCE, when the synthesis resulting from this interaction started falling into place. Another school argues, however, that the Hindus did not possess any self-consciousness as a unified religious tradition, no more than Roman polytheism did, and that such consciousness only began to arise after its encounter with Islam had assumed a solid character, and that it was then that the word Hindu started acquiring a creedal rather than a geographical character. This started happening around the fourteenth century (though some would put it in the sixteenth century) and Hinduism originates during this period. Yet another view holds that this self-consciousness of Hinduism does not really predate its encounter with the West, and that it was this encounter which led to the "invention" of Hinduism. The fact that the word Hinduism was itself coined towards the end of the eighteenth or the beginning of the nineteenth century sits well with this view. We thus have the following range of views regarding the origins of Hinduism to choose from:

1. No discernible origin;
2. *c.* 7000 BCE;
3. *c.* 3000 BCE;
4. *c.* 1500 BCE;
5. 400 BCE;
6. *c.* fourteenth century; and
7. *c.* nineteenth century,

Each is credible in its own way, collectively testifying to the complexity of the issue.

The question of origin is important because it plays a role in the context of imperialism, nationalism and revivalism. British imperial rule over India meant rule by outsiders over Indians, but if Hindus are really also outsiders to India, then the imperial case is strengthened. If it can be demonstrated that India is the homeland of the Indians, then nationalist case is strengthened; and if it can be asserted that the Indian people had a glorious past, either as natives of India or outsiders in India, revivalism is strengthened. All three are undermined to some degree by the modern consensus in genetics that all human beings are ultimately traceable to Africa.

123. Hinduism, Dogmatism in

The six schools of Hindu thought accept Vedic authority; Hindu philosophy therefore could be described as dogmatic. Most scholars are agreed, however, that it would be misleading to do so. The six schools of Hindu philosophy are: Nyāya; Vaiśeṣika, Sāṁkhya, Yoga, Mīmāṁsā and Vedānta. Although the first four of these six schools, as listed above, accept Vedic authority, they do not depend on the Vedas for their teachings, which evolved independently. It also seems to be the case that they accept Vedic authority in terms of *dharma* (social behaviour), rather than *mokṣa* (attainment of the spiritual goal of life), and therefore remain unfettered by Vedic authority where their philosophy is concerned. The two schools of Hindu thought which depend on the Vedas for philosophical content are those of Pūrva-Mīmāṁsā (or Mīmāṁsā) and Uttara-Mīmāṁsā (or Vedānta). It is ironic that they are described as Mīmāṁsā, a term which means rational investigation (with a view to finding solutions). They accept the Vedas as authoritative but they are called Mīmāṁsā because they conduct a rational investigation to determine the purport of the Vedas. Thus while their acceptance of the Vedas could be called dogmatic, their acceptance if its teachings may hardly be so called. The acceptance of the Vedas, even in the case of such an orthodox school as Mīmāṁsā, may be described dogmatic in theory but not in practice, because in practice it was challenged by the schools of Cārvāka, Bauddha and Jaina philosophy, schools which rejected the Vedas, so that Mīmāṁsā was compelled to justify its acceptance of the Vedas on rational grounds. In the case of Vedānta, some schools of it, like that of Advaita Vedānta, ultimately point to a transcendental experience, in which the Vedas are also transcended. So if Hindu thought is described as dogmatic, then one must add that its dogma is such as must be transcended.

124. Hinduism, General Features

Although few features of Hinduism can be described as universal, some of them are general enough to warrant mention:

1. the acceptance of the Vedas as foundational texts;
2. belief in the doctrines of *saṁsāra*, *karma* and *mokṣa*;
3. the centrality of the concept of *dharma*;
4. the acceptance of pluralism; and
5. the sanctity attached to the cow.

125. Hindutva

A term coined around 1923 by a Hindu ideologue, V.D. Savarkar (1883–1966) to get round the divisiveness caused by the use of the Western term "religion" introduced by the British rulers, which was threatening to fragment the comprehensive Indic tradition into separate religions such as Hinduism, Buddhism, Jainism and Sikhism. The use of the term "religion" in the Western sense, as indicating exclusive religious identities, and its imposition on India through the British Census, was creating the danger of fragmenting the various religions of Indian origin, who share considerable common ground, into separate entities. Savarkar invoked the Western distinction between religion and culture, then unknown to India, to counter this effect, by proposing that while these may be classified as different religions, they shared the same culture. The word Hinduism had come into use by now to denote a religion, so he coined the neologism Hindutva, to refer to the shared common culture of these religions of Indian origin.

126. Hospitality in Hinduism

Hospitality is a highly-prized virtue in Hinduism. Paul Thieme even argued that the Indo-European tribes consisted of two kinds – those who were not hospitable to others and those who were. The Aryan tribes distinguished themselves from the rest by virtue of possessing this latter attribute. This might be a speculative point but the instruction to be hospitable is part of the famous graduation speech in the *Taittirīya Upaniṣad* (I.ii.2), wherein one is exhorted to treat mother, father, teacher and guest like a god (*atithidevo bhava*). Not every guest however is an *atithi*. It excludes acquaintances and friends, to whom also one is exhorted to be hospitable, but they are to be described as *abhyāgata*s rather than *atithi*s. The *atithi* is one who arrives uninvited, with whom one is not acquainted, and who stays for just a night (*MS* III.102-03). The only people who could be given precedence over the *atithi* are brides, infants, and sick and pregnant women (*MS* III.114). The hospitality extended has to be in accordance with the status of the guest, but all are to be honoured to the best of the host's ability, according to the *Rāmāyaṇa* (*MS* III.101). It should be done in a manner that all *varṇa*s feel revered and honoured; according to the *Mahābhārata* "even if a *Cāṇḍāla* comes seeking food, at the proper place and time, he should be respectfully welcomed by the householder and offered reverential hospitality", so that the egalitarianism of hospitality even trumps the hierarchy of caste. Indeed, even an enemy may not be turned away, because a tree does not cease to offer shade even to one who comes to chop it, as the text puts it. The sentiment in favour of the *atithi* is very ancient; even a Ṛg-Vedic verse (V.85.7) seeks forgiveness from Varuṇa for wronging a stranger.

127. Icon

The icon may be viewed as a materializing of the spirit, or the spiritual, as *arcāvatāra*, the way Jesus Christ, in official Christianity, is an embodiment of the "Spirit", although the comparison does not go all the way because Jesus Christ was a living being, while the icon is not.

128. Identity

The absolutistic forms of Hinduism, such as Advaita Vedānta, not only emphasize the identity of *Ātman* and *Brahman*, or the identity of the ultimate ground of the individual subject and the ultimate ground of the objective universe, but also emphasize that this is an identity of a very radical kind; it is not the case of two becoming one, or a unity encompassing a variety, but of an identity which is undivisible to begin with. Such radical identity gives way to a more qualified identity in Viśiṣṭādvaita Vedānta, wherein God encompasses everything as its inner controller. Although this system of thought accepts three ultimate realities in the form of God (*Īśvara*), soul (*cit*) and matter (*acit*), the last two are dependent on God, and while distinct, are not separable from God. That is why it is important to emphasize that the philosophically correct English rendering of Viśiṣṭādvaita is not "qualified monism" but "monism of the qualified". The identity is further diluted in the system of Dvaita Vedānta, wherein matter and souls are both distinct and separate, but utterly dependent upon God, and are of and for God so that teleological unity does not imply numerical identity. Yet, although difference has its place, and is dynamically paired with identity in many instances, the overall orientation is one of identity over hierarchy. This seems to hold for not only Hindu philosophy but Hindu sociology as well. It is even true of the caste system, for the fact that the four *varṇa*s emerge from the same *puruṣa*, points to their identity in the *puruṣa*, consistently with their separation as *varṇa*s and the hierarchy that may be involved. It has not often been realized that each *varṇa* lays claim to its own superiority, which again suggests that overall identity may be much more of a pivotal point in Hinduism than hierarchy, and which it sometimes trumps.

129. Indra

The god to whom the largest number of hymns are devoted in the *Ṛg-Veda*. His functions therein are as a weather-god and a war-god. As a weather-god he brings rain, releasing if from its state of captivity in the clouds. As a war-god he leads the Aryans to victory in battle, especially when reinvigorated with a drink called *soma*, still yet to be satisfactorily identified. Sometimes he is even referred to as the one God (*eko devaḥ*). His martial character is often contrasted with the more moral character of Varuṇa. Indra continues to be a god in later Hinduism, specially as the "king of the gods" but yields to gods like Viṣṇu and Śiva in popularity.

130. Indus Valley Civilization

The name by which the culture or civilization, which is now usually called Haṛappan, was referred to earlier. Two Indians, by the name of R.D. Banerji and D.R. Sahni, working under Sir John Marshall, the then Director General of the Archaeological Survey of India, commenced work in the early 1920s on two sites respectively, one at Moheṅjo-Daṛo on the west bank at the Indus in Sind, and the other at Haṛappā, in Punjab, on the eastern bank of the Rāvī. Their archaeological finds led to the identification of a civilization contemporaneous with Egypt and Mesopotamia. This civilization was initially called the Indus Valley civilization, as the earlier archaeological finds were located in the Indus Valley. Subsequent finds indicate that it stretched far beyond this region, so the current trend is to designate it Haṛappan, after its pre-eminent site called Haṛappā. (Also see Aryan–Dravidian Hypothesis.)

131. Iṣṭa-Devatā

Chosen deity: this doctrine may be theologically looked upon as a way of evolving order of the devotional chaos, given the myriads of gods and the myriads of devotees Hinduism is home to. The Hindus respect all gods and deities, but a Hindu may also have a special personal relationship with a chosen deity, as the focus of that Hindu's devotion. This particular deity is known as the *iṣṭa-devatā* (chosen deity). Members in the same family may have different *iṣṭa-devatās*. The doctrine pedagogically mirrors the doctrine of *upāya-kauśalya* (skill in means) in Buddhism, according to which the teaching should be presented at the level of the seeker, and must speak to his condition. So with one's deity. Deities also get created in Hinduism and the emergence of Santoṣī Mātā may be a theological tribute to modern consumerism, just as the worship of Śītalā to avoid the menace of HIV/Aids, is a tribute to Hinduism's ability to invest old deities with new functions. (Also see Hindu Polytheism.)

132. Īśvara (Advaita)

The gradual emergence of the universe out of *Brahman* through *māyā* involves three stages in Advaita Vedānta. *Brahman* as possessing undifferentiated *māyā* is conceived as *Īśvara*, in keeping with the distinction between *Nirguṇa* and *Saguṇa-Brahman*. At this stage of creation, God is in possession of the power of creation and is called *Īśvara*. In the next stage, *Īśvara* is referred to by three optional terms: Hiraṇyagarbha, Sūtrātmā, or Prāṇa. At this stage God is the sum total of all subtle objects. Their differentiation into physical or gross objects occurs in the next stage and the universe emerges. At this point God is called Vaiśvānara or Virāṭ. The process has been explained with the help of some typical examples. It has thus been compared to the three states of consciousness of the individual: deep sleep, dreaming and waking. *Īśvara* could then be seen as God in deep sleep, Hiraṇyagarbha as God in the dreaming state and Vaiśvānara as God awake. The process can also be compared to the way a plant germinates. First comes the seed, comparable to *Īśvara*; then the sprouting or germinating stage, comparable to Hiraṇyagarbha, followed by the stage represented by the plant, comparable to Vaiśvānara. The word *Īśvara* in Advaita is thus used in two senses: in one sense it refers to the immanent aspect of God as *Saguṇa-Brahman* as a whole, the sense in which it is used commonly, and this special sense in which it represents the first of the three stages in the emergence of the cosmos. (Also see Viśiṣṭādvaita Vedānta.)

133. Japa

The constant repetition of a *mantra*.

134. Jāti

The social group one is born into characterized by endogamy, commensality and craft exclusiveness in principle, although in practice these features might manifest themselves in different degrees. This is the word which corresponds to the English word "caste" most closely. Their number has been variously estimated from 4,000 to 8,000. According to the traditional Hindu sociology, the *jātis* arose from the intermixture of the four *varṇas*, but modern sociologists reject this view. The social filiation involved in claiming that the *jātis* arose from the various may be an attempt to integrate the anthropological reality of *jāti* faced by Hinduism as it spread from Punjab over the rest of India, with its own sociological framework of the *varṇas* (classes).

135. Jātrā

From Sanskrit *yātrā*, meaning procession. Just as a person may stay in a house but becomes more accessible when out on a walk, the deities have their shrines but their grace flows over when taken out in a procession.

136. Jñāna-Yoga

The path (*yoga*) of knowledge. It is a very human question to ask: How is the ultimate reality to be experienced, if there is one? Main line Hinduism does accept the existence of such an ultimate reality, which is called *Brahman*, even as it is perpetually debating whether it is best described as *Nirguṇa-Brahman* or *Saguṇa-Brahman*. For those who are inclined to accept the doctrine of *Nirguṇa-Brahman*, the path of knowledge (*jñāna-yoga*) is advocated, for the liberative experiential realization of the ultimate reality. If, according to the doctrine of *Nirguṇa-Brahman*, only a single undivided reality really exists, then how can one be different from this reality, if it alone really exists? It must then be a mistake on our part to think that we are somehow other than this reality. This belief that we are not it represents a state of ignorance, which must be overcome by true knowledge. The path of knowledge is designed to take us out of this state of ignorance in three stages, which are represented by the terms *śravaṇa, manana* and *nididhyāsana*. *Śravaṇa* consists of receiving this teaching of non-duality, preferably from a qualified *guru*, as found in the sacred texts. The teaching is however counter-intuitive, for it asserts non-duality while we live in a world characterized by plurality and diversity. So one has to cogitate and reflect on the point, until its plausibility is established by examples and logic and it no longer seems incredible (*asambhāvanā*). Even after we are intellectually convinced, however, old habits die-hard. So one has to deeply meditate on the truth to overcome these truth-compromising tendencies (*viparīta bhāvanā*). When these are overcome one realizes one's identity with *Brahman* and also realizes that there never was a time the identity did not exist. It was merely obscured by ignorance. (Also see Advaita Vedānta; Bhāmatī School of Advaita Vedānta and Vivaraṇa.)

137. Kabīr

Famous poet-saint of Banaras who flourished in the fifteenth century, but whose exact dates are disputed. Along with Tulsīdās, he is among the celebrated poets of Hindi but unlike him, Kabīr followed the path of *nirguṇa* rather than *saguṇa bhakti*. He belonged to a family of the weaver caste (called *julāhās*) which may have recently converted to Islam; his common names for the ultimate reality, for which he uses eighty-six terms, are Rāma and Hari. These are however used as a general name of God, rather than to indicate a specific incarnation or manifestation. Kabīr was an iconoclast in the best sense of the word, who blasted the formalism and pretensions of both Hinduism and Islam and their followers, and advocated an honest longing for God. His followers, who were both Hindu and Muslim, are called Kabīr-Panthīs, and his message of true love of

God and humanity resonates with modern reformist tendencies. The *Bījaka* is an early collection of his poems and several hymns by him are found in the canon, the *Guru Granth Sahib*. (Also see Bhakti.)

138. Kālī

A manifestation of the Goddess as embracing the darker dimension of life involving death and destruction, who is often depicted in black with fierce eyes and a lolling tongue, somewhat like a female medieval Christian depiction of death. It should not be forgotten, however, that despite the unpleasantness involved, she is universally worshipped as the mother (Kālī Mā or Mātā), a fact which will make her invocation by the great modern mystic, Ramakrishna Paramahamsa (1836-86), less mystifying. She was the focus of Ramakrishna's first major mystical experience. He also uttered her name thrice in a ringing tone just before dying from cancer of the throat. Kālī has been polyvalently interpreted; some see in her presence in the Hindu pantheon the suggestion that one's understanding of life is not complete, until one has faced and come to terms with its most revolting and threatening aspects. (Also see Durgā; Mahādevī; and Ramakrishna Paramahmsa.)

139. Kalpasūtras

The ritualistic orientation of the Brāhmaṇa sections of the Veda finds its continuity in the tradition in the Kalpasūtras, whose goal is to systematize ritual. There are three classes of such *sūtras* (the word *kalpa* standing for ritual procedures):

1. Śrautasūtras,
2. Gṛhyasūtras, and
3. Dharmasūtras.

The great sages of the various branches of Vedic study (*śākhās*), such as Bodhāyana and Āpastamba composed all three of them. The Śrautasūtras take as their province the various public sacrifices, which form the theme of the Brāhmaṇas. The evidence of their performance can be found throughout history; an Aśvamedha was celebrated as late as the eighteenth century, and their persistence among the Nambudirī brāhmaṇas of Kerala to this day has been documented by Fritz Staal. The Gṛhyasūtras are concerned with domestic rites, the daily ones (*nitya*) performed by the family and the occasional ones (*naimittika*, associated with the *saṁskāras*) perhaps with the aid of the family priest, both equally obligatory. The Dharmasūtras equip a person both morally and socially for the ritualistic life, because the "Vedas do no cleanse one devoid of proper conduct" (*VDSū* VI.3). The important Dharmasūtras, apart from those of Baudhāyana and Āpastamba, are those of Gautama and Vasiṣṭha. (Also see Hindu Ritual.)

140. Karavā-cautha

A festival for women, which falls about eleven days before Diwālī, on the fourth day of the dark fortnight of the month of Kārttika (October–Novemeber). Women fast for twenty-four hours without food or water, for securing their husband's longevity as an expression of loving devotion. They receive food and water from the husband to break their fast, after which they partake a special meal prepared for the occasion and then celebrate, the occasion putting on fine clothes and jewellery. It is primarily observed in Punjab. (Also see Women's Rituals.)

141. Karma

The idea of *karma*, in its essential conception, means that one reaps as one sows. This formulation, however, is found in many religions. It receives a typical Hindu extension when it is connected with the idea of *saṁsāra*: that one is, as a living being (*jīva*), born again and again in the phenomenal world, as Hinduism believes this to be the case. Then the question arises: what principle governs the movement of the *jīva* in *saṁsāra*? The answer is provided by the doctrine of *karma*. The question has to do with one's individual destiny in this vast world, and the doctrine of *karma* asserts that an individual's actions (in thought, word and deed) determine the nature of the individual's destiny.

Karma operates virtually like a natural law; like gravity, for instance. *Karma* should however not be confused with fatalism, because it involves a continuously evolving and dynamic movement. Moreover, rarely are all events in life to be attributed to *karma*, for room is sometimes made for natural calamities and medical interventions. The word *karma* is derived from the root *kṛ*, which denotes action. So the doctrine of *karma* in Hinduism has to do with action. More specifically, it explains what happens to us now in terms of how we have acted in the past. One undergoes numerous experiences in life. How are these to be explained? Are these to be explained as mere random occurrences? Do they represent merely a series of statistical contingencies, or is there a deeper logic underlying them, involving cause and effect? The Hindu answer favours the second approach and extends the law of causality from mechanics to the mechanics of life. What then is this law? Very simply it means that the situations we create for others are the kind of situations which will be created for us. One could call it the boomerang effect — what we throw out at the universe, good or bad, ultimately arcs back at us. The doctrine is a comprehensive one and hard to pin down, but a number of oneliners help convey some feel for it: what goes around comes around; you reap as you sow; life is the sum of our choices; *karma* is an unfinished business; it is "the habits that collectively constitute a person's character" and so on.

Karma in Hinduism, it should be emphasized, does not mean just physical action; actually the action of the mind is the key element in its operation. Action here includes all three types of activities: mental (*mānasika*), verbal (*vācika*) and physical (*kāyika*). Thinking ill of someone, or saying a bad things to them or about them, is as much a bad *karma* as physically harming them in some way. Moreover, according to this doctrine, every action produces a double effect: one effect it produces is the result of that action, which is called *phala*; hence the result of *karma* is referred to as *karma-phala*, although often both the cause and effect are subsumed within the term *karma*. The other effect it produces is to leave a mental trace, an impression on the mind. If an act is performed repeatedly, this impression becomes more marked with every repetition. Such a lasting impression is called *saṁskāra*. Thus *karma* produces both what we might call a mechanical effect and a mental effect. The idea that some kind of cosmic justice ungirds the universe is not original with Hinduism. Most religions have it in some form. The idea that our life on earth will be followed by a day of judgement, when we will be sent to heaven or hell in accordance with our deeds, contains the seed idea of *karma*. It has however a different flavour in Hinduism on account of the doctrine of rebirth associated with it. According to this view, our present life is a link in a chain of lives which extends into the past without a beginning and stretches out into the future without an end. What happens to us in the course of these lives depends on our *karma*. In a way, the Abrahamic religion secure cosmic justice vertically and finally: there is a final day of judgement and one is either sent up to heaven or down to hell. In Hinduism, it is secured horizontally and continuously. We go on living, life after life, and within these lives we experience the consequences of our actions as we live these lives. The process of involvement in living out these several lives is called *saṁsāra*, as noted earlier. It is a natural question to ask: when did this process, or alternately *karma*, first begin? According to Hinduism there was never any such original point. According to it, both *karma* and *saṁsāra* are without a beginning (*anādi*). If then what is happening to me now is the result of what I have done in a previous life, or previous lives, then the question arises; why don't I remember those actions? The lighthearted answer to this is: are not the memories of one life enough to make us swoon? The serious answer is that these memories lie buried in our subconscious and can be recovered by certain yogic techniques. There is also the general point that our memories become spotty and tend to fade the closer we get to our time of birth, so that not being able to recall what came before it should not surprise us. Another serious question, certainly from a philosophical point of view, which arises is: If what happens to us now is the result of what we did in our previous lives, then how much freedom do we have? Three broad positions on this point may be identified within the tradition:

1. According to one view, there is no freedom, in the sense that everything is predetermined. But we are still free to react to what happens to us, which then determines our future. Moreover, *karma* may compel us to perform certain acts, like giving money to a beggar, but how we do it is still open to us — we can give the money compassionately or throw it at the beggar rudely.
2. Another view takes an opposite position in this respect: that everything is free will. To grasp this point of view we need to remember that it was own free act, when it was first performed, which ultimately led to whatever was predetermined. So all destiny is free will to begin with. It is important to bear this in mind because this realization enables one to distinguish *karma* from fatalism. In fatalism, it is outside factors, such as the Fates in Greek mythology, who are behind what happens to us; but if what happens is the result of actions we have ourselves performed then only we, and nobody else, is involved.
3. The third view contains both these elements. It is pragmatically evident that one is male, not female or vice versa; or born rich or poor. These could be attributed to past *karma*. But it is also clear that we can learn a new language, or acquire a new skill on the basis of a decision made by us in the present, which thus represents an exercise of our present *karma*. The induction of the idea of time into the discussion of *karma* provides the room for introducing a very important typology of *karma* in Hinduism.

This relates to the division of *karma* into:

1. *prārabdha-karma;*
2. *sañcita-karma;* and
3. *āgāmī* or *kriyamāṇa-karma.*

The word *prārabdha* means "that which has already started", so this form of *karma* refers to that kind of *karma*, within our larger stock of *karma*, which has begun to bear fruit. Our present birth in a particular family would represent the working of this *karma*. The next is *sañcita-karma*; the word *sañcita* means accumulated, so this category relates to all kinds of *karma* stored up by us but still in store. Glimpses of it can be had in our character and our tendencies, or in our likes and dislikes, to the extent that performing those deeds has affected our character; but the deeds have not yet started taking effect. Just as *prārabdha* is patent *karma*; *sañcita* is latent *karma*. Different from both of these is present *karma* or *karma* of the third type. It is called *kriyamāṇa* because it is being performed in the present, like, right now. It is also called *āgāmī-karma* because it includes the *karma* one is going to perform in future. A popular example explains the distinction between these three kinds of *karma* as follows. Think of an archer at an archery contest who is just sent an arrow flying towards the target; he still retains an extra arrow in his hand, and he also has a number of arrows in his quiver. The arrow already speeding away towards the target is *prārabdha-karma*; the arrow the archer holds in his hand is *kriyamāṇa* or *āgāmi-karma* and the arrows in the quiver represent *sañcita-karma*. This distinction is helpful in explaining the situation of a person who has achieved "living liberation" or "embodied liberation" in Hinduism. As soon as one becomes enlightened, one ceases to generate any new *karma*, in the form of *kriyamāṇa* or *āgāmī-karma*. And the flash of enlightenment, as it were, blows up his entire stock of *sañcita-karma*. But the *prārabdha*, which set this life in motion, continues to operate until one dies. This kind of *karma* explains any illnesses the enlightened person might have, honours the enlightened one might receive, and so on, until the enlightened person dies. Just as a free wheel continues to spin for a while even after one has stopped pedalling, even though the enlightened one has stopped generating new *karma*, the momentum generated by previous *karmas* takes some time to subside.

The question of God in relationship to *karma* also needs to be examined. One of the main roles of God is to dispense cosmic justice; but as *karma* plays this role in some schools of Hindu thought, like the Mīmāṁsā dispensed with God, so that Mīmāṁsā, in a sense the most orthodox school of Hindu thought, turns out to be atheistic. The main line Hinduism however looks upon God as the dispenser of *karma*, as presiding over the workings of *karma* impartially. God is described as the supervisor of *karma*, or *karmādhyakṣa* (*ŚvetUp* VI.II) in this role. The presence of God allows the justice of *karma* to be tempered with mercy according to the theistic schools of thought, who see in God's mercy not an attenuation of justice but an expression of it. The factors historically underlying the emergence of the doctrine of *karma* are uncertain. Some scholars attribute it to extraneous, perhaps, tribal influence; other see it as growing naturally within Hinduism out of such concepts as those of *ṛta* and *yajña* within the tradition. (Also see Rebirth and Saṁsāra.)

142. Karmabhūmi

Hindu sacred lore contains the idea, in some of its sections, that the sacred land of India is *karma-bhūmi*, as this is the land where one produces fresh *karma*, while other parts of the globe and the universe are *bhoga-bhūmis* — where one experiences their fruition. *Karma-bhūmi* is thus one name Indians have used for India, and the above-mentioned conception may lie at the root of another strand in Indic thought, that all creatures will perforce have to pass through India, in the course of their several lives, in order to be liberated.

143. Kāśī

A city in India, amongst the oldest in the world, also known as Varanasi or Banaras or Banaras (spelled variously). It emerges in the later Vedic age as the capital of a kingdom; the exact derivation of the name is uncertain. It could refer to a chieftain, or a tribe, or to a kind of grass characteristic of the place. It had become the premier metropolis of north India by sixth century BCE and its location on the western banks of the Ganges further magnified its significance. The Buddha preached his famous first sermon in its environs, a *stūpa* now commemorates the spot. The city is a place of pilgrimage for not only Hindus but Buddhists and Jainas as well; and also for followers of many Hindu denominations such as Vaiṣṇava, Śaiva and Śākta. The city's primary mythical association is with Śiva, who finally got rid of the skull which stuck to his hands, for having chopped off an extra head of Brahmā, which Brahmā had sprouted to ogle at his own daughter. It is famous for its temple dedicated to Śiva, called Viśvanātha (Lord of the World), while Śiva himself is called Kāśīnātha (Lord of Kāśī). The city is also important in medieval Hinduism on account of its association with Kabīr and Ravidās. It has been a major centre of art and learning; one well-known commentary on Pāṇini's famous grammar (*Aṣṭādhyāyī*) by Jayāditya and Vāmana in the seventh century is referred to as the Banaras commentary (*Kāśikā-vṛtti*). The city has over 1,500 temples and numerous small shrines; and it contains several *dharmaśālā*s (inns) where pilgrims can stay free of charge. A centre of the final pilgrimage for many, tradition has it that Lord Śiva himself whispers the liberative *mṛtyuñjaya mantra* into the ears of the deceased. Local priests or guides called *paṇḍā*s are supposed to take care of the pilgrims and sometimes prey on them. Any religious act performed in Kāśī is supposed to be exponentially meritorious. (Also see Śiva and Tīrthayātra.)

144. Khyātivāda (Doctrines of Error)

Indian philosophy is distinguished by the effort it has bestowed on trying to account for error. Almost every major school of thought has its own position on this point. The most discussed among these are:

1. *anyathā-khyāti* or *viparīta-khyāti* of Nyāya-Vaiśeṣika;
2. *akhyāti* of Mīmāṁsā;
3. *anirvacanīya-khyāti* of Advaita Vedānta;
4. *sat-khyāti* of Viśiṣṭādvaita Vedānta; and
5. *ātma-khyati*; and
6. *asat-khyāti* of the Buddhist schools.

According to *anyathā-khyāti* of the Nyāya-Vaiśeṣika school, error consists of taking something to be other than (*anyathā*) what it is. We sometimes think our stationary train is moving when another passes by; the motion of other train is taken to exist other than (*anyathā*) where it is. The snake exists elsewhere but is taken to exist in the rope. The main point to be stressed here is that error always possesses an objective basis. According to *akhyāti* of the Mīmāṁsā school, error is always an act of omission and not commission. There is no mistake really, only a missed take. The rope and the snake represent two separate cognitions and the non-apprehension of their difference is the cause of error. According to *anirvacanīya khyāti* of Advaita Vedānta, the object of illusion is actually present while it lasts. Empirical objects exist prior to being known and also afterwards, like the rope; but illusory objects, like the snake for which the rope is mistaken, endure only so long as we know them. The object of illusion cannot be accepted as real because it ceases to endure, but it cannot be said to be unreal because it did appear, therefore it is described as inexpressible as real or unreal. Opposed to this is the *asat-khyāti* of the Mādhyamika School of Buddhism, according to which that which is thought to appear is altogether non-existent, while according to the *ātma-khyāti* of the Yogācāra school of Buddhism, it is a projection of the percipient. A useful way of classifying these is to differentiate between those theories in which the object of error is real (e.g. *anyathā-khyāti*); those in which the error is unreal (e.g. *asat-khyāti*) and those in which it is neither real nor unreal (*anirvacanīya-khyāti*). (Also see Pramāṇaśāstra.)

145. Kṛṣṇa

One of the incarnations of Viṣṇu, considered by his votaries as a full incarnation of God (*pūṛnāvatāra*) in comparison to others who were partial manifestations of God. He is probably considered a full incarnation on account of the multifaceted role he plays in all stages of life: as a lovable child, who steals butter and plays pranks, and also subdues a serpent; as a dashing adolescent, playfully teasing village belles; as a young hero slaying demons, and saving a village by lifting a mountain; as a rising ruler, who aligns himself with the Pāṇḍavas; as a shrew politician, who guides the Pāṇḍavas to victory; as a benign king, who rules over western India and as a tragic victim, who is shot accidentally to death. He also appears in the contrastive roles as the divine lover of the milkmaids (*gopīs*), and the divine interlocutor of Arjuna in the *Bhagavad-Gītā*. Perhaps a generation awed by the complexity, diversity and richness of his accomplishments had little option but to consider him divine. (Also see Gopīs.)

146. Kumbha Melā

It is not the Muslims gathering for the Hajj in Mecca, but Hindus assembling at the Kumbha Melā, which holds the record for the largest single gathering on earth. Thirty million souls gathered at the 2001 Kumbha Melā held in Prayāga (place for sacrifices), at the most auspicious astrological moment, around the Triveṇī (the point of confluence of three sacred rivers). The gods and the demons are usually at odds in Hindu stories, but in this narrative they combine to churn the legendary ocean for its riches. One such precious item to emerge was a pitcher (*kumbha*) which contained the nectar of immortality. As the gods and demons fought over it, four drops fell on earth, endowing those four places with special salvific potency. These four places, apart from Prayāga, are Haridwar, Ujjain and Nasik. According to some scholars a parallel to the Māgha Melā in the north is provided by the ceremony at Kumbhakoṇam in the south, where people bathe in the sacred waters of the tank during Mahāmakham. (Also see Utsava.)

147. Kuṇḍalinī

The name given to the potential for spiritual realization which is imaged as lying dormant in the form of a coiled serpent at the base of the spine, from which it must be raised to the top of the head for the attainment of enlightenment. Along the vertebral axis lie the various *cakras*, usually visualized in the form of a lotus, and for this reason also called *padmas*. The first *cakra*, called *mūlādhāra*, is located near the organ of evacuation, the next, *svādhiṣṭhāna*, near the organ of generation, followed by *maṇipūraka* near the naval, *anāhata* near the heart, *viśuddha* near the throat, *ājñā* between the eyebrows and *sahasrāra* at the top of the head. This last one is the thousand-blessed lotus, which begins to bloom, when the *kuṇḍalinī* finally pierces it, after having been roused from its dormant state through appropriate yogic practices. This mapping of the subtle body is widely shared within the Tantric traditions.

148. Madhva (1199–1278)

The name of Madhva is associated with the school of Dvaita Vedānta, just as that of Śaṅkara is associated with Advaita Vedānta and that of Rāmānuja with Viśiṣṭādvaita Vedānta. He was born in a village near Uḍupī in the state of Karnataka. Like Śaṅkara, whom he severely criticizes, he wrote commentaries on the principal Upaniṣads, the *Brahma-Sūtra* and the *Bhagavad-Gītā*, to establish his doctrine of Dvaita Vedānta as constituting the correct interpretation of these texts. Additionally, he also commented on the initial hymns of the *Ṛg-Veda*, and expounded the *Mahābhārata* and the *Bhāgavata*. He is also known by other names such as Ānandatīrtha, Pūrṇabodha and Pūrṇaprajña. His natal name was Vāsudeva, and he came to be known as Pūrṇaprajña (or Fully Enlightened) after taking *saṁnyāsa*, while he calls himself Ānandatīrtha in his writings. Jayatīrtha and Vyāsatīrtha are among his important successors. (Also see Dvaita Vedānta.)

149. Mahābhārata

The term refers to both an event and an epic which records the event. The event involves two rival clans, called the Pāṇḍavas and the Kauravas, in contention for the throne of Hastināpur, which is ruled over by the dynasty of the Bharatas, which represented the main dynasty in the northern plains of India, long the seat of political power in India. The two contending powers are thus related to each other as cousins, providing an additional layer of drama to the struggle. Despite repeated attempts at negotiated settlements, the rivalry inexorably ends in a war resulting in such carnage as is said to have decimated the flower of ancient India chivalry. These negative consequences are perhaps what tradition had in mind, when it described the end of the war as making the onset of the Kali-Yuga, despite the fact that the rightful heirs won in the end. The epic records this central event, along with digressions, in over 100,000 verse in its vulgate version, divided into eighteen books called *parvans*. It is thus one of the longest epics in the world, a status it vies for along with the *Kesar* from Tibet and *Manas* from Kyrgyzstan. It is certainly the longest epic of the ancient world. Its most famous section is known as the *Bhagavad-Gītā*, a text of 700 verses in the form of a dialogue between Kṛṣṇa (an incarnation of Viṣṇu who figures in the epic) and Arjuna (one of the Pāṇḍavas). (Also see Abhimanyu.)

150. Mahādevī

The Great Goddess, to distinguish her from numerous other manifestations of feminine divinity, which are ultimately contained within her. She can be viewed as both transcendent and immanent. In the transcendental form, she becomes the equivalent of God, whom she replaces, and it is at her behest that Brahmā, Viṣṇu and Śiva perform their cosmic roles of creating, sustaining and terminating the universe. In her immanent aspect, she embraces the various natural phenomena she has been identified with, such as night (as Rātri), dawn (as Uṣas), mountains (as Pārvatī), rivers (as Gaṅgā) and so on. She also embraces the various other votive goddess figures with positive or negative energies like Sarasvatī and Lakṣmī in the one hand, and Kālī and Durgā (Māriyammaṉ and Śītalā) on the other. (Also see Durgā; Kālī; and Māriyammaṉ.)

151. **Maharishi Mahesh Yogi** (1914–2008)

The moving force behind Transcendental Meditation. Over six million people around the world have been introduced to this form of *mantra* mediation. The movement has established many *yoga* centres, as well as Vedic university in Fairfield, Iowa, while the Maharshi himself lived in the Netherlands. The recent foci of this movement include:

1. reducing crime in an area by achieving a certain degree of collective meditation;
2. producing levitation through meditation; and
3. securing world peace.

Maharishi Mahesh Yogi gained international recognition when Beatles accepted him as their *guru*.

152. **Mahatma Gandhi** (1869–1948)

Mahatma (Great Soul) Gandhi is how Mohandas K. Gandhi was known among the Indian people on account of his reputation for saintliness. He is a major figure of the twentieth century who made contributions in many areas of life: politically, he is known for leading India to freedom against the British rule by evolving a novel mode of non-violent civil disobedience which has been emulated beyond India; socially, he was instrumental in promoting the abolition of untouchability; economically, he was a critic of de-humanizing industrialization and anticipated the environmental crisis; and religiously, he was a vigorous advocate of ecumenism and religious tolerance.

153. **Mahāvākyas**

When trying to identify the basic teaching of a sacred text, it is sometimes helpful to identify some key statements within it, which contain the gist of its message. For instance, in trying to understand the New Testament, it is helpful to use the statement, "Jesus is the Messiah" as a lens. This could be called the *mahāvākya* (great statement) of that text. Advaita Vedānta identifies four such statements, as encapsulating the teachings of the Upaniṣads:

1. All this is verily *Brahman* (*sarvam khalvidam brahma* — *ChāUp* 3.14.1 and *MuṇḍUp* 2.2.1);
2. I am *Brahman* (*ahaṁ brahmāsmi* — *BṛUp* 1.4.10);
3. This *Ātman* is *Brahman* (*ayamātmā brahma* — *BṛUp* 2.5.19);
4. That thou art (*tattvamasi* — *ChāUp* 6.8.7).

Sometimes a fifth *mahāvākya* is identified in the statement as *prajñānam brahma*: Knowledge is *Brahman* (*AitUp* 3.3). If we keep the first four of the list in mind, then the first identifies everything with *Brahman*; the second "I" with *Brahman*; the third *Ātman* with *Brahman*; and the fourth "You" with *Brahman*. If the first in the list is now replaced with *prajñānam brahma*, another classification of *mahāvākyas* can be identified:

1. "Knowledge is *Brahman*" is then described as defining statement about *Brahman* (*lakṣaṇa vākya*);
2. "That thou art", becomes an instructional injunction (*upadeśa vākya*);
3. "I am *Brahman*" serves as basis of practice (*anusandhāna vākya*); and
4. *Ātman* or the Self is *Brahman*, becomes a statement of realization (*anubhava vākya*). (Also see Advaita Vedānta.)

154. Mandir

A common name for temple in the north; the term *devālaya* (abode of god) is more common in the south. The temples are the predominant element in the religious landscape of medieval and modern Hinduism but Vedic Hinduism was characterized by the performance of *yajñas*, more mobile in character. By the time we arrive at the age of Classical Hinduism, however, the temple had become central to the religious imagination. Hardly any temple survives from the pre-Gupta age, probably because of the perishable nature of the material used, despite the fact that the two essential sites in a city used to be the temple and the palace. In medieval times, the temples themselves became a city in miniature, in the sense that, apart from the shrine, one also found halls, stages, inns, workshops and educational institutions within their premises. The staff, apart from the priests, included artists, musicians, servants and even dancing girls called *devadāsīs* to entertain the installed deity, a trend which, according to Al-Bīrūnī (eleventh century) seems to have been unsuccessfully resisted by some as undesirable. They also served as a refuge for the poor and the sick. The temples were often run through vast endowments of lands. The rentals, along with donations, helped in the upkeep of the temples, paying for the services and the priests, as well as the artisans and the artists. Taxes collected from villages were sometimes given to the temples as a grant. The great temple of Kañcīpuram in Tamil Nadu was endowed in this way, with a revenue of 1,000 villages. Forms of indentured labour and bonded service was not unknown, though modern reforms have eliminated this. Modern temples continue the tradition but not on that scale, except for a few new temples built by the Swamiranayan sect in Britain and India. Most simply house an icon and provide for ritual services.

155. Māriyammaṉ

The goddess, who both causes and protects against small pox, is called Śītalā in the north and Māriyammaṉ in the south. Two myths regarding her origin are particularly well known in the south, both involving untouchables. In one she is brāhmaṇa girl who gets married to an untouchable suitor under false pretenses. When the fact is discovered, she immolates herself, turns into fierce goddess and incinerates the untouchable. In the other, she is the pious wife of a holy man with the power to work miracles, a power she loses upon feeling jealous of a divine fair making love. The husband however attributes the loss of power to loss of fidelity on her and gets the son to behead her. She is revived when the mistake is discovered but her head gets attached to the body of an untouchable instead of her own. These stories suggest the interaction of the Great and the Little Tradition in the context of Goddess worship and could represent an attempt to create an imagined community by fusing the Great and Little Tradition.

156. Maṭha (Monastery)

Usually run under an abbot (*mahant*) and to be distinguished from a temple on account of it possessing a monastic and educational orientation. Many traditional orders (*sampradāyas*), founded by famous figures in the tradition such as Śaṅkara, Rāmānuja and Madhva, run their own *maṭhas*, where their followers are schooled and trained in ritual service. Many major medieval and modern religious movements operate through a network of *maṭhas*, which are often built by or around a figure associated with a particular denomination or movement. Some scholars think that the Hindu *maṭhas* were inspired by Buddhist *vihāras*. The formulator of classical Advaita Vedānta, Śaṅkarācārya is supposed to have established four *maṭhas*, at the four corners of India, for the propagation of his doctrines. (Also see Śaṅkara, Rāmānuja; and Madhva.)

157. Māyā

A key doctrine in Advaita Vedānta, which explains the relationship of *Brahman* to the universe. If *Brahman* is the sole undifferentiated reality (without characteristics and without distinctions, i.e. *nirguṇa* and *nirviśeṣa*) then the question arises: how is it related to our empirical world, which is full of distinctions, as illustrated by the various objects and persons found therein? Advaita Vedānta concedes that we do perceive such a world but regards it as falsely true and truly false; just as the snake appears to be so real and menacing when mistakenly perceived in a coiled rope, but disappears upon investigation, to use one stock example. The following points about *māyā* are stressed in Advaita Vedānta:

1. It should not be confused with total non-existence (*asat*), because what is totally non-existent cannot even appear (for example, a barren woman's son who cannot ever be perceived as an object of experience) but the universe is perceived. It is also different from *Brahman*, which is the ultimate reality (*sat*) and the changeless transcendental reality, while the universe is in the grip of change all the time. Thus *māyā* cannot be equated with either total non-existence (*asat*) or absolute existence (*sat*) and hence is described as other than both (*sad-asad-vilakṣaṇa*).

2. From the point of view of *Brahman*, *māyā* does not exist just as from the point of view of the rope, the snake does not exist; it only exists for the onlooker while the onlooker is having the experience. Hence, sometimes the word *māyā* is creatively etymologized as "that which is not" (*yā mā sā*).

3. From our worldly point of view, however, *māyā* appears as a mysterious power which makes something (*Brahman*) appear as something else (the universe). This power has two aspects, referred to as *āvaraṇa* (concealment) and *vikṣepa* (projection). When a rope is perceived as a snake, two things happen: the real nature of the rope as rope is concealed (*āvaraṇa*) and a snake is projected and substituted for it (*vikṣepa*); obscuration or suppression precedes projection or substitution.

4. If one asks: is *māyā* real or unreal, then the Advaitain's answer is that it is indescribable or indeterminate (*anirvacanīya*) in these terms because the world of plurality and diversity does appear to us, thus it cannot be dismissed as unreal, the way a barren woman's son could be dismissed; on the other hand, it cannot be called real because it disappears in the experience of the unitary *Brahman*, the way the snake does when the reality of the rope underlying it is realized. As it cannot be definitively brought within the categories of real

or unreal, it is described as *anirvacanīya* (indescribable). *Māyā* is thus unique in not being describable as real or unreal, but it is not on that account ultimate. It points to the *Brahman* as the ultimate reality, just as the illusory snake points to the rope as its ultimate reality.

5. The main goal of Advaita is not so much to analyse *māyā* as a conception, as to transcend it as a phenomenon. (Also see Bhrama; and Advaita Vedānta.)

158. Mehrgaṛh

The most ancient site of Haṛappan civilization in Baluchistan, which has been dated by Jean-Francoise Jarrige as prior to 6000 BCE, and thus belongs to the Neolithic period. (Also see Indus Valley Civilization.)

159. Mīmāṁsā Darśana

The Mīmāṁsā school takes its cue from the Vedas and attempts to answer two basic questions about them: Why should the Vedas be considered authoritative and, if they are to be considered authoritative, then what is their message? Mīmāṁsā maintains that Vedas are to be considered authoritative because they are eternal (*nitya*). They are eternal because there has always been a succession of teachers and students, who have been transmitting it in an unbroken chain. This transmission is not interrupted by cosmic dissolution because the Mīmāṁsā does not accept a cyclic view of time or cosmology. It maintains a linear view of time, by maintaining that the world has always been as we see it (*na kadācit anīdṛśam jagat*). However, something eternal could be eternally wrong, so the Mīmāṁsā school further maintains that error is extrinsic, and that truth is intrinsic to knowledge. This is known as the doctrine of *svataḥ prāmāṇya* or the doctrine that all knowledge is presumably valid. Error is possible but it caused by a defect, usually traceable to a person who commits the error. But the Veda is infallible, because it is not the work of any person, human or divine (hence called *apauruṣeya*). Nor can it be contradicted by empirical evidence because its authoritativeness is limited to transcendental matters. The core message of this eternal and infallible Veda is to enjoin human beings to ritual action (*codanā lakṣaṇo 'rthaḥ*), as laid down in the earlier portion of the Vedas, namely, the Brāhmaṇas; the school is therefore called Pūrva-Mīmāṁsā because it accepts the earlier part of Vedas as primary, in opposition to the school of Vedānta, which emphasizes the primacy of the latter parts — the Upaniṣads. Mīmāṁsā accepts the Upaniṣads as part of Vedas but views them as analysing the nature of the person who performs the Vedic ritual, and hence auxiliary to the earlier parts, which enjoin ritual. According to this school, the ritual commands of the Vedas are of two kinds: positive (*vidhi*) and negative (*niṣedha*); in other words, classifiable into dos and don'ts. The positive commands are of three kinds: *nitya* (daily), *naimittika* (occasional) and *kāmya* (optional). To the *nitya* category belongs rituals like Agnihotra and *sandhyāvandana*; to the *naimittika* belong the rites of passage known as *saṁskāras*, provisions for bath during eclipses, and so on; to the *kāmya* category belong rites performed to fulfil specific desires, like Jyotiṣṭoma to go to heaven (*svarga*) after death. Although, at one time going to *svarga* was the soteriological goal of the system, it later adopted *mokṣa*, like all other schools of Hindu thought, as the ultimate goal. It could however only be secured by performing Vedic ritual in a salvific way, which ensured purity of self. This goal was secured by neutralizing *karma* in this system too as in others, except that the word here meant ritual action. This school developed the view that by performing *nitya* and *naimittika karmas* one did not gain any merit as one was duty-bound to perform them, but their non-performance entailed demerit. The performance of *kāmya-karmas*, by contrast, generated merit, but their non-performance did not entail any demerit. So *karma*, then, was neutralized by performing *nitya* and *naimittika-karmas* (because their non-performance entailed demerit) and avoiding *kāmya-karmas* (because their performance generated merit). This school is similar to the Nyāya-Vaiśeṣika in its metaphysical orientation.

160. Mīmāṁsā, God in

The Mīmāṁsā school is considered the most orthodox among the various schools of Hindu philosophy but it is atheistic in character, despite the generally theistic nature of Hinduism. God is often regarded as the creator of the universe, but according to the linear view of time in Mīmāṁsā, the world has always existed, so the need for postulating God as its creator does not arise. God is sometimes regarded as the moral custodian of the universe but that task, in this system, is performed automatically by *karma*. God is regarded as the author of the Vedas in some schools of Hindu philosophy, but in this system no author of the Vedas, human or divine, is admitted. Even more to point, even the gods or deities get downgraded in this system and come to be regarded as merely the objects of the sacrifice, the emphasis coming to rest on the sacrifice itself, with the gods coming to be viewed as "grammatical datives". (Also see Īśvara [Advaita].)

161. Mīrābāī (*c.* 1500)

Perhaps the most famous female poet-saint of the Bhakti movement in north India, who flourished in the sixteenth century. She was married to the Rāṇā (ruler) of Mewāṛ but had fallen in love with God and saw herself wedded to Kṛṣṇa, which caused much scandal, as also her willingness to mix with all devotees of Kṛṣṇa, irrespective of their social origins. Her marriage was never consummated, nor did she commit *satī* at the death of her husband. She is believed to have been ultimately absorbed in Kṛṣṇa in Vṛndāvana. Her devotional songs remain immensely popular in India to this day. (Also see Bhakti.)

162. Mṛtyu

The most commonly used Hindu word for death, the certainty of whose occurrence, combined with the uncertainty of the hour, has perpetually beguiled humanity. Although the Hindu belief in rebirth somewhat tones down its otherwise stark finality, it is still to be avoided in the tradition and even dreaded. The most auspicious time for death is in the fullness of years and at a sacred place, specially the banks of the Ganges, preceded by a donation (*dāna*), specially of a cow (*godāna*), to boost one's stock of good *karma* on the eve of one's departure. Death is best encountered with a calm mind, set on God. The last thought is considered very potent in guiding one's future birth, just as the last thought one has on leaving a room usually determines where one goes next. The ability to take the name of God or remember God, at the time of death is a hallmark of a true devotee in the Hindu devotional tradition. From this perspective, Mahatma Gandhi only confirmed his saintly status by uttering the name of Rāma, when he was assassinated.

163. Mukhyā and Gauṇī Vṛtti

The distinction between the two terms on the issue of how the Upaniṣads are to be interpreted: literally or figuratively? Those schools of Hindu philosophy, which evolved after Śaṅkara's school of Advaita Vedānta had developed, claimed that Śaṅkara's school was interpreting the Upaniṣads by resorting to *lakṣaṇā* or *gauṇī vṛtti* (mode of interpretation). That is to say, it took the suggestive and not the literal meaning into account. The school of Acintya-Bhedābheda, associated with the name of Caitanya, emphasized *mukhyā vṛtti* (denotative and direct meaning). If one says a person lives on the Ganges, the statement cannot be taken literally and really means that the person lives on the banks of the Ganges. This is an explanation of *lakṣaṇā*. A form of it is called *gauṇī vṛtti*, when a *guṇa* (quality) is meant. Thus someone may be described as a lion. This obviously means that he shares a trait (*guṇa*) of a lion, namely, bravery. (Also see Caitanya; and Advaita Vedānta.)

164. Mūrti

Image, specially a consecrated image in a temple. The installation of an image in a temple involves a ritual process, at the end of which it becomes infused with life (*prāṇa*). A similar process has to be undergone when it is decommissioned. One should not make the mistake of thinking that the divinity is confined to this place, rather that, though present everywhere, it shines brightly here, just as the same electricity may be present in bulbs of different voltages, and even present in the atmosphere in an unmanifest form. The phenomenon of image worship takes the immanence of God as seriously as its transcendence. Divine omnipresence is not an obstacle to a particularized manifestation, but rather as a confirmation of it. The opening of the eyes of the image is undertaken with special care during the consecration, which once again connects with the role of *darśana* in Hinduism. Such a direct *darśana* of the deity could be too powerful to withstand as the image comes to life, artisans are said to use mirrors for this purpose. In Vaiṣṇava theology, the image actually constitutes the last of the following five forms of God:

1. the transcendental form (*para*);
2. the grouped form (*vyūha*);
3. the incarnated form (*vibhāva*);
4. the immanent form (*antaryāmī*); and
5. the form of an image (*arcā*).

(Also see Viśiṣṭādvaita Vedānta.)

165. Mutiny

Rebellion against the East India Company in north India during 1857-58, which is also called the First War of Independence. One major factor underlying it was the fear of Christian conversion. It was ruthlessly suppressed, with Hindu sepoys (soldiers) being forced to eat beef and Muslim sepoys pork before they were hanged. The next-of-kin were not permitted to remove the bodies, which were left hanging. According to many historians, the Mutiny nevertheless put the fear of God in the British and led adoption of a hands-off policy so far as religion was concerned, during the rest of British rule in India.

166. Mūvāḷakuḻicāmuṇḍī

A goddess in Kerala, who gets her name from the fact that a brāhmaṇa tried to capture her with his magical powers, imprisoning her in a vessel buried in a hole (*kuḻi*), at the depth as three men (*mūvālam*). She broke free, however, and chased the brāhmaṇa, who sought refuge in a temple of Śiva. She spared his life on the condition that she be installed beside Śiva. She thus has both a *teyyam* shrine, as well as a place in the Trikanyalapan Temple for herself. (Also see Mahādevī.)

167. Nāgapañcamī

A festival in honour of serpents, so called because it is held on the fifth day of the bright half of the month Śrāvaṇa (July–August). Hindu folklore is characterized by a certain permeability between the underworld of snakes and the world of human being, and stories of shape shifting abound. Thus snakes, although dreaded, are also worshipped, in good measure perhaps because they are dreaded, but also on account of their positive mythic associations. Apparently snake worship in some form can be traced back to the Indus Valley, where a seal depicts a cobra being supplicated. Cobras are associated with Śiva, and coil around him. Snakes are also associated with rain and with treasures. But more importantly, the serpents who live underground are perceived as having rights on the ground itself. So that their worship takes the form of payment for its use, and part of the idea is to keep them placated against unwanted intrusions.

168. Nāmakaraṇa

The rite of giving the child its formal name. The tradition of giving pet names, before or after the naming ceremony, is common within Hinduism; what sets *nāmakaraṇa* apart is the conferment of the formal name. The name could be drawn from any source; the general rule is that it should be auspicious. The child could be named after a hero, a deity, or the family deity, or on the basis of the horoscope. Children are named after their grandparents in some parts of India. Sometimes amulets are tied to the children with *mantras* on this occasion. (Also see Saṁskāras.)

169. Namaskāra

Popular mode of greeting common in Indic civilization, often accompanied by folding of hands and a slight bow. The gesture had been interpreted at many levels. The bringing of the two palms together has been taken by some to mean: "You and I are one". The gesture of bowing has been taken to mean, "The God, or divine, in me bows to the God or divine in You". The word itself literally means the act of bowing. (Also see Praṇāma.)

170. Nāsadīya-Sūkta

Famous hymn of the *Ṛg-Veda* (X.129), so called because it begins by stating that in the very beginning there was neither non-being nor being (*na asat, na sat*). This hymn is said to contain the "first flash" of the indeterminable Absolute, which plays such a major role in Hindu philosophy. It ends on a note of sublime scepticism and wonders whether even the "highest being in the highest heaven knows how the world came to be".

171. Navya-Nyāya

The Nyāya school is known for its belief in the objective existence on an external world, otherwise called realism. It is also known for its commitment to logic. Hence it may be said to be characterized by logical realism. In due course its commitment to logic came to be foregrounded, even at the expense of other dimensions of the system. This neo-logical movement has heralded by Gaṅgeśa (twelfth century) and came to be called Navya-Nyāya (or the New School), as distinguished from the old school (or Prācīna Nyāya). Many of its exponents, such as Vāsudeva Sārvabhauma and Raghunātha Śiromaṇi, lived in Navadvīpa in Bengal, so it also came to be known not just by its epistemological but also this geographical feature. (Also see Nyāya.)

172. Neti-Neti

"Not so, not so". A famous characterization of *Brahman* by negation, traceable to *Bṛhadāraṇyaka Upaniṣad* (IV.2.4) wherein the Self or *Ātman* is really so characterized, although it has been plausibly applied to *Brahman* because the two are identified in the text and in Advaita Vedānta. The expression has been described as "perhaps the most succinct statement of the unqualified supreme as held by Śaṅkara". The core idea which this short formula captures and contains is that there is nothing in this empirical world which can be used to characterize *Brahman* (ultimate reality), which is also called *nirguṇa* on account of this fact. Space in relation to material objects perhaps provides a useful illustration of this point. We know that material objects are usually characterized by length, width and height. If now one were asked whether space, which is immaterial in nature, could be characterized by any of these we will have to say "not so". The negation does not imply however that space does not exist, only that no description of material objects can be applied to it. Yet, although space is not a material object, all material objects exist in space. Similarly, although nothing in the universe can describe *Brahman*, the universe exists in it. (Also see Advaita Vedānta; and Nirguṇa-Brahman.)

173. Nīlakaṇṭha

Śiva, as the God, who offered to consume the poison which surfaced when the gods and the demons churned the legendary ocean. Śiva held it in his throat, which turned blue on account of its virulence. According to legend, his wife, Pārvatī, put her hand to his throat, to prevent it from descending further. Śiva as Nīlakaṇṭha is taken to represent God's love for mankind, and has been compared to Christ's willingness to take on the cross for the sins of humanity on himself. (Also see Śiva.)

174. Nirguṇa and Saguṇa Bhakti

The distinction should not be confused with the distinction between

Nirguṇa and *Saguṇa-Brahman*. The fact that *bhakti* involves *Saguṇa-Brahman* obviously means that the terms *nirguṇa* and *saguṇa* possess different connotations here. Confusion on this point can be avoided by taking *nirguṇa* to mean without form (*nirākāra*) and taking *saguṇa* to mean with form (*sākāra*). The Bhakti movement in India flowed along two channels: the worship of God in the abstract (without any image or imagery) and the worship of God in the concrete (either through an image or in one of his incarnations such as Rāma and Kṛṣṇa). Those who followed the former trend came to be generally referred to as *sants*, prominent among whom are figures like Kabīr and Nānak. Those who followed the latter trend came generally to be referred to as *bhaktas*, although not without some semantic overlap between two terms. Tulsīdās, Sūrdās, Mīrābāī and Caitanya are examples of *bhaktas*. The *bhaktas* tend to raise their own favoured deities sometimes virtually to the status of God, rather than looking upon them as God's manifestation or incarnation, with the interesting consequence that sometimes the names of these specific deities also began to be used for God in general. This is most apparent in the case of Rāma, a word which has come to mean God in general, apart from referring to God's incarnation as Rāma. (Also see Bhakti.)

175. Nirguṇa-Brahman

The term *Brahman* stands for the ultimate reality in philosophical Hinduism. Hinduism in general is characterized by an ancient and unending debate whether this ultimate reality is more a principle (the Absolute of the philosophers), or more like a person (the God of the theologians). In the idiom of Hindu philosophy, the first position would correspond to the doctrine of *Nirguṇa-Brahman* and the latter to the doctrine of *Saguṇa-Brahman*. What is meant by describing *Brahman* as *nirguṇa* is that it is without (*niḥ*) distinguishing attributes (*guṇas*). More precisely, the doctrine claims that no empirical attribute can be applied to *Brahman*. This is also known as the doctrine of *neti-neti* (not this, not this); that is to say, any attribution of an empirical attribute to *Brahman* has to be dismissed as inapplicable. Example: all material objects contain the property of length, height, breadth, or all of them. But space is totally immaterial and the attributes of length, height or breadth cannot be applied to space. Yet this does not mean that space does not exist; indeed, paradoxically, all material objects exist in immaterial space, to which no material attribute can be applied. Two points specially need to be borne in mind to avoid misunderstanding the doctrine:

1. to say that *Nirguṇa-Brahman* is without characteristics does not mean that it is characterless; the statement should not be taken to mean that it is a substance without attributes but rather that it transcends the distinction between substance and attribute;
2. *Nirguṇa* and *Saguṇa-Brahman* are two aspects of the same *brahman*; the question turns on which of these aspects is ultimately ultimate and not whether *Brahman* is only one and not the other.

(Also see Advaita Vedānta.)

176. Nitya, Vedas as

See Apauruṣeya.

177. Nityatā

Hindu philosophy makes a clear distinction between two kinds of eternality, which may correctly, if crudely, described in English as fixed eternality and fluid eternality. The corresponding Sanskrit terms are *kūṭastha nityatā* and *pravāharūpa nityatā*. The first is exemplified by the unchanging rock and the latter by the ever flowing river. The distinction is important because both the universe and *Brahman* are considered eternal in much of Vedāntic metaphysics; the difference, which makes all the difference is, that *Brahman* possesses *kūṭastha nityatā*, whereas the world of *saṁsāra* is characterized by *pravāharūpa nityatā*.

178. Nyāya

One of the six orthodox schools of Indian philosophy, characterized by logical realism and theism. It believes in the existence of an external world independent of the observer, so that truth means the fidelity with which knowledge depicts its object, otherwise known as the correspondence theory of truth. Such knowledge can be gained by four means (*pramāṇas*):

1. perception (*pratyakṣa*) classified as ordinary (*laukika*) or extraordinary (*alaukika*);
2. inference (*anumāna*);
3. comparison (*upamāna*); and
4. verbal testimony (*śabda*).

The Vedas provide transcendental knowledge, with God (identified with Śiva) as their author, who is always characterized by consciousness unlike the souls, which gain liberation through the knowledge of sixteen logical categories (*padārthas*). This knowledge frees the soul from attachment (*rāga*), aversion (*dveṣa*) and ignorance (*moha*), leading to the cessation of *saṁsāra*, and to a state called *apavarga*, a post-mortem state in which both pleasure and pain are transcended. This school is often hyphenated with the Vaiśeṣika system, with which it became associated early on in its existence. On account of its interest in epistemology, its study is used as a propaedeutic for other schools of philosophy as well. It has been suggested that, as a system, Nyāya could be understood under the four rubrics of:

1. its theory of knowledge;
2. its theory of the physical world;
3. its theory of the self and its liberation; and
4. its theory of God.

(Also see Darśanas.)

179. Nyāya: Pratyakṣa

Nyāya defines *pratyakṣa* (perceptual knowledge), as direct knowledge produced by sense–object contact, which is definite and true; both conditions need to be met because knowledge could be definite (as when we perceive a rope to be a snake) but not true. Some prefer to go beyond defining it as cognition born of sense–object contact, because there was really no snake to be perceived in the example given above. Moreover, Nyāya distinguishes between ordinary (*laukika*) and extraordinary (*alaukika*) perception; it is by the latter that the *yogīs*, for instance, are said to be able to directly perceive atoms, or God everything. Ordinary perception is classified into three kinds: a stage when we know that an object is but not what it is (*nirvikalpa*); when we know what that object is (*savilakpa*) and when we recognize an object to be that which we saw before (*pratyabhijñā*). (Also see Nyāya.)

180. Nyāya: Śabda

The word used for valid verbal testimony in Nyāya, the word valid involving the idea that only verbal testimony given by a trustworthy person (*āpta*), whose meaning has been clearly understood, is valid. *Śabda* possesses not merely a verbal but also a semantic dimension. It has been classified into two, depending on the object and source of knowledge. If the object consists of matters of this world, i.e. of natural perceptible objects (*dṛṣṭārtha*), then the testimony of ordinary dependable people in these matters is valid; but when the object involved is beyond the world as we know it (*adṛṣṭārtha*), then the testimony of experts becomes valid, as of scientist in the case of the atomic nature of matter, or of the scriptures, such as the Veda, in transcendental matters. In other words, the testimony could be Vedic (*vaidika*), or secular in nature (*laukika*). The source of such knowledge is always a trustworthy person — but that person could be human or divine (like God in the case of the Vedas). The trustworthy person (*āpta*) is one who knows what he or she is talking about, and communicates it correctly. (Also see Nyāya.)

181. Nyāya-Sūtra

The foundational text of Nyāya philosophy, ascribed to Gautama (also known as Akṣapāda) and usually assigned to the fourth century BCE. A famous commentary on it is the *Nyāya-Bhāṣya* of Vātsyāyana (*c.* 400); followed by the *Nyāya-Vārtika* of Udyotakara (*c.* 600); the *Tātparya-Ṭīkā* of Vācaspati Miśra (841); and the *Tātparya-Ṭīkā-Pariśuddhi* of Udayana (*c.* 1000), who is also the author of the well-known work of Nyāya school called *Nyāya-Kusumāñjali*. (Also see Nyāya.)

182. Nyāya-Vaiśeṣika

A hyphenated system of these two schools, which results from combining the epistemology of Nyāya with the ontology of Vaiśeṣika; more precisely, by combining the Nyāya doctrine of *pramāṇas* with the Vaiśeṣika doctrine of *padārthas*.

183. Om

Om or *Aum* in its precise phonetic rendition, is an identity-marker in Hinduism (shared to some extent with Sikhism). It is not mentioned in the *Ṛg-Veda* but emerges in the period of the Brāhmaṇa texts, although its origin remains to be adequately explained. It soon came to mark the transition to a holy moment of ritual performance or spiritual discussion and itself acquired a holy property, ending up with a multi-layered symbolism of its own. Already in the Upaniṣads, its constituent units *A*, *U*, *Ṁ* are used to denote the states of waking, the dreaming and the deep sleep respectively, while the silence following it is said to represent a fourth, transcendental state. It thus could be said to really consist of four parts — *A* + *U* + *M* + silence. When used at a cosmic rather than at the individual level, it is a symbol of creation, maintenance and dissolution; at a temporal level of past, present and future; at a Hindu trinitarian level, of Brahmā, Viṣṇu and Śiva; at a sectarian level only of Viṣṇu, or only of Śiva. (Also see Gauḍapāda; and Sacred Sound.)

184. Orientalism

The view, popularized by Edward Said's work of that title, that all historical narration is discourse, i.e. deeply affected by the prevailing power equations, contrary to the academic's self-image of engaging in objective scholarship. Since the relation between the West and the rest of the world was highly asymmetrical during the age of imperialism, the period in which oriental studies emerged, the results of these studies run the danger of being Western "constructions" of reality rather than the reality itself. One scholar who has pursued this line of inquiry in relation to India and Hinduism is Ronald Inden, who, in *Imagining India* identifies Western obsession with caste (as the essence of Indian social life), and with "oriental despotism" (as the essence of Indian political life), as manifestations of Orientalism. (Also see Hindu Studies, Bias in; Subaltern Studies; and Western Tradition of Vedic Study.)

185. Pañcīkaraṇa

"Fivefold combination", or the process of creation as described in Advaita Vedānta. Although there is no unanimity in the Vedāntic texts regarding the exact process by which creation occurs, this is a fairly standard account of how it happens. The five subtle elements (*tanmātras*) as said to arise from *Brahman* in the following order: space or ether (*ākāśa*); air (*vāyu*); fire (*agni*); water (*ap*) and earth (*pṛthvī*). These five, combining in five ways, give rise to the five elements in their gross forms called the *mahābhūtas*, as follows: *ākāśa*, in its physical or gross formation as distinguished from the subtle, is produced by the combination of subtle elements in the following proportions: ½ ether, plus $^{1}/_{8}$ of air, fire, water and earth. This combination of half and one-eighths of the rest produces the corresponding *mahābhūta* and this process is known as *pañcīkaraṇa*. In an interesting parallel, the subtle body (*sūkṣma śarīra*) of human beings is said to be composed of the subtle elements (or *tanmātras*) and the gross or physical body of gross elements (*mahābhūtas*). (Also see Advaita Vedānta.)

186. Parā and Aparā Vidyā

The *Praśna Upaniṣad* (V.2) speaks of higher (*parā*) and lower (*aparā*) *Brahman*; similarly the concept of higher (*parā*) and lower (*aparā*) knowledge (*vidyā*) also evolved. The first distinction is ontological, the second epistemological. The latter is widely deployed in distinguishing between a lower and a higher truth, with the former serving as a stepping stone for the latter. (Also see Advaita Vedānta.)

187. Pāṭhas of Vedas

The Vedas have been transmitted orally for virtually 3,000 years with remarkable accuracy, according to both traditional and modern scholars. This outcome was secured with the help of many modes of recitation, which in effect cross-checked the transmission. Example: while the *saṁhitā-pāṭha* of the Veda is recited along with the euphonic combinations (called *sandhi* in Sanskrit grammar), the *pada-pāṭha* is recited without the euphonic combinations. These various forms of *pāṭhas* ensured the retention of the text in the original form of the language, even when those reciting it began to speak a slightly different form of the language as it evolved as a living reality. One consequence of this was that the reciters later on did not always understand what they were reciting. This divorce between recitation and comprehension is recognized within the tradition and the need to know the meaning is emphasized.

188. Piṇḍa

A ball of rice, or flour, typically as offered to the ancestors, and specially as meant to assist in the formation of the body of the deceased in the other world (*MS* III.237). It is the prospect of the vanishing of this rite which so upsets Arjuna in the *Bhagavad-Gītā* (I.42). If it is true that these rites and the world-view they are part of precede the emergence of the doctrine of *karma* and rebirth (according to which one's actions, and not the ritual actions of one's survivors, would govern one's future destiny), then it is striking that Hindus continue to perform *śrāddha* ceremonies devoutly, while simultaneously subscribing to the doctrine of *karma* without any cognitive dissonance, although attempts to logically reconcile the two are found in Hindu texts. It is striking that the Jainas distinguish themselves from the Hindus precisely on the point, by rejecting *śrāddha*, although willing to accommodate some other Hindu practices. (Also see Hindu Ritual; and Saṁskāras.)

189. Pitṛloka

The world of the fathers, that is ancestors, which is the abode of the departed beings who have led righteous lives. Such a being, however, had to be sustained in the other world, by regular offerings made in this world, through the rite of *śrāddha*.

190. Postmodernism

The discourse which challenges the Enlightenment legacy of focusing on the rational, to the exclusion of other dimensions of human life, with the added implication that what is presented as rational discourse may have underlying non-rational or even irrational elements, the process of identifying these being labelled as deconstruction. The Enlightenments emphasis on rationality sharply contrasted it with irrationality, which one was exhorted to eschew. However, life as it is lived, includes not just the rational and the irrational, but also the non-rational. A person's emotional life and family life in general have major non-rational components, so does the way one relates to existential issues of life and death, which may not be capable of being reduced to the rational. The emphasis on the rational, and the contrasting of it with the irrational, to the exclusion of the non-rational, meant that the non-rational was conflated with the irrational and dismissed along with it. The deeper roots of the erosion of social and spiritual life in the West may lie here. This tendency of conflating the non-rational and the irrational may also have encouraged the equation of religion with superstition. (Also see Hindu Studies, Bias in; Orientalism; and Subaltern Studies.)

191. Pradakṣiṇā

Circumambulation, specially of a sacred site such as icon, *stūpa*, or temple, bearing to the right in the clockwise manner. It is considered auspicious and may have originally been connected with warding off evil influences. It could also be an atoning gesture, as the king's wives circumambulate the horse which is sacrificed in the Aśvamedha, by way of making amends for its killing (*ŚataBrā* XIII.2.8.4). It is connected with the Hindu cultural perception of the body, which privileges the right side as the pure side, with the right hand used for eating, the left being for washing after answering calls of nature. The opposite or anti-clockwise circumambulation is called *prasavya*, and is the mode used in funerary rights. (Also see Abhicāra.)

192. Pramāṇaśāstra

The word for epistemology as it occurs in Hindu philosophy. It addresses two basic questions:

1. What is valid knowledge (*pramā*)? and
2. What are the means of valid knowledge (*pramāṇa*)?

Epistemology has been an important component of Hindu philosophy and there is a tradition of listing the various schools of Indian thought by the number of *pramāṇa*s they subscribe to. Thus the Cārvāka school only accepts perception (*pratyakṣa*); the Buddhist school approves of two: perception (*pratyakṣa*) and inference (*anumāna*); the Vaiśeṣika school accepts these two as well, prior to its merger with Nyāya; Jaina, Sāṁkhya and Yoga schools accept three: perception, inference, as well as verbal testimony (*śabda*); the Nyāya school accepts four: perception, inference, comparison (*upamāna*) and verbal testimony; the schools of Mīmāṁsā and Vedānta accept six: perception, inference, comparison, verbal testimony, postulation (*arthāpatti*) and non-apprehension (*anupalabdhi*). The Tamil novel, *Maṇimekalai* of Cattanār (*c.* 500), alludes to such a classification. (Also see Darśanas.)

193. Praṇāma

Prostration, an advanced version of which is called *sāṣṭāṅga-praṇāma*, when one falls prostrate on the ground. The eight elements which constitute it are said to be the knees, the feet, the hands, the chest, mind, head, speech and sight; but in its common form it involves a simple bow, almost like a *namaskāra*, which includes touching or grasping the feet (called *caraṇa-sparśa*) specially of the elders, parents, priests and *guru*. Touching the feet of anyone is considered a special act of veneration. (Also see Namaskāra.)

194. Prapatti

"Self-surrender" is an important soteriological concept in Viśiṣṭādvaita Vedānta. Devotion to God (*bhakti*) is said to lead to liberation in Hinduism but sometimes the practice of such devotion was hedged in with considerations of qualifications and so on, specially if it was meant to be practised in accordance with the Śāstras (scriptures). *Prapatti* then marks not only the culmination of *bhakti* but, equally importantly, emerges as an alternative to *bhakti* for those who may not be entitled for the practice of formal *bhakti*. It is open to all and is said to be immediately effective. It consists of the following sixfold resolve in relation to God:

1. following the will of God,
2. not crossing his purposes;
3. believing that he will save;
4. seeking help from him and him alone;
5. casting oneself on God; and
6. cultivating meekness.

Those who have surrendered to Viṣṇu abide in his Vaikuṇṭha after death. This concept is said to reflect the influence of the Vaiṣṇava or Bhāgavata creed on the Viśiṣṭādvaita system. (Also see Bhakti; and Viśiṣṭādvaita Vedānta.)

195. Prasāda

Food, offered in *pūjā* (worship) to the deity, is not consumed by the deity but offered back to the devotees, as an act of tangible and even edible grace. The wafer in the Eucharist could be considered the *prasāda* of Christ from a Hindu perspective. The word can be applied both to the act of grace, and object sanctified by it, specially if it is a food item. Some deities favour certain pabulums. Gaṇeśa's fondness for sweets (specially what are called *laḍḍūs*) is well known; the planet Saturn, worshipped as a deity, prefers sesame. (Also see Pūjā.)

196. Prasthāna-Traya

Also known as *prasthāna-trayī*; the terms refer to the following three texts collectively:

1. the Upaniṣads;
2. the *Brahma-Sūtra;* and
3. the *Bhagavad-Gītā.*

(Also see Vedānta.)

197. Prātiśākhya

A class of texts which describe the changes required to obtain the Saṁhitā text from the *pada-pāṭha* of the Vedas. (Also see Pāṭhas of Vedas.)

198. Preta

Literally one who has "gone over". The word is usually applied to a ghost, who has "gone over" to the other world. It refers also to the process by which one becomes a ghost, if the proper rituals are not performed. According to popular belief the departed inhabits in this state from about twelve days to a year, until one becomes ready to move on and resume the post-mortem passage, through a "body" constructed ritually by those who survive him or her. (Also see Pitṛloka.)

199. Printing

Printing emerged in China, where the written language unites the country, in opposition to India, where Sanskrit united the country as a spoken language, although written in each region in its own script (until recently, when the Devanāgarī script was adopted by foreign missionaries to print Sanskrit texts to advance proselytization). Modern printing, once introduced towards the end of the eighteenth century on a firm basis, was readily adopted as a means of popularizing their teachings by various Hindu reform movements, which arose after 1800. A prominent figure who exploited the opportunities offered by the print medium was Raja Rammohun Roy (1772/74–1833). The life of Dayananda Sarasvati (1824-83), the founder of the Arya Samaj, is instructive in this respect. Until his visit to Calcutta in 1872, Dayananda Sarasvati relied largely on the spoken word to spread his word and engaged in oral debates, called *śāstrārthas*, to advance his point of view. After the visit to Calcutta, he changed his strategy. He switched primarily to the print medium to spread his message, and as a corollary, rarely wasted time in verbally duelling with his opposition. Lithography has produced an effect similar to printing. Just as printing helped standardized manuals and translations, use of standard posters has had a similar effect in terms of images.

200. Proofs of the Existence of God

The main line Vedānta position is that the existence of God cannot be established by reason, because someone can always come up with a better argument. The firm proof of the existence of God is thus provided by scripture. The Nyāya school, however, does offer reasons for the existence of God, both independently of and in relation to the Vedas. Udayana (CE 1000) is the Nyāya thinker best known in this regard. Some of the arguments are summarized below:

1. While atoms may said to be the material cause of the world, the world needs an efficient cause. That efficient cause is God,

as it is difficult to imagine all the individual souls collectively playing that role, for the cause must be equal to the task in terms of knowledge and power.

2. The created universe is an ordered universe, showing signs of design and therefore pointing to a designer. This argument is similar to the teleological argument in Western thought.
3. The world displays not only natural but moral order in the light of the doctrine of *karma*. There must be someone who is responsible for such moral supervision, and that someone is more likely to be one than many, as it would be against the principle of parsimony to posit a plurality of gods.
4. Udayana additionally offers a negative proof, namely, that no one has proven the non-existence of God.
5. Udayana also offers an experiential argument, namely, that God is a fact disclosed by experience (*suprasiddhānubhava*).
6. Udayana also relies on the Vedas to establish the existence of God, but as Nyāya accepts God as the author of the Vedas this could be said to involve circular reasoning, if one established God's existence on the basis of the Vedas, and the authority of the Vedas on the basis of God. Udayana argues, however, that reciprocal dependence need not involve a circular argument when the universe of discourse is different. Thus Vedas depend on God for their *existence* by being reiterated at the beginning of each cycle, but not for our *knowledge* of them which comes from a succession of teachers. Similarly our knowledge of God comes from the Vedas but His existence is independent of them.
7. The rational theology of Udayana also contains a feature at superficially similar to Karl Rahner's doctrine of the anonymous Christian. Udayana argues earnestly that though Cārvākas, Buddhists and Mīmāṁsakas do not ostensibly believe in God, they do so without realizing it. (Also see Nyāya.)

201. Pūjā

A keyword used to denote worship in Hinduism. It has been suggested that the word and the rite it represents may be of Dravidian origin, as the word is not found in Indo-European languages outside the Indian subcontinent. However, the core model, which replicates honouring a guest, or a king, goes back to early Vedic times, for this is the way the *devas* were worshipped in the *Ṛg-Veda*. The main difference between Vedic and present-day *pūjā* turns on the invisible presence of the gods in Vedic times and the visible presence of the gods, in the form of an image at home or in the temple, today. The process has been felicitously described by one observer as follows:

> The presence of the deity is invoked (*āvāhana*); a seat is offered (*āsana*); the feet are washed (*pādya*); an offering of sandalwood paste and rice as a sign of respect is made (*arghya*); the sacred thread is put on the idol (*upavīta*); sandalwood paste is smeared (*candana*); flowers (*puṣpa*) are offered; incense (*dhūpa*) is burnt; the lamps (*dīpa*) are waved; food (*naivedya*) is offered and then betel (*tāmbūla*); next camphor (*nīrājana*) is burnt and gold is given as a gift (*svarṇa-puṣpa*); finally the deity is bidden farewell to (*visarjana*).

The model of a guest is apparently more suitable for domestic worship and that of a king for temple worship. The king is roused in the morning from sleep with a hymn of praise which serves as the celestial alarm bell. The hymn is used to rouse God at the Tirupati Temple, with each stanza ending with *suprabhātam* (literally, "good morning") is widely known. The king is then given a ceremonial bath and dressed up in regalia, after which he holds court and gives audience, even as he is plied with sweets. At noon he has his lunch and then retires for an afternoon siesta. He again takes up his position in the evening, as worshippers come to pay him respect. Later in the evening he is entertained with performances also watched by the worshippers, which might explain the development of dancing by the *devadāsīs*. He is of course accompanied by his divine consort, specially during the evening activities, until he turns in for the night with due ceremony.

202. Pūjā: Mūrti-Pūjā

"Image worship", a pervasive feature of Hinduism, which shocked the French traveller, Francois Bernier, as much in the seventeenth century as it might a foreign visitor to India now, leading him to ask the *paṇḍits* for an explanation, which they offered as follows:

> We have indeed in our temples a great variety of images. . . . To all these images we pay great honour; prostrating our bodies, and presenting to them, with much ceremony, flowers, rice, scented oil, saffron, and other similar articles. Yet we do not believe that these statues are themselves Brahmā or Viṣṇu but merely their images and representations. We show them deference only for the sake of the deity whom they represent, and when we pray it is not to the statue, but to that deity. Images are admitted in our temples, because we conceive that prayers are offered up with more devotion when there is something before the eyes that fixes the mind; but in fact we acknowledge that God alone is absolute, that He only is the omnipotent Lord.

This explanation may not apply to those forms of Hinduism which hold the image to actually be God, as in *arcāvatāra* (see Arcā), although no Hindu would consider God as confined to image, or the image exhausting the being of God. There is also a strand within Hinduism which looks upon image worship as a stepping stone to a higher conception of God, and as an inferior form of worship in terms of this higher conception. The *Śiva Purāṇa* contains the following verse:

> The highest state is the natural realization of God's presence, the second in rank is meditation and contemplation, the third is the worship of symbols which are reminders of the Supreme, and the fourth is the performance of ritual and pilgrimages to sacred places.

There is also a Sanskrit verse to similar effect:

> One begins with the worship of idols; next comes the muttering of *mantras* and the offering of prayers; above that is mental worship and the contemplation of the Absolute excels them all.

(Also see Hindu Polytheism.)

203. Pūjā: Pañcāyatana

"Fivefold worship", a rite by which multiple deities are worshipped simultaneously while primacy is accorded to one, comparable to the Vedic henotheism after a fashion. The figure five refers to the five gods involved:

1. Viṣṇu,
2. Śiva,
3. Gaṇeśa,
4. Sūrya, and
5. Śakti.

Each deity is represented by an object, usually stone, and the arrangement of the stone represents a constellation of priority and coexistence. For example, when Viṣṇu is placed as the centre as a black stone, then the gods Śiva, Gaṇeśa, Sūrya and Goddess Śakti are respectively represented in the north-east, south-east, south-west and north-west directions by a white stone, red stone, crystal and metallic ore. The ritual can be shared by the followers of these five deities collectively, as any of deities could occupy the central place. This is a good example of the application, within Hinduism, of the principle of rotating hierarchy to maintain a dynamic pluralism.

204. Pūjā: Vaiśvadeva

A Vedic household ceremony performed for the well-being of the whole family, unlike the *sandhyā-vandana*, which is performed by the person for himself or herself.

205. Purāṇas

A genre of sacred literature in Hinduism popular with the masses.

The etymology of the word is explained by Yāska as *purā navaṁ*, (that which is old but ever new). The Purāṇas are supposed to deal with five topics (*pañcalakṣanam*):

1. creation (*sarga*);
2. dissolution (*pratisarga*);
3. genealogy of gods and sages (*vaṁśa*);
4. the periods of the various Manus (*manvantarāṇi*); and
5. the accounts of the royal dynasties (*vaṁśānucaritam*).

But they overflow the boundaries of these topics. They are divided into two categories: The eighteen main Purāṇas, and another set of eighteen subsidiary Purāṇas, called Upa-Purāṇas.

The main Purāṇas are the following, in accordance with a famous verse which lists them:

1. *Brahma Purāṇa,*
2. *Padma Purāṇa,*
3. *Viṣṇu Purāṇa,*
4. *Śiva Purāṇa,*
5. *Bhāgavata Purāṇa,*
6. *Nārada Purāṇa,*
7. *Mārkaṇḍeya Purāṇa,*
8. *Agni Purāṇa,*
9. *Bhaviṣya Purāṇa,*
10. *Brahmavaivarta Purāṇa,*
11. *Liṅga Purāṇa,*
12. *Varāha Purāṇa,*
13. *Skanda Purāṇa,*
14. *Vāmana Purāṇa,*
15. *Kūrma Purāṇa,*
16. *Matsya Purāṇa,*

17. *Guruḍa Purāṇa*, and
18. *Brahmāṇḍa Purāṇa.*

The subsidiary Purāṇas are listed below in a similar fashion:

1. *Sanatkumāra*,
2. *Narasiṁha*,
3. *Nāradīya*,
4. *Śiva*,
5. *Durvāsā*,
6. *Kapila*,
7. *Mānava*,
8. *Anuśānasa*,
9. *Brahmāṇḍa*,
10. *Vāruṇa*,
11. *Kālikā*,
12. *Maheśvara*,
13. *Sāmbha*,
14. *Nandī*,
15. *Sūrya*,
16. *Parāśara*,
17. *Bhāgavata* (probably a misreading for *Bhārgava*), and
18. *Vasiṣṭha.*

There are also Purāṇas of other kinds, nor are they linguistically confined to Sanskrit. Some Tamil works, which deal with the celestial activities of Śiva are also called so, the best known in the genre perhaps being the *Periya Purāṇam*. There is also the tradition of various significant sites in Hinduism possessing a local or *Sthala Purāṇa*. The major Purāṇas gained great importance during the period of classical Hinduism, most of which are to be assigned in their present form to a period *between* the fifth and the tenth century. Their context is provided by the rise of devotional deities in Hinduism, which may have some links with Vedic deities, but come into their own during this period and are worshipped either at home or in large temples, along with their celebrated devotees. They are known as the fifth Veda, like so many other texts which gained sanctity in Hinduism, and perhaps crucial to their role in Hinduism is the fact that they cater to the religious needs of the people in Kali-Yuga, which commenced around 3102 BCE, according to the most widely accepted sacred chronology. This age is said to represent a decline in the spiritual capacities of individuals. These texts claim to address this new situation by providing a religion for the masses based on devotion. (Also see Smṛti.)

206. Purohita

Literally the one placed in front and actually meaning the family priest, who guides family through the various domestic rites, or performs special *pūjās* for it. This could be a relationship which goes back through many generations, or now increasingly a recently acquired one. The *purohita* receives *dakṣiṇā* for his services.

207. Puruṣa and Prakṛti

Just as Hinduism possesses a full-fledged male theology on the one hand, and a full-fledged female theology on the other, it also contains a strand which strives to give both the male and the female elements their due. This is most obvious in some schools of philosophy which are frankly dualistic, like Sāṁkhya, where the male (*puruṣa*) represents spirit, and the female (*prakṛti*), matter. It is when we move to theology from philosophy however that this vision acquires more colour. In the case of Śaivism, Śiva and Pārvatī acquire prominence as a pair, and in the case of Vaiṣṇavism, the pairing of Viṣṇu and Lakṣmī is profiled. If we include Brahmā, as the third member of the Hindu trinity, then he is paired with Sarasvatī, although she is also sometimes affiliated to him as a daughter. These pairings could be the result of either an underlying empirical realization that ignoring the gender equation can be dangerous, or a recognition of a profounder natural fact that the male and the female may not be as far apart essentially as they appear biologically, because one becomes a male or a female on account of the relative dominance of this particular feature rather than on account of a complete absence of the other. (Also see Sāṁkhya.)

208. Puruṣārtha

From *puruṣa* (human beings) and *artha* (pursued goal), hence the doctrine of the legitimate goals of human behaviour. These were once considered three (*trivarga*) but were subsequently standardized as four:

1. *dharma*;
2. *artha*;
3. *kāma;* and
4. *mokṣa*.

Dharma represents the pursuit of virtue or righteousness and represents the moral, and in some contexts, social norms, subject to which the goals of *artha* and *kāma* should be pursued. *Artha* stands for wealth and power, or material gain and worldly success, and *kāma* for the pleasures of life. *Mokṣa* stands for liberation or salvation. (Also see Dharma and Mokṣa; and Śāstra.)

209. Puruṣa-Sūkta

Famous hymn of the *Ṛg-Veda* (X.90), so called because reality is holistically presented as a primeval person (*puruṣa*), from whose sacrifice the universe emerged. It thus hints at the organic unity of the whole universe and contains the first description (*ṚV* X.90.12) of what later on came to be called the four *varṇa*s of brāhmaṇa, kṣatriya, vaiśya and śūdra, although the word *varṇa* does not occur in the hymn. It thus provides the first scriptural justification of the "caste system", with some interpreters emphasizing the hierarchy involved in the enumeration and others the organic unity or harmony of society, as all are parts belong to the same *puruṣa*. The temple in Hinduism is also designed in the likeness of a *puruṣa*, making the text a part of the ceremonial founding of a temple. (Also see Varṇa.)

210. Radha Soami Satsang

A modern religious movement within Hinduism, pioneered by Swami Shiv Dayal Singh (d. 1878) of Agra, who was popularly known as Soamiji Maharaj. His basic teachings included vegetarianism, teetotalism, morality and meditation. Radha symbolized the soul in search of its master (Soami), union with whom was the ultimate spiritual goal. Swami Shiv Dayal did not appoint a successor, and the movement split after his movement, with some breakaway units establishing themselves in other parts of India, notably in pre-partition Punjab, on the banks of River Beas. This wing of the movement is said to be the largest, which claims a following of about two million people. The satsang at Agra is known for its educational activities.

211. Raja Rammohun Roy (1772/4–1833)

Hailed as the father of modern India, Rammohun Roy was the first Indian to respond fully to the new situation created by the establishment of British rule over India and the consequent exposure to modernity. He was also the first Hindu to make English a primary linguistic vehicle of this response, a step which has led to Hindus using English more for intrafaith purposes than perhaps any other religious tradition (with the possible exception of Judaism). Roy felt the need to reform Hinduism both theologically and socially, and to defend Hinduism against attacks on it by Christian missionaries. He critiqued Christianity in return, criticizing its doctrines of vicarious atonement and the Trinity. Theologically, Roy preached a non-idolatrous monotheism which he found rooted in the Upaniṣads; socially, he attacked caste discrimination, superstition, and subjugation of women, specifically symbolized by the rite of suttee, which he vigorously opposed. He founded, in 1828, an organization to promote his ideals, called the Brahmo Sabha, which was renamed Brahmo Samaj in 1841, the name by which it is known today. Several organizations sympathetic to its ideas were also formed across India. The theological agenda of Roy made little headway but his social reformist agenda is now part of the Indian constitution. (Also see Printing; and Suttee.)

212. Ramakrishna Mission

An organization founded in 1887 by Swami Vivekananda to propagate the teachings of his *guru*, Ramakrishna. The Mission and the Ramakrishna Math (monastic order) constitute the foundational institutions of the Ramakrishna movement. In 2007, the Ramakrishna Mission was running sixteen hospitals, 120 dispensaries, and 6,500 educational institutions throughout India, and had centres in over fourteen countries outside India. Its headquarters are located at the Belur Math near Calcutta.

213. Ramakrishna Paramahamsa (1836-86)

A major mystic of modern India, Ramakrishna became the central figure of a movement started by his disciple, Swami Vivekananda (1863–1902), which has done much to spread his teachings. Ramakrishna has been described as religious genius inasmuch as after his first mystical experience of Kālī, he devoted himself to exploring the various religious modalities within Hinduism, confirming their validity. He then extended his practice to embrace Christianity and Islam as well, so that in the end he could offer his personal witness to the ecumenical claim that not only all forms of Hinduism, but Christianity and Islam as well, represented valid approaches to the divine. This position has become virtually an article of faith within modern Hinduism, along with its corollary that if all paths are valid, then proselytizing has no place in interfaith relations. Ramakrishna, as the guru of Swami Vivekananda, also provides an exception to the rule that many of the major figures of modern Hinduism did not have a traditional *guru*, Swami Dayananda Sarasvati being the other exception. (Also see Kālī; Ramakrishna Mission; and Vivekananda.)

214. Rāmānanda

A pivotal figure in the history of the Bhakti movement in India, who is said to have settled in Banaras early in the fifteenth century (1400?-1470?), although hailing from the south India, where he may have belonged to the order founded by Rāmānuja. He was a devotee of Rāma, and, like Caitanya who was devoted to Kṛṣṇa, is associated with promoting the worship of his chosen god more through personal charisma than literary activity. One of his famous statements: "Do not inquire into caste or creed; whosoever worship God is God's" indicates how devotion was meant to trump caste. Both the *sant* and the *bhakta* traditions of medieval India claim him as one of their own. He founded the Rāmānandī order, to which most of the present-day *sādhus* belong, and promoted the use of the local language (in this case, Hindi), in practice. His disregard for caste resonates with modern reformist tendencies, while the persistent tradition that Kabīr was his disciple marks him out a potential bridge-builder between Hinduism and Islam. (Also see Bhakti; and Kabīr.)

215. Rāma-Rājya

Rāma-rājya or *Rām-rāj* embodies the concept of the ideal ruler and ideal rule in the Hindu imagination. Mahatma Gandhi promised *Rāma-rājya* (*Khudāi Rāj* in Muslim idiom) in place of the British Raj during his campaigns and the words continue to evoke idea of a blessed government. The concept should be distinguished from that of Hindu Raj, which is more political, while than that of *Rām-rāj* is largely utopian.

216. Rāmāyaṇa

Along with the *Mahābhārata*, one of the two main epics of Hinduism, although the tradition itself views it as the first example of belles-letters. The stage is set in this epic for the descent of God Viṣṇu on earth, as Rāma, on account of the depredations of the demonic figure of Rāvaṇa, who although a great scholar and a devotee of

Śiva, now oppresses the worlds, armed with a boon that no god or demon could kill him. Viṣṇu therefore has to appear as a human being to accomplish this task, by being born as Rāma, the son of King Daśaratha. The *Rāmāyaṇa* is an account of Rāma's life (see Rāma). The epic is popular not only throughout India but also in South Asia, the narrative proving malleable enough to be cast in different moulds. (Also see *Mahābhārata*.)

217. Ravidās

Also known as Raidās, Ravidās was a saint-poet of the fifteenth century. Not much is known of his life, apart from the fact that he was born into an untouchable tanner family, a fact alluded to in his songs. He emphasized the fact that the ultimate reality transcends human conceptual categories; and therefore those who seek it, by implication, transcend man-made social boundaries, such as those represented by caste. His verses refer to brāhmaṇas coming to him for spiritual guidance, even as he refers to their pride and hints that the lowly status of the untouchable makes him particularly suitable for spiritual progress, because it is not obstructed by one's ego. The spiritually nourishing and socially egalitarian thrust of the teachings has made him a popular figure in reformist Hinduism and an organization called All India Adi Dharma Mission, founded in 1957, acknowledges him as its founding figure. (Also see Bhakti.)

218. Rebirth

Belief in rebirth is a corollary to that of *karma*. Logically the two can be separated; it is possible to have *karma* (cosmic moral justice) without rebirth, as it is clear from the eschatology of the Abrahamic religions, and it is possible to have rebirth without *karma*, as is the case with many primitive societies. But the two dovetail in Hinduism.

The idea of multiple births and deaths differs diametrically from the more usual idea of a single birth and a single death found in the Abrahamic religions (followed by the last judgement). Such rebirth in Hinduism can occur in the form of any one of sentient beings, including animals. As a consequence, the distinction between humans and animals is less watertight within it than in the Abrahamic religions. Some schools believe that fresh *karma* is only generated in a human birth and other forms of life, sub-human or superhuman, are only meant for working out past *karma*. Theosophists believe that once one is born a human being, there is no sliding back.

The mechanism of rebirth is identified in terms of *liṅga-śarīra* or *sūkṣma-śarīra*; both terms denote a subtle body, which leaves the physical body at the moment of death and is reincarnated in another physical body. Vedānta works with an even more elaborate scheme of the human person and speaks of the three bodies (*tri-śarīra*): the causal body (*kāraṇa-śarīra*); the subtle body (*sūkṣma-śarīra*) and the gross or physical body (*sthūla-śarīra*). In terms of this scheme, the causal and subtle bodies migrate simultaneously at the moment of death. Al-Bīrūnī identifies the belief in rebirth or metempsychosis as the "shibboleth of the Hindu religion", on par with the Shahadah in Islam, the Trinity in Christianity and the Sabbath in Judaism. (Also see Karma.)

219. Revelation

The Vedas enjoy the status of revelation in Hinduism, although there are different ways in which they are understood as such within the tradition. According to a major strand, the Vedas have no author, human or divine; that is why they are called *apauruṣeya* and *nitya* (authorless and eternal). One finds here the unusual concept of a revelation without a revealer; it should be noted however that, in this form of Hinduism, the universe is itself without a beginning. This is the prevailing view in the Mīmāṁsā school of Hinduism, which does not subscribe to a cyclical cosmology, so characteristic of the rest of Hinduism. It accepts the Vedas as a natural fact. The Vedānta school accepts a cyclical cosmology but still regards the Vedas as *apauruṣeya* and *nitya*. The universe is continuously recycled no doubt, but this process has no beginning and the Vedas are recited, exactly as they were, by Brahmā, at the beginning of each cycle. The Vedas are eternal, in the sense in which a beginningless series of like things is, according to Vedānta. While the Vedas do not have any author according to both Mīmāṁsā and Vedānta, they do have one according to Nyāya, which regards God as their author. The commonly held view is that the entire corpus is revealed simultaneously at the beginning of a cycle of creation, and contrasts with the modern academic understanding of the Vedas as revealed over a period of time, usually seen as extending from *c.* 1500 BCE to *c.* 400 BCE. The two views could be reconciled by introducing the idea of progressive revelation. Similarly, revelation is considered beginningless in Hinduism as the Vedas are called *anādi*, but this could also be reconciled with the modern stance through the idea that the earliest texts have no visible origin, in the sense that although we can say that by 1500 BCE the *Ṛg-Veda* was in existence, it is virtually impossible, according to Max Müller who first seriously tried dating it, to state when it came into being. (Also see Vedas.)

220. Ritual: Historical Background

Two major classifications of Hindu ritual, first as Vedic and Āgamic, and then as Śrauta and Smārta, encapsulate the historical background of Hindu ritual. Hindu ritual was originally Vedic, as is clear from the organization of the Vedic corpus into the categories of Mantra or Saṁhitā, Brāhmaṇa, Āraṇyaka and Upaniṣad. The *mantras* were meant to be used in sacrifices which originally seem to have been simple, inasmuch as the offering was spread out, or offered in fire, and the gods invited to partake of it. As ritual became more complicated, a class of priests or brāhmaṇas evolved to address this complexity. Later developments involve a questioning of the ritual and meditation on it, which leads to the evolution of the Āraṇyakas and the Upaniṣads. This is an extension in the direction of the exploration of the philosophical meaning of the ritual; their technical aspect was taken up by the tradition embodied in the Kalpasūtras. The distinction between *śrauta* and *smārta-karmas*, or rituals within the Vedic tradition now comes into play, with the *śrauta-karmas* referring to those rights which are ordained in the Śruti, and *smārta-karmas* referring to those rituals whose knowledge is obtained from the Smṛti but which are said to be have been enjoined by Śruti texts now lost. The later portions of the Vedas represent an in-house or loyal opposition to ritualism; the critique of such ritualism by the new religious movements represented by Buddhism and Jainism, religions co-eval with the Upaniṣadic period within Hinduism, was not so constrained and more extreme. These religions came to be patronized by royal dynasties. Thus Aśoka's patronage of Buddhism is well known but his grandson, Samprati, was as an enthusiastic supporter of Jainism, as Aśoka was of Buddhism. The cumulative effect of these developments, and the assertion of what would in modern parlance be called animal rights in the face of their slaughter in Vedic ritual, let to a rapid contraction (but not total elimination) of public Vedic rituals in the public square; the domestic Vedic rites being relatively less affected or not affected at all. As Vedic public Vedic ritual fell into disuse, its place was taken by the rise of temple worship, with one major difference between the two gaining obvious prominence. Vedic worship was aniconic, whereas images were central to temple worship. The manner whose construction and maintenance of these temples and associated worship is spelled out in texts known as Āgamas, sometimes also called Tantras. (Also see Hindu Ritual.)

221. Ritual Symbolism

The ritualistic world-view of the Brāhmaṇa texts was, for a while, the dominant world-view within Hinduism, and perhaps that very dominance led people into interrogating its unquestioned acceptance. This prompted reflection on the ritual. Such questioning, on the one hand, led to its allegorization, and, on the other hand, to its interiorization. The Āraṇyakas and the Upaniṣads are the texts wherein this happens. The example of allegorization is provided by the *Bṛhadāraṇyaka Upaniṣad*, which actually begins by comicizing the horse sacrifice:

Aum, the dawn verily is the head of the sacrificial horse. . . .

There is also an implied transvaluation of values — the horse sacrifice confers sovereignty over the world, but spiritual sovereignty requires the abandonment of the world. The other early Upaniṣad, usually considered as old as the *Bṛhadāraṇyaka*, is the *Chāndogya*. Within it the life of a human being is interpreted in terms of the Soma sacrifice. But such symbolism is not necessarily merely an accommodation to changing reality, for the mental performance of a ritual is still considered as efficacious as its physical performance. There is however a recognition of the inefficacy of mere ritual or the perfunctory observance of ritual. Thus the *Kaṭha Upaniṣad* opens with Vājaśravas performing the Viśvajit sacrifice, in which all possessions are given away. But the precocious son, Naciketā, observes that the father is only giving away cows as good as dead, like giving away one's junk furniture to the Salvation Army. Since a son is supposed to one's most precious possession, he asks his father, perhaps sarcastically, "To whom do you give me", and the father tells him to go to hell, which he does, but that's another story. The point is that mere ritual observance has no purchase on spirituality. This point is made with great force by the *sant*s in medieval India but a certain ambivalence about ritual seems to lie at the core of religion. Ritual, on the one hand, provides the social glue which holds the community together, but on the other, its rapid observance has no spiritual spin-off. (Also see Vedānta.)

222. Roop Kanwar

The name of the eighteen-year old bride, who reportedly committed *satī* on 4 September 1987. Although more than forty cases of *satī* have been recorded in post-Independent India, her's is the best known on account of the controversy surrounding it in two key respects: was it a voluntary act and are such voluntary acts acceptable. Roop Kanwar was married to Mal Singh and lived with her husband's family in Deorālā, Rajasthan, but her husband passed away seven months into the marriage. When the funeral pyre for the husband was lit, however, she also perished along with his body as a *satī*. Five hundred people witnessed the event, a ceremony held thirteen days after her reputed *satī* was attended by 50,000 people. She was raised to semi-divine status of Satī-Mā. All this happened while *satī* remained forbidden by law as it is now, the original prohibition going back to 1829. The question of whether she committed *satī* of her own free will was crucial to the case and constituted the defence of members of Mal Singh's family, who were ultimately released and no charges filed for want of witnesses. The case is a lightning rod in the tussle between secular reformists who equate *satī* with murder, and Hindu traditionalists who ask: should the state not respect freedom of religion, if a woman freely chooses to go the way it is claimed Roop Kanwar went? (Also see Suttee.)

223. Ṛṣis

The word means a "seer", from the root *dṛś* (to see) but is specifically applied to one who sees the ultimate truth, and specially to the people to whom the Vedas are supposed to have been revealed. They are depicted as seeing the Vedas or as hearing them, hinting at synesthesia. The fact that the word *veda* is cognate with English video is suggestive. The word has several important connotations:

1. The Vedas represent the record of the spiritual experiences of the seers.
2. They are the medium through which divine wisdom is transmitted, just as the Qur'ān, for instance, was transmitted to the Prophet.
3. The seers thus discover the truth, the way Newton might have discovered the law of gravity and Einstein that of relativity, they do not "invent" it.
4. The personal foibles of the seers do not compromise the validity of the revelation, no more than the marital shortcomings of Einstein compromise his theories of relativity.

5. Revelation in Hinduism is mediated through multiple individuals rather than a single one.

This feature, which brings Hinduism closer to Judaism, has been used by Hindus to make the point that their scripture is a product of a community of minds, rather than of one, and may therefore have greater purchase on us on account of the objectivity achieved thereby, over against the claim of just one individual, just as one might is guided by the position of the scientific community, rather than of a single scientist. *Ṛṣis* are, *sensu stricto*, not the composers of the hymns but only their receptors.

224. Ṛta

An important philosophical concept in the *Ṛg-Veda*, considered by many to be the precursor of both *karma* and *dharma*. The word originally meant the ordered course of things such as the alternation of day and night, and the sequence of the seasons. The word for a season in Sanskrit, significantly, is *ṛtu*. This sense of natural order paved the way for a sense of moral order. The *Ṛg-Veda* gods share some physical attributes, as entities, for instance, which shine (*deva*), but they are also all described as guardians of the moral order (*ṛtasya gopāḥ*— *ṚV* VII.64.2). In the Brāhmaṇas, the word becomes a synonym of *yajña*, so that to the sense of natural and moral order, that of sacrificial order is also added. As the law of nature, or one's nature, *ṛta* has been connected with *dharma*. The same Ṛg-Vedic verse (X.124.5) which distinguishes *ṛta* (true) and *anṛta* (false), also states that it is ever-changing. Moreover, as a *yajña* connects ritual action with reward, and the word *karma* itself also means ritual-action, the concept could have paved the way for the emergence of the doctrine of *karma*. (Also see Vedic Religion.)

225. Sacred Cow

The cow is considered sacred in Hinduism and killing it is a heinous sin; even a crime in some states of India. She roams about freely in India, although the sentiment does not always extend to the bull or the buffalo but often does. Her divinity is explained and manifested in various ways. According to one Pūraṇa, all divinities exist in her; according to another, her is a divinity herself, and an incarnation of the Goddess. In many Purāṇic accounts, the earth assumes the form of a cow when ruled by oppressive tyrants, and appears in the conclave of the gods for relief in this form. She is sometimes used to symbolize "Mother India", or a "Hindu India" and Gandhi called it a poem in pity. When Raja Ranjit Singh (d. 1839) conquered Afghanistan he abolished the slaughter of cows and sale of beef in the country. All parts of her body and its functions are said to be of use; the dried cow dung is used as a cleansing and purifying agent, and otherwise used as a fertilizer, leading to her being a dubbed fertilizer factory on legs. She consumes refuse and stray vegetation; and produces the calf, which, when gelded, serves as the primary means for cultivation and transportation. Five products produced by her, called *pañca-gavya*, are considered therapeutic both medicinally and spiritually: milk, butter, curd, urine and dung, the last two often used in expiatory rites within Hinduism. Some anthropologists have explained the sanctity of the cow, which the modern mind may find hard to comprehend, as the apotheosis of her integral and even crucial role in the economy, but other elements may also be involved. In a village society one's cow is almost part of the extended family, arousing the sentiments associated with a pet and she has also been dubbed the foster mother of humanity, a description, which, if pushed too far, could lead one to equate killing her with matricide. This is a bit rich, but may point to the web of sentiments in which her reverence is nestled within Hinduism. (Also see Hinduism: General Features.)

226. Sacred Sound

The concept of sacred sound is said to constitute one of the continuities of Hinduism because one finds the tradition attending to it from the very beginning. Given the early role of chanting in Vedic studies, Hinduism is not merely an oral but also an aural tradition, and hearing a sacred word is as potent as seeing a holy person. This tradition of *veda-pāṭha* (recitation of the Vedas), also finds a minimalized expression in the *mantra*, just as it finds a maximalized expression in the *anāhata nāda* (the view that the universe is resonating with a divine sound). In some religions, the written word has been the medium of revelation, as in Judaism and Catholic Christianity, but in some others, such as Islam and Hinduism, sound can have precedence over word. (Also see Om.)

227. Sādhana/Sādhanā

From the root *sadh* (to finish or accomplish), it means the course one follows to achieve the spiritual goal of life. The idea of dedicated disciplined pursuit towards this goal is a key semantic component of the word. The exact mode of spiritual practice may vary from person to person, in keeping with one's preferences and background, but it is not the specificity but the intensity of the pursuit which is denoted by the word. Every system of *yoga* one pursues, or every sect to which one belongs, will have its own spiritual regimen to pursue, but it is its vigorous pursuit, in whatever form, which is indicated by the word. Common to all the practices which might be said to constitute *sādhanā* is the idea that one must "liberate oneself through discipline". (Also see Yoga.)

228. Sādhana-catuṣṭaya

"Fourfold means", the name given to the fourfold qualifications in Advaita Vedānta, required for anyone seeking knowledge of *Brahman*, preparing one for the audition of the scriptural texts (*śravaṇa*), reflection on them (*manana*) and meditation on them (*nididhyāsana*). These are:

1. the ability to discriminate between the eternal and the transient (*nityānitya-vastu-viveka*);
2. giving up all desire for anything in this world or the next (*ihāmutra-phala-tyāga*);
3. developing six qualities (*śama-damādi-sādhana-sampat*); and
4. intense longing for liberation (*mumukṣatva*).

The six qualities under item three are:

1. *śama* (calmness);
2. *dama* (self-control);
3. *uparati* (spirit of detachment);
4. *titikṣā* (patience);
5. *śraddhā* (faith); and
6. *samādhi* (concentration).

(Also see Advaita Vedānta).

229. Saguṇa-Brahman

There is a long-standing debate within Hinduism about the nature of the ultimate reality, which is called *Brahman*, as to whether it possesses or does not possess distinguishing attributes. Those who advocate the doctrine of *Nirguṇa-Brahman* argue that ultimately *Brahman* does not possess any distinguishing attributes, just as one might say of a blank screen that it possesses no distinguishing images until the movie starts. Those who advocate the doctrine of a *Saguṇa-Brahman* argue the opposite, that the ultimate reality does possess distinguishing attributes such as majesty, power and so on, which we associate with God. According to them, the concept of *Nirguṇa-Brahman* is a mere abstraction. These two descriptions of *Brahman* have been associated with two distinct soteriological orientations within Hinduism — one represented by the path of knowledge (*jñāna*) and the other by the path of devotion (*bhakti*). According to the path of knowledge, when one achieves liberation one realizes one's identity with *Brahman* and no distinction remains between the *Brahman* and *Ātman* (one's true Self). According to the path of devotion, the *Ātman* and *Brahman* are two distinct entities and liberation does not consist in realizing the identity of *Ātman* and *Brahman* but in developing the proper relationship between *Ātman* and *Brahman*, as one of loving devotion on the part of the *jīva*. (Also see Nirguṇa-Brahman.)

230. Śaiva-Siddhānta

"Śaiva doctrines", is one of the three main philosophical systems associated with Śaivism in India, the other two being the Liṅgāyata and Kashmir Śaivism. Although Śaiva-Siddhānta is now associated with south India, its origin has been traced to Kashmir and there is tradition of Tirumūḷar, sometimes described as the earliest Tamil Śaiva, of bringing Śaivism to the south from the north, particularly Kashmir. Śaiva-Siddhānta is considered a realistic school compared to the more idealist school of Kashmir Śaivism. The system of Śaiva-Siddhānta may be presented in terms of the three fundamental categories (*padārtha*): *pati* (God), *paśu* (souls) and *pāśa* (bond). The word *pati* stands for Śiva, the Supreme Lord. He performs the five functions of:

1. creation,
2. preservation,
3. destruction,
4. concealment, and
5. bestowal of grace.

He performs the function of creation by acting as the efficient cause, while *māyā*, activated by Ananta, serves as the material cause. *Māyā* in this system accounts for both the celestial and the material world and is therefore called pure (*śuddha) māyā* in the former context and *aśuddha-māyā* in the latter. The total number of elements (*tattva*s) involved in the process is thirty. From *śuddha-māyā* arise the five pure principles: *śiva-tattva, śakti-tattva, sadaśiva-tattva, īśvara-tattva* and *śuddhavidyā-tattva*. Śiva functions through these and also provides for the functioning of pure souls in the celestial realm. The world as we know it emerges from *aśuddha* (impure) *māyā*, from which arise the twenty-four *tattva*s as envisaged in Sāṁkhya. The *jīva*s are called *paśu* in an imagery suggestive of the shepherd, so common in Christianity. The soul suffers from three bonds called *āṇava, karma* and *māyā*, for which the word *mala* (impurity) is used, which emphasizes the role of *samaya-dīkṣā* in this system. *Mala* is a substance which must first be removed by ritual action, before proceeding to *nirvāṇa-dīkṣā*, which leads to liberation. This liberation is required because the *jīva*, although possessing a pervasive soul, regards itself atomic in size and this "original sin" makes it fall into the trap of *karma*, both good and bad, for the working out of which the third *mala*, that of *māyā*, provides the theatre. The souls are classified in three ways in this system, in relation to the *malas* (impurities):

1. those with all the bonds in place (*sakala*);
2. those who become free of *māyā* at the time of dissolution or *pralaya* (*pralayākala*); and
3. those whose *māyā* and *karma* are washed away but *āṇava* remains (*vijñānākala*).

The process of liberation starts once the *jīva* realizes the futility of *saṁsāra* and turns towards God. The four stages involved in the process are called:

1. *caryā*,
2. *kriyā*,
3. *yoga*, and
4. *jñāna*.

Each has a corresponding devotional attitude and a salvific state associated with it. *Caryā* consists of external acts devoted to Śiva like collecting flowers for Śiva and so on. The corresponding devotional attitude is of a servant of God (*dāsa-mārga*) and the salvific state it secures is a residence in God's realm (*sālokya*). *Kriyā* consists of a more intimate devotion to God; the corresponding attitude is that of a devout son (*sat-putra-mārga*) and the salvific state is nearness to God (*sāmīpya*). Yoga consists of contemplation of God; the corresponding attitude is that of a friend (*sakhā-mārga*) and the salvific state involves sharing the form of God (*sārūpya*). *Jñāna* involves knowledge of God and therefore leads directly to salvation; the attitude involved is that of a seeker of truth (*sanmārga*), and one achieves the state of union with Śiva (*sāyujya*). Although the word *advaita* is used to describe this state, it does not mean ontological identity with *Brahman* as in Advaita Vedānta, but rather non-separation from Śiva. The soul shares in the nature of Śiva (*śiva-tattva*), while remaining entitatively different. Perhaps one could describe it as indicating equality rather than identity with Śiva. The clear connection between devotional states and states of salvation envisaged in the form of Śaivism contrasts with the case in Vaiṣṇavism, wherein a larger range of emotional attitudes is identified but no clear pattern of their relation to salvific states in general is indicated, although some attempt to grade the emotional states (*bhāvas*) is evident in the school of Caitanya. Dīkṣā in this system is not open to women but they can find a place in Śiva's world vicariously, through the merit earned by their husband. (Also see Śiva.)

231. Śaiva-Siddhānta: Texts

The textual sources of Śaiva Siddhānta consist of the twenty-eight Śaivāgama texts, along with the *Tirumurai*, compiled by Nambi Āṇḍār Nambi (eleventh century). The *Tirumurai* contains the contributions of the sixty-three Nāyaṉārs, just as the *Divyaprabandham* contains the poetic outpourings of the twelve Āḻvārs. This includes the *Tirumandiram* of Tirumūlar; the *Tevāram* of Appar, Sundarar and Sambandhar, and, finally the *Tiruvācakam* of Māṇikkavācakar. The Āgamic and the Bhaktic sources are supplemented by philosophical ones, in the form of *Śiva-Jñāna-Bodham* of Meykaṇḍār (thirteenth century), whose underlying message has been summarized as follows:

> *Śivam* is one; *jñānam* is the knowledge of its true nature; *bodham* is the realization of that knowledge.

This entire textual tradition, inclusive of the Vedas, is summarized in the following verse:

> The Veda is the cow; its milk is the true Āgama; the Tamil sung by the four is the ghee extracted from it; and the virtue of the Tamil work, full of wisdom (*bodham*), of Meykaṇḍar of the celebrated [city of] Vennai is the fine taste of the *ghī*.

Other later important works include Arulnandi's *Śiva-Jñāna-Siddhiyar* and Umāpati's *Śiva-Prakāśam* and *Tiru-Varuṭ-payan*. Śaiva-Siddhānta as a system rests on the Vedas and the Āgamas. Nīlakaṇṭha, in his commentary on the *Vedānta-Sūtra*, in the fourteenth century, tries to reconcile these two. In the same way, both Sanskrit and Tamil texts figure as textual sources of Śaiva-Siddhānta.

232. Śaivism

The beliefs and practices associated with the followers of Śiva.

233. Śākhā

Literally branch, here standing for a branch of Vedic transmission. The task of carrying on the oral transmission of the Vedic corpus was divided among families, who specialized along a particular line of transmission. For instance, one following the Vājasaneyī Śākhā of the *Yajur-Veda* would specialize in the *Śatapatha Brāhmaṇa*, an Āraṇyaka of the same name, the *Bṛhadāraṇyaka Upaniṣad*, the *Kātyāyana-Śrauta-sūtra* and the *Pāraskara-Gṛhyasūtra*, which incidentally allows for the initiation of śūdras of good moral standing into Vedic studies (comparable to a similar statement made in the *Āpastamba-Gṛhyasūtra*). (Also see Pāṭhas of Vedas; and Prātiśākhya.)

234. Sākṣī

"Witness"; a key concept in Advaita Vedānta. It represents the *jīva* in its true character, that part of it which is identical with *Brahman*, whereas other parts of it are made up of adjuncts (*upādhis*) which are themselves part of the universe, such as mind and body. The witness is the implication of all empirical thought, without being implicated in it, just as a screen is implied in all images that are projected on it, but is not implicated in them, in the sense that they can change or disappear without affecting the screen at all. (Also see Advaita Vedānta.)

235. Samādhi

States of profound absorption which constitute the last stage in the system of *yoga* spelled out by Patañjali. It consists of two subdivisions: *asamprajñāta* and *samprajñāta*. In the former, also known as *samāpatti*, the mind is entirely absorbed in the object and assumes its form, but in the latter all mental modifications cease and nothing is thought of or known by the mind. The Self abides in its own essence as pure consciousness. The world of objects dissolves. *Asamprajñāta samādhi* can be of four kinds:

1. *savitarka*: when the mind is concentrated on a concrete physical object, such as an image;
2. *savicāra*: when the mind is concentrated on the subtle essential form of it, constituted by *tanmātras*;
3. *sānanda*: when the mind is concentrated on a subtler object, like a sense;
4. *sāsmita*: when the object of concentration is the ego itself.

This final stage of *asamprajñāta samādhi* is also called *dharmamegha samādhi*.

236. Sāṁkhya

One of the six schools of Hindu philosophy, with ancient roots. However, although Sāṁkhya is one of the oldest schools of Indian philosophy, the basic text of this school, the *Sāṁkhya-Kārikā* of Īśvarakṛṣṇa is relatively late, and assigned to the fifth century. It was among the books the Buddhist monk, Paramārtha, took with him to China in 546. In its classical formulation, it appears as an atheistic system (Nirīśvara Sāṁkhya), although subsequently a theistic version of it also attested (Seśvara Sāṁkhya). It is a dualistic system, in that it accepts the reality of both spirit (*puruṣa*) and matter (*prakṛti*) as ultimate entities. But while it brings all the diversity of matter under one category in the concept of *prakṛti*, it insists on the ultimate reality of multiple centres of consciousness, called *puruṣas*. These are subject to suffering on account of their entanglement with matter, and, once freed from it, achieve the *summum bonum* of life in the state of sublime isolation, called *kaivalya*. The Sāṁkhya view of material evolution has been quite influential in Hinduism, well beyond the confines of the school. It reduces the world of matter to twenty-four elements (*tattvas*), a description widely used in Hinduism. It also describes *prakṛti* as constituted as well as characterized by qualities or strands called *guṇas*. These are three in number and are called *sattva, rajas* and *tamas. Sattva* stands for all that is pure, light and sublime; *rajas* for passion and energy, and *tamas* for darkness and stolidity. This trichotomy has been applied to gods, human beings, temperaments and even diet. This classical system of Sāṁkhya is characterized by epistemological realism, fundamental dualism, material monism and spiritual pluralism. It is realistic in the sense that it believes in the existence of an external world independent of the individual subject and accepts the correspondence theory of truth, like the Nyāya-Vaiśeṣika school. It, however, introduces a new element in this epistemology with its concept of *vṛtti*, which may be translated into English as mode or mental modification. The intellect (*buddhi*) assumes the form of the object through this process of modification, so that perception is no longer direct but mediated by *vṛtti*, which holds true not just in the case of perception but also of inference. Its fundamental dualism consists of the fact that it accepts the independent existence of two ultimate realities: *puruṣa* and *prakṛti* (spirit and matter). The Nyāya-Vaiśeṣika school accepts a number of ultimate constituents of matter but they are all unified in Sāṁkhya under the concept of *prakṛti* (nature), whose evolutes they are. It is constituted of three strands (*guṇas*) referred to earlier, which remain in equilibrium in the state of cosmic quiescence. These dynamically reproduce themselves even in the state of quiescence;

creation is set in motion when their dynamic equilibrium is disturbed. Then *prakṛti* evolves into what is called *mahat* (great) or *buddhi* (intellect); which evolves into *ahaṁkāra* (ego), but here more properly stands for the principle of individuation. Further evolution bifurcates along the lines of the subjective individual and the objective world. On the subjective side, the process gives rise to the mind (*manas*), the five organs of perception: smell, taste, sight, touch and sound (*jñānendriyas*), and the five organs of action: speech, prehension, movement, evacuation and generation (*karmendriyas*). On the objective side, first the subtle (*tanmātras*) and then the manifest (*mahābhūtas*), forms of the five elements appear: earth, water, fire, air and ether. These evolutes of *prakṛti*, along with *prakṛti*, add up to twenty-four in number. The category of spirit (*puruṣa*), when placed alongside that of matter (*prakṛti*), and it evolutes, completes the list of the twenty-five *tattvas* of Sāṁkhya. Although the *puruṣa* is often used in the singular, it still stands for the plurality of souls as centres of consciousness, justifying the description of this system as characterized by spiritual pluralism, which contrasts with its material monism, as it aggregates all matter into the single category of *prakṛti*. It is the identification of *puruṣa* with *prakṛti* which is responsible for suffering; the *puruṣas* are really free but in their ignorance (*avidyā*) misidentify with *prakṛti*. When they achieve proper discrimination (*viveka*) between the two, they achieve the state of *kaivalya* (isolation) from *prakṛti*. The state of *kaivalya* should not be equated with pleasure, which a result of the working of *sattva*, a *guṇa* of *prakṛti*, which is now transcended; but one experiences the peace that passes all understanding, which comes from recognizing oneself as pure consciousness. This state of liberation can be achieved in this life (unlike the state of liberation in Nyāya-Vaiśeṣika school) and is called *jīvan-mukti* (living liberation). (Also see Yoga.)

237. Saṁsāra

Around the age of the classical Upaniṣads, that is roughly from the eighth to fourth centuries BCE, a major change came about not only in Hinduism but in the Indic world-view, which replaced the sacrificial world-view of the Brāhmaṇa texts. Life, in the Brāhmaṇa texts, consisting of living in this world and then moving on to other worlds after death, although the importance attached to ancestral rites maintained a kind of connection between the two. During the Upaniṣadic period, this view was replaced by the idea that one is born again and again into this world, or in other worlds, and that liberation consisted in being liberated from this cycle. The word *saṁsāra* encapsulates this new paradigm. This new paradigm, in main outline, is shared by all the four religions of Indian origin: Hinduism, Buddhism, Jainism and Sikhism. (Also see Karma; and Rebirth.)

238. Śaṅkara

The *ācārya* of Advaita Vedānta, at whose hands the system received its classical formulation. He is assigned the dates 788–820 but these may convey a false sense of precision and somewhat earlier dates have been proposed. He is credited with a short lifespan of thirty-two years by tradition, during which he laid the foundations of intellectual and institutional structures which survive to this day. He wrote commentaries on the three basic texts of Vedānta namely, the Upaniṣads, the *Brahma-Sūtra* and the *Bhagavad-Gītā*, interpreting them as expounding the doctrine of Advaita Vedānta, as well as well-known manuals of the system such, as the *Vivekacūḍāmaṇi* and the *Upadeśasāhasrī*. He also established *maṭha*s (monasteries) at four corners of India to propagate the teaching: at Badrīnāth in the north, Dvārakā in the west, Purī in the east and Śṛṅgerī in the south. (Also see Gauḍapāda; and Advaita Vedānta.)

239. Śaṅkara: Post-Śaṅkara Advaita

After Saṅkara had established the school of Advaita Vedānta on firm grounds, rival positions developed within Advaita Vedānta itself on such issues as: Is the *jīva* or *Brahman* the locus of *avidyā*? How precisely does the one become the many? Are the *mahāvākyas* capable of generating *jñāna* by just being heard (*śravaṇa*) or is further reflection and meditation also required? The followers of

Śaṅkara differed on such issues and this divergence got formalized in the appearance of two schools in the post-Śaṅkara period, known as Vivaraṇa and Bhāmatī. According to the Vivaraṇa school, *Brahman* is both the locus (*āśraya*) and subject (*viṣaya*) of *avidyā*, but the Bhāmatī school regarded the *jīva* as its locus. Similarly, the Vivaraṇa school explained the relationship of multiple *jīvas* on the model of "reflexionism" (Pratibimbavāda), as one single object produces many reflections like the sun reflected in many ports of water, while the Bhāmatī school explained it on the model of delimitation (Avacchedavāda), like infinite space getting confined with the limits of a pot. Similarly, the Vivaraṇa school held that mere audition or the *mahāvākyas* could trigger realization, but, the Bhāmatī school felt that audition (*śravaṇa*) had to be followed up by reflection (*manana*) and meditation (*nididhyāsana*). The Vivaraṇa school probably has a largely philosophical following but the Bhāmatī school has also not been without its advocates. Madhusūdana Sarasvatī (sixteenth century) accepts all such conflicting positions, which, according to him, may be resorted in accordance with the fitness of the student (*adhikāra*) because the main goal after all is to realize *Brahman*. (Also see Bhāmatī School of Advaita Vedānta; and Vivaraṇa.)

240. Śaṅkarācārya

See Śaṅkara.

241. Sanskritization

A term coined by the Indian sociologist, M.N. Srinivas, to describe the adoption of the norms of the higher castes by the lower castes to achieve upward mobility, while the upper castes may themselves be adopting Western norms for the same purpose, a process described as Westernization. The affirmative action policies of the Indian government has made it advantageous to be a member of the backward classes or castes. The attempt on the part of some higher castes to identify themselves as lower to take advantage of these benefits is now being referred to as reverse Sanskritization.

The term is a useful one and has also been applied to theology. It then used to describe one aspect of the interaction between local or regional tradition and the pan-Indian Brāhmanical tradition, specially as reflecting divine upward mobility, as when a local Goddess, such as Māriyammaṉ, is identified with a Goddess of the pan-Indian tradition such as Durgā.

242. Sant

See Bhakti movement.

243. Sarva-Darśana-Saṁgraha

A famous compendium of Indian thought prepared by Mādhva Vidyāraṇya, an Advaitin, in the fourteenth century, during the Vijayanagara Empire. It literally means the summary of all philosophical systems. The author uses one school to demolish the other, clearing the way for the primacy of Advaita Vedānta. Thus the Cārvākas are worsted by the Buddhists, who are undone by the Jainas. They are taken care by the system of Rāmānuja, which is accounted for by the system of Madhva, while the four Śaiva schools: Pāśupata, Śaiva, Pratyabhijñā and Raseśvara cancel each other out. The Vaiśeṣika system is accounted for by the Nyāya system, which in turn are overcome by Mīmāṁsā. The system of Pāṇini follows them but is overcome by Yoga, which is close to the truth, which is realized in its fullness in Advaita Vedānta. It is significant that the author does not adopt or confine himself to the "six-system mode" of presentation. (Also see Darśanas.)

244. Śāstra

One way of understanding the significance of this category would be to place it within the larger perspective that each of the four *puruṣārthas*. Each of these have certain texts associated with them to assist in their pursuit. Some of these pursuits, like *kāma* (sex) for instance, human beings also share with the animals. However, such pursuit is instinctive in the case of animals; what makes *kāma* a goal of human endeavour is its conscious pursuit. This fact of conscious pursuit holds the key to the notion of *puruṣārthas*. Such conscious pursuit presupposes guidelines and this is where the concept of Śāstra becomes important; for these texts provide such guidelines. Thus this word denotes the relevant literature in relation to all the *puruṣārthas*. Hence the bodies of literature known as Kāmaśāstra, Arthaśāstra and Dharmaśāstra. There is no corresponding Mokṣaśāstra as such, but the entire philosophical tradition of India will fall under this rubric. (Also see Puruṣārthas.)

245. Sathya Sai Baba (1926–2011)

Sathya Sai Baba is an immensely popular figure in India, specially in its middle class, and in the Hindu Diaspora, although he left the country only once in 1968 to visit devotees in East Africa. His appeal was based on the supernatural feats with which he is credited, which include materializing objects out of thin air, appearing before devotees in a crisis, multiple location and the ability to manifest enormous amounts of sacred ash called *vibhūti*, specially associated with Śiva, although he was also said to unite Śiva and Śakti in one. Sathya Sai Baba created a vast network of educational and ameliorative services on the basis of the devotion his supernatural feats have inspired in individuals. These include numerous hospitals, four colleges (three for women, one for men) and volunteers who perform various social services. Sathya Sai Baba opposed the erosion of Hindu values through Western cultural influences and emphasized the quintessentially Hindu lifestyle which includes vegetarianism, the regular reading of scriptures such as the *Bhagavad-Gītā* and practice of *yoga*.

246. Satsaṅga

A gathering for a holy purpose such as reading a sacred text, meeting a holy person or participating in devotional chanting. Social distinctions tend to dissolve during a *satsaṅga* and spirituality acts as the solvent of hierarchy. Once it is over, one reverts to the status quo. It is usually open to whosoever cares to attend. (Also see Bhakti.)

247. Satyanārāyṇa-Pūjā

This is a ritual performed by the Hindus on various auspicious occasions such as a house warming, graduation and marriage as a way of celebrating good fortune or securing it. The full-moon day (*pūrṇimā*) is considered particularly auspicious for its performance. Historians connect it with the figure of Satya Pīr, who was worshipped by Hindus, Buddhists and Muslims in Bengal towards the end of the nineteenth century. The story (*kathā*) now forms part of the Revā Khaṇḍa of the *Skanda Purāṇa* and could be a recent addition to it. The narrative describes the origin and benefits of the *pūjā*. The stories emphasize promise-keeping, spiritual egalitarianism and giving thanks to God. For instance, Kalāvatī, in the excitement of reunion with her husband, forgets to thank God and therefore faces situations which require her to think of God. This *pūjā* is quite popular, across the social spectrum. It may be undertaken to gain any of the three goals of life (*trivarga*). (Also see Pūjā.)

248. Secular State, India as a

Although the word "secular" was included in the preamble of the Indian Constitution only during the period of emergency (1975-77) imposed by Indira Gandhi, the movement for Indian independence led by the Indian National Congress was secular from its very inception, if secularism is taken to the stand for the separation of Church and state. This was partly due to the fact that the anti-colonial leadership was committed to the model of secular democracy; partly due to the fact that it offered the best policy option in a religiously plural India, and partly due to the fact that Hinduism countenances it *de facto* in separating the role of the brāhmaṇa from the kṣatriya. How deeply both the leaderships of the Indian National Congress and the Muslim League were committed to this ideal is obscured by the fact of the obvious religiosity of Gandhi as the leader of the Congress and the League's demand for a separate state for the Muslims of

India. Gandhi's religiosity was too spiritual and ecumenical to be opposed to the secular state, which he explicitly endorsed; while although Qaid-i-Azam Jinnah demanded a separate state for the Muslims, he wanted to keep Church and state apart within it. The bid to keep Pakistan secular failed early, but the attempt to keep India secular continues, with a strange twist. The secularists of India, who include the Congress party and the minorities, are accused by Hindu political organizations of being pseudo-secularist because these organizations feel, as representatives of the Hindus, that the secularism practised by successive governments since Independence has been asymmetrical, in the sense that secularism is understood and applied differently in relation to the majority and the minority religious communities in India. It is remarkable however that almost all political parties in India accept the need for the state to be secular in India, although the semantics might vary. (Also see Hindutva.)

249. Siddha

A person who has discovered the path to *mokṣa* through an intensely personal quest and can therefore form a lineage by initiating others, without the need for recycling traditional orthodoxy. It also often involved praxis into which the disciple is initiated.

250. Sikh Separatism

When the British dominions in India were partitioned into India and Pakistan, there were some cries raised for a homeland for the Sikhs as well, but, by and large, the Sikhs threw their lot with the Hindus. The demand was revived, however, in the 1980s, in the form of the demand for Khalistan. This demand could be seen in the perspective of an ongoing assertion of an independent Sikh identity, which began with the Singh Sabha movement and, in 1925, resulted in the formation of the Shiromani Gurudwara Prabandhak Committee (SGPC). The SGPC took over the running of Sikh institutions which had fallen into the hands of Hindu *Mahants*. Unlike the Hindu community, the Sikh community also has a religious apex body in the Akal Takht, located at the Golden Temple in Amritsar, otherwise known as Har Mandir. At issue was the extent to which the assertion of a distinct identity was to be given political expression. Thus an attempt was made, in the 1980s, to create a homeland for the Sikhs, perhaps on the model of the creation of Pakistan as a homeland for the Muslims of British India. The tactics employed were certainly comparable and the problems involved similar, in the sense that although Sikhs constituted a majority in the Punjab, they were also, like the Muslims, spread all over the country. An attempt to carve out a *de facto* state, by exacting payments from Sikhs and driving Hindus away, was made under Sant Bhindranwale. But when his forces occupied the Golden Temple in 1984, events went into fast forward: the Indian army marched in and flushed out the militants in June 1984. Indira Gandhi was then assassinated by her Sikh guards in October 1984. Delhi was convulsed by anti-Sikh riots in November 1984 in revenge, in which 3,000 Sikhs lost their lives. The movement gradually lost steam. After this sanguinary denouement, Sikh extremist excesses alienated the majority of the Sikhs and comparatively moderate Sikhs gained control. The different destinies of the Muslim and Sikh separatist movements highlight the difference the central government, whether imperial or national, can make in affecting such outcomes.

251. Sikhism

A religious tradition which arose in the sixteenth century in Punjab, whose followers are called disciples (*sikh*, most probably from the Sanskrit *śiśya*) of the Ten Gurus, hence the name Sikhism. These Ten Gurus are:

1. Guru Nanak (1469–1539);
2. Guru Angad (1504-52);
3. Guru Amar Das (1479–1574);
4. Guru Ram Das (1534-81);
5. Guru Arjan (1563–1606);

6. Guru Hargobind (1595-81);
7. Guru Har Rai (1630-61);
8. Guru Har Krishnan (1656–64);
9. Guru Tegh Bahadur (1621-75); and
10. Guru Gobind Singh (1666–1708).

Guru Gobind Singh, who declared that the Sikh holy scripture, the *Guru Granth Sahib*, will henceforth be the *guru*. Sikhism, like Islam, opposes image worship and rejects the idea of divine incarnation; but, like Hinduism, it accepts the doctrine of *karma* and rebirth. Although many Hindus like to consider Sikhs as members of the larger Hindu family, most Sikhs prefer to consider themselves as members of a separate religious tradition.

252. Śiva

The three major streams of devotion within Hinduism are Vaiṣṇavism, Śaivism and Śāktism, or the worship of Viṣṇu, Śiva and Śakti respectively. Among these, the worship of Śiva (along with probably that of Śakti) could go back to Haṛappan times of the middle of the second millennium BCE, if one of the seals discovered during that period is considered a representation of proto-Śiva. Śiva has been connected with the Vedic God Rudra but it is in classical Hinduism that he emerges as one of the two main gods towards whom Hindus direct their devotion. The figure of Śiva seems to reconcile antithetical tendencies. He is the lord of death and destruction but also of immortality, and combines elements of both asceticism and eroticism in his personality, brought out well in the pact entered into with his wife Pārvatī, according to which they would spend one half the year devoted to asceticism and the other half to conjugal life. He thus has a wife Pārvatī and two sons, Gaṇeśa and Kumāra, the family lives on the Kailāsa Mountain with Nandī (the bull), who is Śiva's vehicle. He is sometimes depicted in person, but more often worshipped in the form of a conical stone or object called the *liṅga*. It is often referred to as a phallic symbol but if it was so in origin, the origin has been lost sight of, and it is regularly viewed as aniconic symbol of Śiva by the worshipper. To describe it as phallic is potentially as misleading as to describe Jesus as an illegitimate son of God. The Śivaliṅga is usually explained within the tradition as representing the world's cosmic pillar in general, or that pillar of light in particular, the form in which Śiva appeared when the gods were disputing who among them was the greatest. The wrathful side of Śiva is more pronounced than that of other Hindu gods but he compensates for this by being extremely easy to please.

253. Śiva as Naṭarāja

Śiva's depiction as the cosmic dancer, or Naṭarāja, was given a plastic manifestation in south India during the Coḷa Period (*c.* 1000–1300), which, on account of its evocative quality, is celebrated as one of the great achievements of Indian art. The image, usually cast in metal, depicts the Śiva with four arms — two outstretched and two upfront, while one foot stamps on a demon and other is raised gracefully. The whole image is often covered with an orb. The image pulsates with symbolism. Śiva bears a drum in the outstretched upper right hand and a tongue of fire in the other. The drum symbolizes the beginning of spatio-temporal creation, either with the beginning of time (the count of the dreambeat) or of space (the medium through which sound of the drumbeat moves). The upper left hand, with the flame, symbolizes the end of the universe in fire, which may also be interpreted as Śiva rescuing one from the fire of the pyre, or by extension from that of *saṁsāra*. Both hands are arrested in their perpetual motion, representing the ceaseless movement as well as integration of creation and destruction. The gesture of protection also integrates the function of preservation with that of creation and destruction. This gesture of protection or fearlessness, called *abhaya-mudrā*, is made with the lower right hand, while the lower left hand points towards the upraised foot of God, where one should seek refuge. The other foot stamps on the demon of forgetfulness or heedlessness, called Apasmāra in Sanskrit and Muyalaka in Tamil. The orb of flames circling the dancing figure has been interpreted both as the fiery circle of *saṁsāra* or as the light of enlightenment. Thus the image can be seen as balancing both *saṁsāra* and *nirvāṇa*, just as it is seen as balancing life and death. One might here distinguish between worshipping the image and participating in it, although it is possible to overdo this distinction. One worships Śiva for his grace sought at his feet, but by entering into the dance one transcends the limitations of time and space, and of opposites, in the manifestations of the Great God (Mahādeva).

254. Śivarātri

Śivarātri (the night dedicated to Siva) falls on the fourteenth day of the dark half of the month of Māgha (January–February), when a rigorous fast in honour of Śiva is supposed to be observed throughout the night. It is during a Śivarātri that Dayananda Sarasvati (1824-83) had a conversion experience in reverse, when as a boy he observed that his father had dozed off during the vigil and a mouse was nibbling away at the offerings made to the Śivaliṅga. Dayananda became sceptical of a God's ability to save him, when he discovered that God could not protect the offering made to it and turned against idolatry. Most people however feel fortified in their faith after observing the fast. Śiva is the patron saint of ghosts and similar beings, which occupy the lower "echelons" of the Hindu pantheon, which is a sign of his power; but he is also an ascetic and the patron of ascetics. (Also see Dayananda Sarasvati.)

255. Smṛti

A basic distinction is drawn in Hindu sacred literature between two bodies of literature, one of which is called Śruti (revelation) and the other called Smṛti (tradition), although there has been a constant tendency for the border between the two to get fudged. Nevertheless, in the main, the four Vedas, with the four divisions within them, have been taken as Śruti; the rest of sacred literature is Smṛti. The word *smṛti* itself can be used in a narrow and a broad sense. In the broad sense, any body of literature considered sacred, which is not Śruti, is Smṛti, so that this category includes Dharmaśāstras, Itīhāsas, Purāṇas, Darśanas and Āgamas; in the narrow sense, it the word refers to Smṛti proper, to the texts which bear that name, like the *Manu-Smṛti*, which are usually referred to as Hindu law books. The relationship of the Śruti to Smṛti needs to be clarified, both in regards to nomenclature and precedence. Śruti is so called because it is heard, i.e. divinely auditioned by the seers (*ṛṣis*) who are its receptors and not authors. It has no author as such, either in the form of man or God. Smṛti, however, is a work whose author can be "remembered", i.e. identified. Śruti takes precedence over Smṛti in case of a conflict between the two. This has been interpreted by modern Hindus to mean that because Śruti is eternal and fixed, while Smṛti can vary, that social usages embodied in the Smṛtis must be consistent with eternal values and when "time makes ancient good uncouth", then new ones are composed to reflect those eternal values more clearly. This explains why different Smṛtis have been recommended for different *yugas*. Thus according to the *Pārāśara-Smṛti*:

> The Smṛtis of Manu are intended for the Kṛta-Yuga; that of Yājñavalkya is for the Tretā-Yuga; that of Śaṅkha and Likhita are for the Dvāpara-Yuga; and that of Parāśara is for the Kali-Yuga.

The Smṛtis associated with the following names have been singled out within the tradition:

1. Viṣṇu;
2. Parāśara;
3. Dakṣa;
4. Samvarta;
5. Vyāsa;
6. Hārīta;
7. Śātātapa;
8. Vasiṣṭha;

9. Yama;
10. Āpastamba;
11. Gautama;
12. Devala;
13. Śaṅkha-Likhita;
14. Bharadvāja;
15. Uśanas;
16. Atri;
17. Śaunaka; and
18. Yājñavalkya.

256. Śrī-Yantra

A famous Tantric *yantra* symbolizing the union and interpretation of opposites. It consists of downward triangles interwoven with upward triangles, representing the union of *prakṛti* (matter) and *puruṣa* (spirit), fire and water, or male and female. The dot at the centre represents the original unity of opposites. (Also see Tantra.)

257. Subaltern Studies

A branch of the historical studies pioneered by Ranajit Guha (b. 1923), based on the premise that the voices of the oppressed and the underprivileged have either been excluded from history, or presented only negatively, and that this bias is reflected all the way from the very themes chosen as part of the master narrative of Indian history to the way the narrative is shaped. The aim of subaltern studies is to allow these suppressed voices to be heard. (Also see Hindu Studies, Bias in; and Orientalism.)

258. Śuddhādvaita Vedānta

"Pure non-dualism" is a school of Vedānta founded by Vallabha (1475–1531), also known as Vallabhācārya, on account of possessing the title of *ācārya*, which was conferred on him by the Vijayanagara court. He travelled widely in India, but spent most of his life in the north, at Banaras and Adel (a place near Allahabad), although he hailed from the south. Upon feeling divinely commanded to interpret the Prasthāna-Traya correctly, specially against what he regarded as their misrepresentation by Śaṅkara, he wrote his commentary on the *Brahma-Sūtra* called *Aṇubhāṣya*, the word suggesting that he may also have written a more extended commentary. According to him, Śaṅkara's concept of *māyā* adulterated Śaṅkara's non-dualism, reducing it to what he labelled Kevalādvaita (mere Advaita) and which he distinguished his own position, which he called Śuddhādvaita (pure Advaita) because Śaṅkara's Advaita was impure in so far as it had to depend on *māyā*, the principle of illusion, to explain the world. Śuddhādvaita is also different from Nimbārka's Dvaitādvaita, because while, in the latter the relationship of *Brahman* with the world is one of difference-cum-non-difference, for Vallabha it is one of non-difference, as cause and effect were to be considered identical. His system is also known as Puṣṭi-Mārga (path of divine grace), which leads to the experience of the bliss of God's own nature (*svarūpānanda*) characterized by *rasa* (sentiment), which was considered even superior to *brahmānanda*. A striking textual feature of the school is its acceptance of the *Bhāgavata Purāṇa* as on the same level as the Upaniṣads, the *Brahma-Sūtra* and the *Bhagavad-Gītā*, which are listed in the following order in this school:

1. Upaniṣads,
2. *Bhagavad-Gītā*,
3. *Brahma-Sūtra*, and
4. *Bhāgavata*.

The order is important, as the former text is supposed to be understood in the light of the latter. The *Bhāgavata Purāṇa*, which is said to provide a record of the meditational experience of sage Vyāsa (and therefore also referred to as *samādhi-bhāṣā*), is therefore the ultimate authority for this school. This school also tends to understand the texts literally, accepting even apparently contradictory statements. The supreme reality is described in this system as Śrī Kṛṣṇa, identified with the Upaniṣadic *Brahman*, who is perfect (*pūrṇa*) and the supreme person (*puruṣottama*), and is described as *sat* (existence), *cit* (consciousness), *ānanda* (bliss) and also *rasa*. At the level of the ultimate reality, this school distinguishes between *para* (supreme) *Brahman* and *Akṣara* (immutable) *Brahman*, the latter possessing only limited bliss, as compared to the infinite bliss (*ānanda* of *Para-Brahman*), equated with Kṛṣṇa. One who possesses knowledge of *Brahman*, without it being associated with devotion, gets absorbed in *Akṣara-Brahman*. The expression *nirguṇa* means that the supreme reality is devoid of material qualities rather than meaning that it possesses no qualities. The universe is created by God though his *māyā-śakti* for the sake of sport (*līlā*), and it is a transformation of the very essence of God (*svarūpa-pariṇāma*) in the course of which God is not affected at all (*avikṛta-pariṇāma*), and represents the *sat* aspect of God. In this system, it is not the world (*jagat*) which is unreal, but the *jīva*'s involvement in it known as *saṁsāra*, which arises solely from I-ness (*ahantā*) and My-ness (*mamatā*). The *jīvas* are metaphysically of two kinds: those which arose like sparks from *Akṣara-Brahman*, when the One desired to be many, and those which he specially brings out from himself for playful company in eternity (*nitya-līlā*). Ordinary souls are atomic in size and while neither omnipresent nor coterminous with the body, pervade the body through the quality of intelligence (*caitanya*). They fall under three categories:

1. those wallowing in the stream (*pravāha*) of *saṁsāra* and hence called *pravāha*;
2. those on the Vedic path (*maryādā*); and
3. those who have received God's grace (*puṣṭi*).

The path of *maryādā* is restricted to male members of the first three *varṇas*, but the Puṣṭi-Mārga is open to all. Any follower on this path can undertake the sacrament of *brahma-sambandha*, by undertaking which one commits one's body and property to God. The entire family is supposed to participate in serving the Lord (*sevā*), the highest form of which is supposed to be mental, and Vallabha advises preferring service to the Lord (*bhāgavat-dharma*) over *varṇāśrama-dharma* if necessary. The supreme exemplars of this path are the *gopīs*, hence the description of God as Gopīvallabhava (or beloved of the *gopīs*) is of special significance in this school. (Also see Advaita Vedānta.)

259. Sūrdās (*c.* 1485–1563)

The two great poet-saints of *saguṇa bhakti* in the medieval times in the north are Tulsīdās (1532?–1623) and Sūrdās, whose poetic devotion was respectively focused on Rāma and Kṛṣṇa and who respectively wrote in Awadhī and Brajabhāṣā. Sūrdās is traditionally considered to have been blind, though his vivid descriptions have led some to wonder if he was born so. He was formerly a follower of Vallabhācārya school and is the author of the memorable statement: "whether through passion, anger, love or friendship, if a man thinks of God constantly, he becomes God". (Also see Bhakti; and Nirguṇa and Saguṇa Bhakti.)

260. Sūtaka

Impurity caused by childbirth (or abortion). Childbirth is an occasion for happiness but it is accompanied by the release of substances such as blood and placenta, which are ritually polluting. The term "happy pollution" encapsulates both these dimensions. This impurity lasts for ten days during which religious activities and interdining with others are suspended. At the end of the period the house is cleaned, family members bathe, the father shaves and the occasion is celebrated. (Also see Untouchability.)

261. Suttee (Satī)

Suttee is an anglicized form of the word *satī* (a chase virtuous woman). In its anglicized form it denotes the act of being burnt upon the funeral pyre of the husband as a display of her virtue.

Although optional in principle, it had acquired a coercive customary character by the eighteenth century. It was therefore abolished within the British dominions in 1829 and had already been abolished in certain Marāṭhā dominions earlier. It was also discouraged during the Mogul Empire. Modern Hindu reformers of the time, such as Raja Rammohun Roy in Bengal and Swaminarayan in western India actively opposed it. Nevertheless, cases of suttee continue to occur and over forty have been reported in post-Independence India.

262. Swadhyay Movement

This movement founded by Pandurang Athavale (1920–2003), affectionately known as Dādā (elder brother), who ran a *pāṭhaśālā* (Sanskrit school) in Bombay (Mumbai). According to tradition he gave a talk in Japan in 1956, in which he held up the *Bhagavad-Gītā* as providing the key to the solutions of the modern world. Upon being asked whether he had tried this himself, he was forced to admit that he had not. He then started a movement upon his return, for the uplift of the poorest low-caste people, specially fisher folk, based on the teachings of that text. He was awarded the Templeton Prize for progress in religion in 1997. A feature film has also been made illustrating the approach of his movements. By the end of the century, the movement had touched the lives of 20 million people in about 100,000 villages. The movement has 350 centers in America.

A unique feature of this movement is that it asks the volunteer to donate not money but time and skills. This is the underlying concept of *bhakti-pherī* (devotional visit), for the person is meant to develop personal rapport with the downtrodden and the disadvantaged and to see the divine in them. Similarly, instead of handing over money to those who need help, the people are encouraged to generate their own funds or resources, as for instance by fisherman putting the catch of a particular day into a common pool operated by their own committee. The movement offers an interesting reinterpretation of Advaita Vedānta. According to Advaita Vedānta all beings possess the same reality, the differences among them being entirely the result of adjuncts (*upādhis*). But for these adjuncts, which are ultimately unreal, and whose attachment to an *ātman* is illusory, everyone is identical with one another and with *Brahman*. The Svadhyaya movement focuses on the identity of everyone with each other, and uses it that as intellectual capital to promote equality and fellow feeling.

263. Tantra

Literally "warp and woof", or that which is woven or interwoven, which could then refer to interweaving of the various texts, or the interweaving of the teachings, or the interweaving of the teachings and the texts, or the "interweaving" of the *guru* and disciple, or all of them. The word thus has many connotations. At its widest, it refers to the Āgamas or texts which lay down how the six cultic deities of Hinduism, usually referred as *ṣaṇmata*, are to be worshipped, namely, Gaṇeśa, Kārttikeya, Sūrya, Viṣṇu, Śiva and Śakti. In a somewhat narrower sense, it is used to refer to the texts involving the last of these, namely Śakti. A third sense narrows the semantic circle even further, by using the word to refer to those texts which deal with what is known as left-handed worship of Śakti, called *vāmācāra*. This form of worship employs means conventionally forbidden in worship, such as the use of wine or sex. Scholarship became aware first of the association of Tantric practices with sex, which thus led to an association of the word Tantra with sex, an association which survives in popular usage to this day. Tantra, which has been traced back to around the fifth century, marks a distinct phase in the development of Indian religiosity, characterized by a certain catholicity. Thus Tantra is open to the participation of all *varṇas* (classes), as well as women. It is also catholic in the sense that this development characterizes not only Hinduism, but Buddhism and Jainism as well, and thus may be considered Indic rather than Hindu in character. It was also catholic in the sense that it spread beyond the geographical boundaries of India. One text, for instance, divides Bhāratavarṣa or "India" into three parts called Krāntas namely, Viṣṇukrānta, Rathakrānta and Aśvakrānta, to each of which as set of sixty-four Tantras is allotted. Viṣṇukrānta is then described as extending to the east from the Vindhyas, up to Java in Indonesia; Rathakrānta as extending north of the Vindhyas including China (Mahācīna), and Aśvakrānta as extending westward. According to Tantric self-understanding, Śruti or the Vedas were meant for Satya-Yuga, Smṛti for Tretā, Purāṇas for Dvāpara and the Āgamas for Kali. Thus the Tantras are specifically meant for the Kali-Yuga or the present age. (Also see Āgamas.)

264. Tantra: Left-Handed

Left-handed Tantra consists of making use of those elements in worship, whose use in worship is normally forbidden. There is a standard list of five, which are called the five *makāras* because they all begin with the letter *ma*. They are also called *pañca-tattvas* or the five elements, although Abhinavagupta speaks of three. These are (1) *madya* (wine); (2) *matsya* (fish); (3) *māṁsa* (meat); (4) *mudrā* (parched grains, considered as an aphrodisiac, or hand gestures); and (5) *maithuna* (copulation); the word *mithuna* denotes a couple in Sanskrit. There has been a debate within the Tantric tradition whether these instructions are to be taken literally or figuratively. Lakṣmīdhara (sixteenth century) frowns upon a literal understanding, but Bhāskarācārya (eighteenth century) approves of it. Taken literally, the logic is that "one rises by what one falls". Just as something, which is normally poison, can serve as a medicine once treated properly, the use of the five elements, once ritualized, is said to lend them salvific potency. Thus a kind of sublimation seems to be involved. Its literal use was also like that of a "controlled substance", in the sense that the Tantric text distinguish between three kinds of aspirants: the *divya* (who is predominantly *sāttvika* in nature); the *vīra* (who is *rājasika*) and the *paśu* (who is *tāmasika*). The literal practice of the rite was only meant for the *vīra*, "the *paśu* was not fit for it; the *divya* did not require it". When not taken literally, the *makāras* were taken as code words for other substances or yogic positions, so that substitution and internalization took the place of sublimation. The substitute (or *pratinidhi*) for wine was milk or coconut water; for meat or fish, sesamum or ginger; for sex, flowers. In terms of yogic positions, eating meat, or even beef, when prescribed, meant placing the tip of the tongue at the base of the throat. Tantra developed a whole vocabulary along these lines, represented by a *sandhā-bhāṣā* (intentional language).

265. Tattva-Traya

The three ultimate realities in Viśiṣṭādvaita Vedānta: *Īśvara* (God); *cit* (soul) and *acit* (matter). *Īśvara* in this system is identified with Viṣṇu and his role in this system is summarized in the following passage from the *Bṛhadāraṇyaka Upaniṣad* (III.7):

> He who dwells in the world, and is within it, whom the world does not know, whose body is the world, and who controls the world from within, is the self, the inner ruler, immortal.

The idea that the world is God's body suggests that God is its soul, in the sense of constituting an organic unity with it. Moreover, as the body exists for the sake of the soul, the world exists for the sake of God and just as the soul controls the body from within, God controls the world from within. It also indicates that God is both immanent and transcendent in relation to the world, just as the soul is both immanent and transcendent in relation to the body. And just as the body changes but not the soul, and the soul is not affected by the changes of the body, God himself does not change even though the world does. And God is also not affected by changes in the world. God exists in various forms as:

1. *para* (transcendental);
2. *vyūha* (grouped);
3. *antaryāmī* (immanent);
4. *vibhava* (incarnations); and
5. *arcā* (image).

In the transcendental form, he possesses the six auspicious qualities (*bhāgas*), on account of which he is called *bhagavān*, or the possessor of these qualities, which are *jñāna* (knowledge), *aiśvarya* (lordship); *śakti* (power); *bala* (strength); *vīrya* (virility) and *tejas* (splendour). The second *tattva* is *cit* (souls), also called *jīvas*, which is also looked upon God's body in the sense that God is immanent in it and guides it from within. The soul is atomic in size but possesses *dharmabhūta-jñāna* (attributive knowledge); that is to say, it both is and has knowledge. These *jīvas* are infinite and can be classified into three categories:

1. *nitya* (eternal), who were never bound;
2. *mukta* (free), who have achieved liberation; and
3. *baddha* (bound), who are still in *saṁsāra*.

The third *tattva* is *acit* (insentient matter): it is also called *prakṛti* and the three *guṇas* — *sattva*, *rajas* and *tamas* — are its attributes (and not constituents as in Sāṁkhya). During the period of dissolution it continues to exist in subtle form, so that creation and dissolution involve its appearance and disappearance and not its destruction. The effect is latent in the cause and causation implies transformation (*pariṇāma*) but although this doctrine is also designated as Satkāryavāda it differs from the standard version in the sense that it is not the substance (say, clay) which is taken as the material cause but is mode (say, lump), which is transformed into another mode (say, pot). (Also see Viśiṣṭādvaita Vedānta.)

266. Teej (Tīja)

The name of a festival celebrated by women on the third day of the bright half of the month of Bhādrapada (August–September). It is celebrated by married women for the health and long life of they husbands, and by the unmarried women to obtain a suitable husband. It is based on the paradigm of Pārvatī undergoing fasting and purification, in order to win the hand of Śiva in marriage. Women usually spend the night at a holy place, usually a temple and close to the presence of holy water, as in a tank or river. The night is spent in fasting, followed by immersion in water. (Also see Women's Rituals.)

267. Teyyam

The name for shrines for local gods and goddesses in Kerala and neighbouring regions, where they are represented by artistes as deities and worshipped. The artistes are drawn from the lower castes but all castes participate in the worship. The word is derived from Sanskrit *devam*. (Also see Hindu Ritual.)

268. Theory of Causation

Western philosophy contains a fourfold schema of causation, which goes back to Aristotle, involving the distinction between material cause, efficient cause, formal cause and final cause. A restaurant is built of bricks and so on, they are its material cause; the builders are the efficient cause; the concept of a restaurant, which is embodied in the restaurant, is the formal cause and the purpose for which the restaurant is made, to earn a profit by running a restaurant, the final cause. The Hindu theory of causation, at its most manifest level, focuses on the material cause especially analysing its relation to the effect it produces. The key area investigated is the analysis of material cause (*upādāna-kāraṇa*) in terms of cause (*kāraṇa*) and effect (*kārya*), and the key issue addressed becomes: does the effect pre-exist in the material cause or not? In other words, when threads are woven together to produce a piece of cloth, has something new come into existence, which did not exist earlier, or should the piece of cloth be looked upon as having pre-existed in some way, as latent, in the threads? The Nyāya-Vaiśeṣika and the Sāṁkhya-Yoga schools of thought answer the question differently. According to the Nyāya-Vaiśeṣika school, the effect does not pre-exist in the cause, and is a new creation. Hence this view is known as Asatkāryavāda (*a-sat-kārya-vāda*: the doctrine that the effect does not pre-exist in the cause) and as Ārambhavāda, as the word *ārambha* having the connotation of a new beginning. According to this view, when the threads are woven together to produce a piece of cloth, the piece of cloth should not be seen as pre-existing in the threads but should be seen as a new product, apart from and in addition to the threads. The relationship of the new product and threads is described as one of *samavāya* (inherence). The Sāṁkhya-Yoga school of philosophy however maintains that if the effect did not pre-exist in the cause, any cause could produce any effect and one could obtain oil from sand. It prefers therefore to believe that the effect is latent, or pre-exists, in the material cause. This doctrine is known as that of Satkāryavāda (*sat-kārya-vāda*: the doctrine that effect [pre]-exists [in the cause]). It is also called Pariṇāmavāda, or the doctrine that the effect is a transformation of the cause. If then the material cause is thus related to the effect, the question arises — what is the nature of this relationship, or, more, precisely, does the effect represent an actual transformation of the cause (the way milk actually changes into curd) or is merely a phenomenal manifestation (the way a rope may appear to be a serpent). On this point, the school of Advaita Vedānta ultimately parts company from Sāṁkhya-Yoga. It initially favours the doctrine of Satkāryavāda over Asatkāryavāda and regards it valid at the plane of empirical existence, as explaining causal relationships within the universe, but insists that the universe as such cannot be considered an actual transformation of ultimate reality into this world, but only as its phenomenal appearance, the way a rope might appear as a snake. Indeed it argues that in relation to *Brahman*, the universe is an illusory appearance and that while causation as a principle might apply to relationships within the universe, it cannot be applied to the relationship between the universe and *Brahman*. (Also see Darśanas.)

269. Tilaka

Also called *ṭīkā*, the mark made on the forehead between but above the eyes, with a powder, usually red, mixed with water and grains of rice. It is often applied to the foreheads of the devotees after the *darśana* of the image, and is worn by married woman as a mark of their status. It also served as a marker of Hindu identity in the history of Hinduism. In his confrontation with the Mogul emperor Aurangzeb, the Sikh Guru, Tegh Bahadur (1621-75), is said to have been acting as the defender of the frontal marks of the Hindus.

270. Tīrthayātrā

Or pilgrimage, is integral to Hinduism. The landmass of India is considered sacred, and sanctified by the presence of gods, goddesses and sages. Thus *darśana* (act of religious viewing), is extended in a sense to cover not just images, and pious or powerful persons but also places charged with sacred power. The word *tīrtha* means a ford or river crossing and takes on metaphysical overtones in a pilgrimage, as the pilgrim reaches out for at least a glimpse of the other shore, if not the shore itself. During a pilgrimage one observes a pious lifestyle and performs the rituals considered appropriate for the place. Centres of pilgrimage exert a powerful call and Hindus often go on pilgrimage to far-off lands, even when political vicissitudes have allowed these sites to fall into foreign hands. Ironically, what is now called Pakistan, or land of the pure, virtually coincides geographically with the region originally occupied by the Ṛg-Vedic Aryans and the realization could have further implications for the way pilgrimage is perceived in modern Hinduism. Pilgrims often carry sacred memorabilia for relatives and friends, which often takes the form of *prasāda* or *vibhūti* (sacred ash) and rosary beads. Originally these pilgrimages were performed mainly on foot but modern transport has not only expanded the reach of such pilgrimages but also made them more convenient. The centres of pilgrimage in Hinduism include such places as Mathurā, Ayodhyā, Triveṇī, Prayāga, Gayā, Rāmeśvaram, and so on.

271. Tradition and Modernity

The encounter between the Hindu religious tradition and modernity needs to be viewed in historical perspective. The Hindu tradition has had to face three major challenges over its long history:

1. The emergence of the heterodoxies of Buddhism and Jainism, in the sixth century BCE;
2. the encounter with Islam from *c.* 1000 onwards, although presaged already in the eight century; and
3. the encounter with modernity in the form of British rule, Christianity and now globalization.

The first may be bypassed for the moment as an issue internal to India, both geographically and culturally, but the other two stand out as major religious and political intrusions. How did the Hindu tradition deal with these crises? One point becomes immediately apparent that, on the whole, while in facing the Islamic challenge it retreated into a defensive posture, in facing modernity it has adopted a more assertive position. For instance, one Narasiṁhācārya is said to have advised the participants in a Kumbha Melā, in medieval times, that Hindus have to respond to the challenge of Islam by adopting the *karmaṭha-vṛtti* (mode of the tortoise), who contracts his limbs, and retreats into its shell when threatened. However, in the face of modernity, the Hindu tradition virtually stepped forward to meet, or if necessary, confront it, from the time of Raja Rammohun Roy onwards. This does not mean that such a move was free from tension, for it did involve a negotiation between tradition and modernity, but this was treated as a creative tension, and not defensive tension as in the earlier case of Islam. This tension led to the rise of numerous new religious movements in India during 200 years of British rule. As the engagement with modernity continues, so does the rise of new religious movements, some with their early roots in the pre-Independence period. The rise of the middle class in modern India after 1800 is important in this context. The origin of this class may be traced to Macaulay's dream of creating a class of people "Indians in blood and colour, but English in opinion, in morals, in tastes and in intellect", who would serve as a go-betweens, between the ruling British class and the masses. Thus it was envisaged as a middle class in a cultural sense, but with the growth of the modern economy it has increasingly became a middle class in the economic class as well. As this class emerged from the "native" Indians, rooted as they might have been in loyalties to caste, kin and region, it was exposed to modernity and had to deal with the new world of science and technology and new kinds of social and political arrangements. Nowadays it has to contend with the Internet, CNN and so on. The traditional ties had to be adjusted to these new developments. Most of the modern religious movements from 1800 onwards, and the contemporary religious movements as well, seem to have arisen within this middle class, or at least arisen to meet its religious needs, whatever their origin.

272. **Tulsīdās** (d. 1623)

A major figure of the Bhakti movement like Sūrdās, but while Sūrdās's poetry is centred particularly on Kṛṣṇa, that of Tulsīdās was centred on Rāma. He is particularly known for his rendering of the story of the *Rāmāyaṇa* into the popular language of north India known as Hindi, under the title of *Rāmacaritamānasa* (Lake of the Deeds of Rāma). Its success was immediate and it continues to enjoy immense popularity to this day at many levels of society.

273. Ubhaya-Vedānta

"Dual Vedānta", a doctrine developed by Rāmānuja, which is crucial for understanding the textual foundations of Viśiṣṭādvaita Vedānta. Like many other systems of Vedānta, the school of Viśiṣṭādvaita Vedānta relies on the Upaniṣads, as the word Vedānta indicates. It, however, accepts another body of sacred literature on par with the Upaniṣads, hence the name Ubhaya-Vedānta. This other body of literature consists of the *Nālāyira-Prabandham*, also known as the *Divyaprabandham*. This is a collection of the poems of the Tamil Āḻvars made by Nāthamuni (tenth century) whose tradition was carried on by his grandson, Yāmānujācārya, also known as Ālavandār. He wrote various manuals on Viśiṣṭādvaita Vedānta, while Rāmānuja wrote a commentary on the *Brahma-Sūtra* called *Śrībhāṣya*. Thus both the Tamil and the Sanskrit traditions equally contributed to the emergence of the system. This doctrine of

Ubhaya-Vedānta recognizes and sacralizes this fact. (Also see Viśiṣṭādvaita Vedānta.)

274. Untouchability

The practice of considering the touch of certain kinds of people as polluting, which requires ritual purification. It sometimes consists of not consuming food from certain people, rather than avoiding their touch. A family where a death has occurred, or women after childbirth are so considered temporarily but the word is primarily associated with a class of people called by various names who share the common fact that their touch is considered polluting because of engaging in work which involves dealing with human waste, dead animals and other activities considered ritually polluting. Certain disabilities, like those suffered by blacks for instance in the United States, were associated with being an untouchable. Mahatma Gandhi vigorously agitated for its abolition throughout his public life and it was constitutionally abolished in 1950, although traces of it persist. Although a noticeable feature of Hinduism for centuries, there is no evidence of its prevalence in either the *Ṛg-Veda*, or in the Hindu community in Bali, Indonesia.

275. Upamāna

Comparison, recognized by the Nyāya school as an independent means of valid knowledge (*pramāṇa*), as explaining the connection of a word to what it denotes. The standard example is provided by someone wanting to know what a wild cow (*gavaya*) looks like, and is told that it is an animal comparable to a cow. When it subsequently sees one and identifies it as such, this knowledge is set to arise through *upamāna* (comparison). Nyāya maintains the claim of it being an independent means of knowledge, in the face of criticism from the Jaina school which sees it as a form of recognition (*pratyabhijñā*); some Buddhist schools, which think it can be reduced to perception and testimony; the Sāṁkhya school, which sees it is a form of inference; and the Mīmāṁsā and Vedānta schools, who have their own take on it, namely, that one concludes from the similarity of the wild cow to the cow not just that the wild cow is like the cow, but that the cow is also like the wild cow, and that these similarities are distinct: if *A* and *B* are similar, then the similarity of *A* to *B* may not be identical with the similarity of B to A. (Also see Pramāṇaśāstra.)

276. Upaniṣad

Usually explained etymologically as *up-ni-ṣad*, or knowledge derived while sitting up close to, or at the feet of the preceptor. It has however semantically been directly translated as knowledge of reality (*tattva-jñāna*) or more often, as secret or esoteric knowledge (*rahasya*). The two approaches can of course be connected, with devout proximity likely to be involved in the transmission of both transcendental and/or esoteric knowledge. Śaṅkara's detailed gloss of the word in the light of this, although more explicit, also seems more laboured:

> To destroy ignorance by revealing the knowledge of the supreme Spirit and cutting off the bonds of worldly existence.

Upaniṣad as a category is rather elastic. More than 200 Upaniṣads have been identified, although one Upaniṣad, the *Muktikopaniṣad*, itself claims their number to be 108. It therefore becomes important to list the classical Upaniṣads, whose place within that rubric is unquestioned, which are considered so by virtue of being commented upon by the *ācāryas* of the tradition, such as Śaṅkara, who is among the earliest to comment on them. These are usually minimally listed as follows: *Īśa*, *Kena*, *Kaṭha*, *Praśna*, *Muṇḍaka*, *Māṇḍūkya*, *Taittirīya*, *Aitareya*, *Chāndogya* and *Bṛhadāraṇyaka*. The sequence is not chronological; the last four are among the oldest according to modern scholars. (Also see Vedānta.)

277. Utsava

Festival; Hinduism abounds in festivals such as Holī, Vasanta-Pañcamī, Nāgapañcamī, Guru-Pūrṇimā, Daśaharā, Diwālī and so on. They interrupt the flow of mundane time and allow interaction with sacred time to charge one's religious and spiritual batteries, as it were. They are so numerous that almost every Hindu will have the experience of participating in them, and adjusting his or her personal and/or professional life to do so. Hindus in the diaspora usually congregate to celebrate these festivals, if for nothing else, as markers of a Hindu identity. The salvific deeds of the heroes or gods are often enacted, sometimes by children, and *kathāvācaka*s (narrators of these divine stories) are invited to commemorate them. The normal dietic pattern gives way to either feasting or fasting, or both, depending on the nature of the festival.

278. Vaikuṇṭha

The paradise of Viṣṇu. The word appears as an epithet of Indra in the *Ṛg-Veda* but comes to denote the Heaven of Viṣṇu, or Viṣṇu-loka, in Vaiṣṇavism. It is located, in sacred geography, either at the bottom of the ocean, or more probably, on a peak of Mt. Meru or on top of *brahmāṇḍa* (cosmic egg), to which true devotees of Viṣṇu go after death. Sometimes Śivaloka, like Viṣṇuloka, is also placed alongside at the top of the cosmos. (Also see Viṣṇu.)

279. Vaikuṇṭha Ekādaśī

Also known as Mokṣadā Ekādaśī, it occurs on the eleventh day of the bright half of the Hindu month of Mārgaśīrṣa (November–December), it is particularly sacred to Viṣṇu. It is claimed that it is particularly auspicious to die on this day as the doors to Vaikuṇṭha are supposed to remain open.

280. Vaiśeṣika School of Philosophy

The Vaiśeṣika school of Hindu philosophy is known for its doctrines of categories (*padārtha*s), into which the world is analysed. These were six to begin with, with the last one being added later. These seven categories are the following:

1. substance (*dravya*);
2. quality (*guṇa*);

3. action (*karma*);
4. generality (*sāmānya*);
5. particularity (*viśeṣa*); inherence (*samavāya*); and
7. non-existence (*abhāva*).

The Vaiśeṣika world-view reduces the material and spiritual world to the nine substance (*dravyas*) of:

1. earth;
2. water;
3. fire;
4. air;
5. ether;
6. time;
7. space;
8. self; and
9. mind.

The first four are reducible to impartite and eternal atoms, while ether, although a substance like the other four, is infinite rather than atomic in nature, along with time and space. The self is spiritual in nature but consciousness is adventitious to it, while the mind is inert, atomic and eternal. The logic behind this classification is interesting. In order to be ultimate something must be indivisible, and this property is shared, at one end of the spectrum, by the infinitesimal, and, at the other end, by the infinite. The second category of qualities consists of twenty-four items, both material and mental in nature. The third category of activity covers five motions: upward, downward, contraction, expansion and locomotion. Generality (*sāmānya*) is the generic element in all members of a class by virtue of which the class, such as that of human beings, for instance, remains eternal, though human beings live and die. Particularity (*viśeṣa*) is that which differentiates the eternal substances, as well as that property on account of which atoms, otherwise similar to one another, nevertheless remain distinct entities. Inherence (*samavāya*) is more than mere conjunction (*saṁyoga*), inasmuch as conjoining elements can separate in conjunction, while *samavāya* binds inseparable entities like:

1. substance and quality;
2. substance and activity;
3. particularly and generality;
4. eternal substance and particularity; and
5. whole and parts.

The cast category, *abhāva* (non-existence) consists of negative facts. Such non-existence must be distinguished from absolute nothing, as it is the absence of something particular. The concept of bondage and release in Vaiśeṣika is similar to that in the Nyāya school, and is also brought about by the knowledge of *padārthas*. These *padārthas* consist of logical categories in Nyāya, in Vaiśeṣika they consist of the categories just discussed. Their knowledge leads to a state of freedom from both misery and bliss; in this system too, as in Nyāya, the absence of misery does not imply of bliss. (Also see Atomic Theory; and Nyāya-Vaiśeṣika.)

281. Vaiṣṇavism

The beliefs and practices associated with the followers of Viṣṇu.

282. Varṇa

The sociological division of society into four classes (*varṇas*), usually listed as consisting of:

1. Brāhmaṇas,
2. Kṣatriyas,
3. Vaiśyas, and
4. Śūdras.

(Also see Jāti.)

283. Vasanta-Pañcamī

Also called Śrī-Pañcamī, this festival is dedicated to Sarasvatī, the goddess of learning. It is a day for wearing bright yellow dresses, specially for women and girls. It is celebrated on the fifth day of the bright half of the month Māgha (January–February), when people visit temples dedicated to Sarasvatī and seek blessings. Some save this day to instruct children in writing the letters of the alphabet for the first time.

284. Veda

The word Veda by itself means knowledge or wisdom and is cognate with the English words wit, wisdom and video. It has the meaning of a book containing wisdom, when applied to the Hindu scriptures. Whether this wisdom is only spiritual and can also be conventional is debated within the tradition; the Vedāntic component of the tradition emphasizes its spiritual character. The Vedas are four in number and each of them may be said to possess four layers, so that collectively the Vedic corpus can be laid out on the following primary grid. Tradition attributes this arrangement to Vyāsa:

Ṛg-Veda	*Yajur-Veda*	*Sāma-Veda*	*Atharva-Veda*	*Timeline*
Mantra or Saṁhitā				1500–1200 BCE
Brāhmaṇa				1200–1000 BCE
Āraṇyaka				1000–800 BCE
Upaniṣads				800 BCE

The horizontal and vertical axes possess with their own logic. The *Ṛg-Veda* is the first to be mentioned because it is also perhaps the oldest as well as largest, the *Yajur-Veda* being two-thirds of it in size, and the *Sāma* and the *Atharva* half in size. The other Vedas borrow considerably from the *Ṛg-Veda*, with the *Atharva* only having a fifth of its material in common. In a sense then, the *Yajur-Veda* represents a liturgical development of the *Ṛg-Veda* and the *Sāma-Veda* a musical one, while the *Atharva-Veda* has little connection with the sacrifices, except in its concluding parts. This textual development along the horizontal line may be complemented with the chronological development along the vertical axis. The hymns of the Mantra or Saṁhitā portions (to which sometimes the word Veda is restricted in modern usage) are devotional invocations of the gods, which take on a pronounced ritualistic dimension in the Brāhmaṇas, in which ritual exegesis predominates. The widespread use of ritual and the ritualistic world-view, which made even the daily arising of the sun dependent on proper ritual, naturally led to a questioning of it. In due course philosophical explanations of ritual came to be developed in the Āraṇyakas (forest books), indicating by their name the environment into which the people retreated to reflect on ritual. This interrogation of ritual soon expanded into an interrogation of the existential situation itself in which ritual is embedded, leading to the Upaniṣads or esoteric treatises which emerged as masters disclosed their teachings to the disciples who sat up close (*up-ni-sad*) to the masters. From an existential point of view, apart from the textual and chronological, the four divisions of the Vedas can also be connected with the four stages of life or (*āśramas*) as biography recapitulates history. In the first stage of *brahmacarya*, the celibate student learns to recite the Saṁhitā or Mantras, even as Vedic knowledge to equip oneself for the rest of life is acquired. In the second stage of *gārhasthya*, or that of the householder, one of the key duties of the householder is to tend to the sacred fire and perform the sacrifices, for which one draws on one's knowledge of the Brāhmaṇas. In the third stage of *vānaprastha*, one's attention turns to the Āraṇyakas, which explore the deeper symbolic meaning of ritual. Indeed, the Āraṇyakas prescribe substitutes for ritual and develop the doctrine that their mental enactment of the ritual could be as efficacious as their physical performance. Finally, in the stage of *saṁnyāsa*, once self-realization becomes the main focus of one's life, one turns to the Upaniṣads for guidance. Finally, if in addition to the textual, the historical and the biographical perspectives, one also considers the soteriological, then the Vedic corpus is classified into

1. the ritual section (*karma-kāṇḍa*);
2. meditation or worship section (*upāsanā-kāṇḍa*); and
3. knowledge section (*jñāna-kāṇḍa*).

In terms of this triptych, the *karma-kāṇḍa* is constituted by the Mantras (or Saṁhitās) and the Brāhmaṇas; the *upāsanā-kāṇḍa* by the Āraṇyakas and the *jñāna-kāṇḍa* by the Upaniṣads.

285. Veda: The "Fifth" Veda

The Vedas are traditionally recognized as four in number; there is a tradition of describing any other piece of sacred literature, which is deemed worthy of the holy status of a Veda, as the "fifth" Veda. It is famously applied to the *Mahābhārata*, in such Purāṇas as the *Brahmāṇḍa*, the *Skanda* and the *Bhāgavata*. Madhva makes the further assertion, on the basis of these Purāṇic statements, that not only is the *Mahābhārata* the fifth Veda, it is even superior to the Vedas. Sometimes instead of calling such a text the fifth Veda, it is called a Veda itself. Thus the *Divyaprabandham* is called the Tamil Veda and the *Guru Granth Sahib* is referred to as the Veda of the Sikhs.

286. Veda: The "Lost" Veda

The Dharmasūtras develop the view that, in some cases, the words of the Brāhmaṇa texts, on the basis of which some of the rites have been promulgated were apparently lost, and the connection had to be inferred. In other words, it had to be assumed that they are based on procedures prescribed in the Vedas (*ĀpDhSū* 1.4.12.10). This doctrine has been appropriated within the Hindu tradition in both a conservative and a liberal way. The famous Nyāya scholar, Jayanta (tenth century), is willing to accept Buddhist texts as authoritative by invoking the "Lost Veda" argument in support. But Kumārila (*c.* seventh century) took a different position and argues that Smṛti provisions, for which no Śruti text is available, could be the result of a Vedic *śākhā* being lost, or may only appear lost, because the Vedas are scattered and people negligent. In other words, the texts are not lost, we are at a loss. He adduces this argument to prevent

Buddhist texts from gaining legitimacy. However, it was on the basis of this doctrine that the Tantras are perceived as connected to the Vedas. Those rituals and practices which are found in the Tantras, but are not directly traceable to the Vedas, are believed to be derived from Vedic texts lost to us.

287. Vedāṅga

Literally "limbs of the Vedas", and actually the six branches of study considered auxiliary to the Vedas. These are:

1. Śikṣā, science of correct pronunciation or phonetics;
2. Chandas, science of prosody;
3. Nirukta, science of etymology;
4. Vyākaraṇa, science of grammar;
5. Jyotiṣa, science of astronomy; and
6. Kalpa, ritual science, laying down rules for rituals and prescriptions for ceremonies.

Thus even the secular sciences thrived in relation to religion, a phenomenon some view negatively as science not being able to free itself from religion, and others positively, as suggesting a holistic view of knowledge. From a modern point of view, the first grammar in the world came to be formulated in India in the form of Pāṇini's *Aṣṭādhyāyī* (*c.* fifth century), while the *Chandaḥśāstra* of Piṅgala (*c.* second century BCE) anticipates the binary principle of computing.

288. Vedānta

The word can be used in a narrow and a broad sense. Used narrowly, it devotes the schools of Hindu philosophy which treat the end-portions (*anta*) of the Vedas (hence the term Vedānta) as the foundational texts of their system. These texts are also called Upaniṣads. The schools of Vedānta usually include two other texts along with them as part of their canon: the *Vedānta-Sūtra*, or *Brahma-Sūtra*, which try to summarize the teachings of the Upaniṣads in a series of aphorisms, and the *Bhagavad-Gītā*, which calls itself an Upaniṣad, although technically not part of the Vedas. These three texts are collectively called the Prasthāna-Traya, that is to say, the set of three foundational texts, or more imaginatively, the three points of departure. It is a fundamental assumption of the Hindu philosophical tradition that the Upaniṣads themselves, as well as the two other texts, have to be understood coherently. In other words, despite apparent divergences and even contradictions, the texts collectively deliver a single message. What that one message is, however, a consistently and persistently debated issue within the tradition, giving rise to the various schools of Vedānta.

The word Vedānta originally stood for the Upaniṣads but, with the passage of time, has now come to denote, in its widest sense, the entire body of thought which developed out of it. If the word is taken in the sense of "what comes last" (*anta*) in the context of the Vedas then it can be taken to mean:

1. The texts which constitute the last section of the Vedic corpus.
2. The texts which figure in the last stage of life. In the first stage of life, as a student, one is devoted to learning the Saṁhitā or Mantra portion by heart; the second stage, as a householder, one is devoted to performing ritual as explained in the Brāhmaṇas; the third stage, as a hermit, one studies the Āraṇyakas and in the fourth and the last stage as a renunciant one studies the Upaniṣads. The word Vedānta can also connote this fact.
3. It can also be taken to mean the last stage, or culmination, of Vedic speculation about the nature of ultimate reality. In the Saṁhitā portion the questions such as "Who is the God to whom we offer sacrifice?" are raised. Now the tradition begins to feel that this long quest for the answer to these questions has come to an end in the Upaniṣads.
4. If we take the word *veda* to mean spiritual knowledge in

general, rather than the texts in which it is embodied, and take the word *anta* to mean a conclusion, as it comes at the end of a carefully argued presentation, then Vedānta could also mean conclusions about spiritual knowledge, in its more general sense, "found in the end portions of the Vedas".

The fact that, in this sense, schools of Vedānta abound and often differ from one another, should not blind us to the fact that there is virtual unanimity among them in rejecting the following positions:

1. The world is the product of material elements, which combined on their own to produce it;
2. that the world emerged spontaneously out of a single entity called Nature;
3. that the world was created by an efficient cause, out of a material cause independent of it;
4. that the world has an unconscious cause; and
5. that knowledge of God could be obtained in a purely rational manner alone.

The influence of Vedānta is pervasive but variable. Most scholars think that Vaiṣṇava thought has been affected by it much more than Śaiva thought and Śākta even less. Its influence has also varied over time; at one time, in the early history of Hinduism, Mīmāṁsā was arguably more influential than Vedānta, while modern Hinduism is deeply dyed in Vedānta.

289. Vedānta-Sūtra

This text, attributed to Bādarāyaṇa and often placed in the fifth century, is also known as *Brahma-Sūtra*, *Śārīraka-Sūtra*, *Śārīraka-Mīmāṁsā* and *Uttara-Mīmāṁsā*. Its context is provided by the fact that the Upaniṣads developed in various different Vedic schools (*śākhās*) as they are called, and their teachings represented a variety of opinions despite a certain unity of outlook. This led to the need to harmonize them and the *Vedānta-Sūtra* is an effort to do so, although the cryptic Sūtra style, in which it is composed, meant that its aphorisms could, and were, interpreted in different ways, so that those schools of Vedāntic thought which arose later had to harmonize their teachings with those of the Upaniṣads and the *Bhagavad-Gītā* in turn, thus partly explaining the emergence of the Prasthāna Trayī. The text of the *Vedānta-Sūtra* is divided into four chapters: the first, called *samanvaya*, is concerned with demonstrating the coherence of the Upaniṣadic teachings and establishes *Brahman* as the ultimate reality, which is the concern of the Upaniṣads; the second, called *avirodha*, is devoted to overcoming contradictions; the third, called *sādhana*, is devoted to an examination of the means of the realization of *Brahman* and the fourth, called *phala*, deals with the fruits or results of the knowledge of *Brahman*. The text has been interpreted by the major schools of Vedānta in their own way, through the various commentaries written on it, and also through the various sub-commentaries which followed. (Also see Prasthāna-Traya.)

290. Vedic Religion

Early Vedic religion consisted of fire sacrifices called *yajña* or *homa*, to the gods. The offerings included clarified butter and grains, as well as the flesh of animals, which were spread around or poured into a sacred fire. The fire then carried the offerings to heaven in the form of smoke. Indra was the main God, to whom one-fourth of the total number of hymns in the *Ṛg-Veda* are addressed. Then came Agni, followed by Soma, in terms of this criterion. The importance of Agni is obvious, that of Soma needs to be explained. Soma was a drink prepared from a plant whose exhilarating and conscious-transforming properties are celebrated in the *Ṛg-Veda*. The word was used for the plant as well as the deity; after a time the identity of the plant was lost to the Aryans. Modern scholarship has not yet succeeded in identifying it beyond dispute. Another important god in the *Ṛg-Veda* is Varuṇa, whose moral quality contrasts with the heroic quality of Indra. While Indra boasts of his achievement, every hymn addressed to Varuṇa asks for forgiveness. These gods faded into the background in later Hinduism, in which Indra became a ruler of heaven, Agni became an agent of ritual, Soma came to be identified with the moon and Varuṇa became the lord of the oceans. The attribute shared by the various gods was that of being the guardians of *ṛta* (or of physical and moral order), a concept for which the word *dharma* came to be used. (Also see Ṛta.)

291. Vedic Ritual

The central feature of modern-day Hindu ritual is *pūjā*, which may be combined with some Vedic elements such as *homa*, but is different from the Vedic in the sense that the deity is visible in *pūjā* in the form of the image but was invisible in the Vedic setting, as Vedic worship was aniconic. When it comes, however, to the point of the main models employed for offering worship to the deity — as a "beloved guest" or an "honoured king" — they converge. The keyword in the context of Vedic worship is ritual (*yajña*), which corresponds to the *pūjā* ritual in temple worship. The *yajña* is a sacrificial ritual in which an offering is made to a deity, after the deity has been invited, either by spreading the offering out at the sacrificial altar, or committing them to fire. In the first case the deity comes to take it, in the latter it is sent to the deity, for, in the Vedic imagination, the fire carried the offerings to the deities, who lived in the atmospheric regions or in heaven. Sometimes the aroma could achieve that effect and perhaps explains the use of incense later. The method which used Agni as a mediator was by far the most popular and also made Agni, or fire, all the more important as a god, so that Agni itself is approached to carry on the process of mediation not only by taking things to the gods but also by bringing gods to the worshipper: "O Agni, bring hither Varuṇa to our offering. Bring Indra from the skies and Maruts from the air." The purpose of the offering could be construed as twofold — to please the gods or to appease them, or both, as the gods both have a mellow and a fierce side to their personality. The idea underlying the ritual, in later literature, is clearly mutual exchange, as in the

Brāhmaṇa texts, while the motives earlier on may have been simple adoration or fear. This mutual compact could be viewed as a crass act — something along the lines of "I scratch your back and you scratch my back", or more of a class act as depicted in *Bhagavad-Gītā* (III.10-12):

> The creator said, creating the people and the sacrifice: may you propagate through this. Let this be the wish-fulfilling cow to fulfil your wishes. Cherishing the gods by this the gods will cherish you — in this way you will achieve the great good by cherishing each other.

The offerings ranged from grains, melted butter and *soma* juice to animals. Animal offerings, although became widespread at one stage, did not always carry scriptural sentiment with them, for a verse in the *Sāma-Veda* runs as follows:

> O ye gods! We use no sacrificial stake. We slay no victim. We worship entirely by the repetition of sacred verses.

This offering of speech is also hinted in the *Ṛg-Veda*: "Utter a powerful speech to Indra which is sweeter than butter or honey". In due course, this speech itself took the form of *stotra* in later literature, which, in later Hinduism became a genre of literature used in worshipping God.

292. Vīraśaivism

"Heroic Śaivism", an important development in the Hindu religious tradition: historically, sociologically, philosophically and religiously. Its followers are also known as Liṅgāyata, although it has been suggested that this may be a name given to them by others. The historical context is provided by the Cāḷukyas of Kalyāṇī in the twelfth century, when Cāḷukya power declined and Bijjala Kaḷcūrī (ruled *c.* 1160-67), a rebel held the throne. It was during his reign that Basava (*c.* 1106-67), his brāhmaṇa minister, who is said by some to have been originally a Jaina, founded the Vīraśaiva sect by introducing social and theological reforms. These included an egalitarianism which cut across caste lines, culminating in the marriage of a young outcaste with a brāhmaṇa girl, which offended the king so much that he ordered the execution of the parents. This caused a riot leading to the death of the king. Basava, who was opposed this violent response, is said to have spent the last years of his life away from the community. The community does not practise cremation as it believes that a member of it is immediately raised to the company of Śiva upon death; nor does it employ brāhmaṇas. Members of the community do not worship images but only wear the *liṅga*, which also replaces the sacred thread. Vīraśaivism opposed child marriage and approved of widow remarriage. An important Vīraśaiva is the woman-saint, Akkā Mahādevī, a junior contemporary of Basava, who moved about clothed only in her hair and whose Kannaḍa poems, called *vacanas*, are a cherished legacy. Scripturally, the sect now accepts the Vedas (although it apparently started out by rejecting them), along with the Āgamas and the Purāṇas, the hymns of the Nāyanārs (who are called the ancient ones — *purātana*), in addition to the sayings of the Kannaḍa mystics like Basava and Akkā Mahādevī, referred to above. Philosophically, the Vīraśaiva system of thought is now known as Śakti-Viśiṣṭādvaita, or the non-duality of God as qualified by his *śakti* (power), the idea being that God and soul are inseparable on account of being bound together by God's inalienable power. It also ensures that the ultimate reality in this system, Para-Śiva (Supreme Śiva), brings about the creation of the world through the inseparable *śakti*, also called *māyā* or *mūla-prakṛti*, which evolves into the universe but leaves God unaffected by the process. The *jīva* (individual soul) is a part (*aṁśa*) of God, in the sense that it proceeds from God, shares His essence and returns to Him as a part might to the whole. This return involves the overcoming the ignorance (*avidyā*) of the fact that the soul is totally dependent on God, which results in union (*aikya*) with God, a state described as *liṅgāṅga-sāmarasya* (harmonization of *liṅga* 'Śiva' and *aṅga* 'soul'). The union is soteriological but not ontological, the two remain entitatively different and the relationship between the two is described as one of identity-cum-difference (*bhedābheda*). At a more technical level, *Brahman*, understood here obviously as *Saguṇa-Brahman* and identified with Para-Śiva is called *sthala* (location or abode), because Śiva is the abode of all. The word *sthala* is of course grammatically related to the root *stha* with a suffix, but in keeping with the Indic tradition of providing philosophical rather philological etymologies, the word is explained as applying to God because in Him everything exists (*stha*) and to Him it returns (*la*). Thus Para-Śiva divides himself into *liṅga* and *aṅga*, and so does His *Śakti* into *kalā* (part) and *bhakti* (devotion), the former being connected with Śiva whom it enables to project the world, and the latter with the soul, whom it guides back to Śiva. In order for this to be achieved, eight rules called *aṣṭāvaraṇa* (reminiscent of the Eightfold Path) have to be observed:

1. obedience of the *guru*;
2. worship of *liṅga*;
3. reverence for the *jaṅgama*;
4. smearing of the sacred ash (*vibhūti*);
5. wearing of a rosary of *rudrākṣa* beads;
6. *pādodaka*, sipping the water in which the feet of the *guru* or the *jaṅgama* have been washed;
7. *prasāda*, offering food to a *guru*, *jaṅgama* or *liṅga*, and partaking sacramentally of what is left over; and
8. *pañcākṣara*, uttering the five-syllabled formula *Namaḥ Śivāya*.

The three key terms in Vīraśaivism are *guru*, *jaṅgama* and *liṅga* as is obvious from the above. The *guru* is of course the preceptor who assumes personal responsibility for making one see the light; the *jaṅgama* at one level is the perfected soul, and, at another, the person who replaces the brāhmaṇa priest, while the *liṅga* stands for Śiva. Abbe Dubois (eighteenth century) mentions the curious custom that when the *jaṅgama* visited a householder's home, all the men left, leaving the womenfolk to look after him. Religiously the sect's appearance is important as an example of strictly ethical monotheism emerging in the context of Śaivism, and the presence of a kind of sectarianism within Hinduism. (Also see Basavanna.)

293. Viśiṣṭādvaita Vedānta

The term, Viśiṣṭādvaita Vedānta, is difficult to render in English. It is usually referred to as "qualified monism", but scholars of the system point out that it would be more accurate to describe it as "the monism of the qualified" rather than as "qualified monism". This point underlies the suggestion that it should be called "organismal non-dualism". It is one of the three pre-eminent schools of Vedānta, along with Advaita Vedānta, in relation to which it is more dualistic, and Dvaita Vedānta, in relation to which it is more monistic. It thus falls in the middle both historically and philosophically, as it were, in terms of these three major formulations of Vedānta. The word "qualified" needs be understood with care in this system, which posits three ultimate entities: God, soul and matter. God is qualified by the soul and matter and it is the qualified or the embodied that is one (as God), while the factors qualifying or embodying it are quite distinct, though inseparable from it, namely, soul and matter, which are totally dependent on God for their existence, while God enjoys independent existence. One way of furthering one's understanding of "qualified monism" or Viśiṣṭādvaita would be to contrast it with the system of Advaita. Thus while Advaita Vedānta accords priority to *Nirguṇa-Brahman*, Viśiṣṭādvaita Vedānta accords priority to *Saguṇa-Brahman*. Similarly, while Advaita Vedānta relies on the path of knowledge (*jñāna*) to ultimately secure liberation, the system of Viśiṣṭādvaita ultimately relies on the path of devotion (*bhakti*) to secure that outcome. And while Advaita Vedānta believes that *jīvan-mukti* (living liberation, or embodied liberation) is possible, which is to say that liberation is a pre-mortem state, according to Viśiṣṭādvaita Vedānta, only post-mortem liberation, or what is called *videha-mukti*, is possible. To elaborate on the comparison: The history of Hindu philosophy, from one point of view, is a continuous debate on the question whether *Brahman* is ultimately *nirguṇa* or *saguṇa*, i.e. is it more like a principle, or more like a person. Śaṅkara argued for the ultimacy of *Nirguṇa-Brahman* but Rāmānuja (1017–1137) thought that his *Nirguṇa-Brahman* was a mere abstraction. Śaṅkara identified it with *nirviśeṣa caitanya* (undifferentiated consciousness) but Rāmānuja pointed out that, consciousness, as we know it, always has an object, so that Śaṅkara's undifferentiated or objectless consciousness is only an abstraction. Thus, in this system, *Brahman*, the ultimate reality, comprises three eternal realities (*tattva-traya*), namely, God (*Īśvara*), soul (*cit*) and matter (*acit*), the last two qualifying the first, so God is *viśiṣṭa* (qualified) in this sense as well, apart from possessing many qualities. A key component of the philosophy of Viśiṣṭādvaita Vedānta is its analysis of the nature of the relationship between these three, which is described by the term *apṛthak-siddhi* or inseparability. The point to note is that it is an internal rather than an external relationship. For instance, the relationship the body has to the coat it wears is very different from the relationship it has with the soul. The relationship of the body with the coat, even if one is seen constantly wearing it, is an external relationship and both can exist without the other, but the relationship between the body and the soul is in internal one and, is for the body, an inseparable relationship. Rāmānuja argues that this kind of deep internal relationship exists in two cases:

1. In the case of a relationship between substance and attribute; and
2. In the case of a relationship between body and soul, and is characterized by inseparability, although the elements involved are distinct.

To cite a popular example, we might refer to a blue lotus. The lotus is however a substance, and the colour blue is an attribute, but "blueness" and "lotusness" have been identified with each other. In the case of body and soul, the same soul is characterized at different stages of life as old or young in terms of the body. In the case of substance and attribute, such identification was simultaneous, here it is successive, but in both cases it is characterized by inseparability; blueness and lotusness being inseparable from the flower and the states of the body from the soul. But it should be noted that God persists and stands independently on its own from the qualifiers, which are dependent on it, though inseparable from it. In this way God (*Īśvara*), is the qualified, while souls (*cit*), and matter (*acit*) are the qualifying elements. The Advaita (monism) of Viśiṣṭādvaita consists of the fact that it is same one God who is qualified by soul and matter. This is why the system should be described as "the monism of the qualified". Rāmānuja was thus able to reconcile those statements in the Upaniṣads, which describe *Brahman* as distinct from the souls and the world, and those which describe them as identical, by arguing that, in the former case, the Upaniṣads were asserting the separateness of the three *tattvas*, but in the latter case, only meant that the soul and matter were inseparable from God and not literally identical as Advaita Vedānta took them to be. It is God (*Īśvara*), as qualified by the soul (*cit*) or matter (*acit*), which is non-dual (*advaita*). (Also see Tattva-Traya.)

294. Viśiṣṭādvaita Vedānta: Mokṣa

Mokṣa in Viśiṣṭādvaita Vedānta is achieved through the paths of *karma*, *jñāna* and *bhakti*. *Karma-yoga* purified the mind and prepared it for *jñāna-yoga* (path of knowledge). The knowledge involved here is however that of one's utter dependence on God. This leads to love of God (*bhakti*), which is defined by Rāmānuja as the constant recollection of God (*dhruvānusmṛti*). One is then led to a vision of God, but actual liberation only takes place after death (*videha-mukti*). This means that one must perform *karma* in the sense of ritual, and one's duties, till the very end.

295. Viṣṇu

One of the two primary gods of Hinduism, along with Śiva. Viṣṇu as a god is often said to represent the confluence of three entities. One of them is the far-striding Viṣṇu in the *Ṛg-Veda*, usually identified as a solar deity, with the three strides representing his movement through the skies. This divinity merged with the figure of Nārāyaṇa as a cosmic god, whose conception is well-developed in the Brāhmaṇas. A third layer is then provided by the Bhāgavata cult, associated with Kṛṣṇa, resulting in the composite figure we have. One important feature is his incarnations of *avatāras*, when he intervenes to prevent the premature dissolution of the universe and to establish justice. Śiva, by contrast, does not typically incarnate himself; he either appears as himself or animates a body through which he speaks.

296. Vishwa Hindu Parishad (VHP)

An organization, formed in 1964, to bring all Hindus under one umbrella. This council for all Hindus hopes to speak for all Hindus, a category which, for its purposes, includes Buddhists, Jainas and Sikhs. It may thus be seen as a response to the need felt by Hindus to offer a common front and undertake joint action, made difficult by the inherently plural nature of Hinduism. The need seems to arise from some common pressures to which the Hindus in India have been subjected, such as attempts at proselytization by Islam and Christianity (in the face of which a non-proselytizing religion such as Hinduism might feel helpless) the continuing need to carry on the Gandhian agenda to uplift the untouchable classes among the Hindus, and to combat the apolitical nature of Hinduism, which makes it vulnerable to state policies directed against it, such as the appointment of Marxists as vice-chancellors of Sanskrit universities, or the presence of communists on governing boards of the temples. The VHP is an international organization, with centres in twenty-five countries, and maintains fraternal relations with other Hindu organizations such as the Rashtriya Swayamsevak Sangha (RSS), and the Bharatiya Janta Party (BJP), although tensions have sometimes surfaced on policy matters.

The VHP vision of India's history and destiny, with which many Hindus could sympathize but which others vehemently oppose, runs somewhat like this. India was a leading civilization until around 1000, after which it succumbed to Turko-Afghan and Moghul rule, and then, after 1800, to British rule. These rulers had their own religion which they tried to impose on the Hindus, a people they tried to destroy in the process. Hindu self-assertion is therefore required to restore national confidence and dignity and resume the forward march of Indic/Hindu civilization, now that the country is politically independent and no longer under Muslim or British rule, but the process is being thwarted by a misplaced secularism, which is just a cover for continuing the anti-Hindu policies of the earlier foreign rulers. Some spokespersons of the VHP have openly called for a Hindu state; to the extent the call is not rhetorical it is an acknowledgement of the difficulty of mobilizing Hindus along political lines, compared to the Muslims, the Chriṣtians, the Sikhs and even the Communists. The VHP has been trying to infuse Indian politics with a political, and down the line, an electoral awareness of Hindu identity. The year 1983 was an important one in this respect, when processions from different parts of the country converged on Nagpur, the RSS headquarters, which is located in the state of Maharashtra but geographically stands at the centre of India. These processions eulogized Mother India, the Ganges and the Hindus. Another important year was 1992, when Karsevakas were mobilized from all over the country to press for the building a temple to Rāma in Ayodhyā, on the site where a mosque stood, allegedly constructed during the reign of the Mogul Emperor Babur by demolishing a Hindu temple. Consecrated bricks for use in the construction of this temple has been collected from Hindu communities all over the world. This agitation has not succeeded in building a temple but the mosque was demolished by a mob on 6 December 1992. (Also see Hindutva.)

297. Vivāha

The *Kāmasūtra* recommends a marriage by mutual consent between the parties as the best, because it is based on affection, but most marriages in India are still arranged by the parents, although more and more people are now getting married on their own. In most middle-class families, even when the marriage is an arranged one, the suitors are taken into confidence and can exercise a veto. Marriages used to be not just a bond between individuals but also their families in India, and hence were arranged by the families. The emergence of a geographically and professionally mobile middle class, the increasing urbanization of population, and the steady replacement of joint family system by the nuclear family are now altering this reality.

298. Vivaraṇa School of Advaita Vedānta

A sub-school of Advaita Vedānta, based on the text *Pañcapādikā* by Padmapāda, a direct disciple of Śaṅkara, which was commented on by Prakāśātma (thirteenth century) in *Pañcapādikā-Vivaraṇa.* Sarvajñātma (*c.* 900), the author of *Saṁkṣepa-Śārīraka*, is also associated with the Vivaraṇa school. The teachings of the school are summarized by Bhāratītīrtha Vidyāraṇya (fourteenth century) in the *Vivaraṇa-Prameya-Saṁgraha.* (Also see Bhāmatī School of Advaita Vedānta; and Śaṅkara: Post-Śaṅkara Advaita.)

299. Vivekananda (1863–1902)

Swami Vivekananda enjoys iconic status as a representative of modern Hinduism. He was a disciple of Ramakrishna, who, after his master's death in 1886 devoted himself to spiritual life, disappointing his family who had hoped to see him make good on his Western education. He then travelled throughout India but appeared, on his own initiative, as a representative of Hinduism at the Parliament of Religions at Chicago in 1893, where his stirring speech has become a part of his legend in India. The assessment that when he finished speaking, "Hinduism has been created" is not wide off the mark, as his formulation of Hinduism has profoundly influenced modern Hinduism. (Also see Ramakrishna Paramahamsa.)

300. Vrata

A religious or pious vow, whether recommended or voluntary. These vows could cover a wide range, all the way from vow to observe a day's silence, or fast, to temporary or lifelong celibacy, although most *vratas* are short-lived and typically last for a day. They may also be observed out of devotion for a deity to secure a boon. Thus one might fast for Goddess Lakṣmī for financial success, or for Goddess Sarasvatī for educational success. One could also fast for the well-being of others, like wives fasting for the health and long life of the husband.

Vratas often include a nocturnal vigil, a phenomenon which may draw inspiration from *Bhagavad-Gītā* (II.69):

> The person with self-control stays awake in what is night to all creatures; and treats as night wherein the creatures stay awake.

Vratas of all kinds abound in Hinduism, include those for sunshine in winter (*māgha-maṇḍala-vrata*) and for good harvests (*pauṣa-vrata*).

301. Vyāsa

According to the unanimous Hindu tradition, the Vedas, as we have them, were organized in their present form by a person, who rescued them from obscurity and disarray. His name is given as Vyāsa and he is said to have performed this feat, according to most accounts, at the end of the Dvāpara and beginning of Kali-Yuga, that is to say, *c.* 3000 BCE. He is said to have divided the existing inchoate mass of material into the four Vedas of *Ṛg*, *Yajur*, *Sāma* and *Atharva,* and to have taught it to his four disciples: Paila, Vaiśampāyana, Jaimini and Sumanta, to ensure their proper transmission. Hence his name Veda-Vyāsa, or the arranger or classifier of the Vedas. According to one scholar, "This tradition is so strong among Hindu scholars that it cannot but be accepted as having some historical basis". While the Purāṇas claim that the eternal Veda was arranged into four parts by Vyāsa, they do not say that Vyāsa divided them into *maṇḍalas* or *kāṇḍas*. (Also see Vedas; and Mahābhārata.)

302. Western Tradition of Vedic Study

Modern Western study is said to have been initiated by Eugene Burnouf in Paris (1801-52), around the time Colebrooke offered the first clear picture of the Vedas in English. Two pupils of Burnouf, Rudolf Roth (1821-95) and Friedrich Max Müller (1823–1903) provided the lead in insisting on an Indo-European rather than an Indian context for the Vedas, while two other Western scholars, R. Pischel (1849–1908) and K.F. Geldner (1852–1921) insisted on respecting the Indian provenance of the Vedas. (Also see Orientalism.)

303. Women's Rituals

The tradition of separate women's rituals is very ancient in India, with the wife of Indra herself claiming to be a trendsetter in the matter. This point is also supported by the *Atharva-Veda*, although the androcentric nature of much of the existing literature obscures this from view. Thus just as boys are initiated into *upanayana*, girls are initiated into womanhood with the onset of menstruation. Although ritually considered unclean, anthropological evidence indicates that its onset is also celebrated in some parts of India, although girls are secluded for a week thereafter. Elders in the family initiated the younger generation into the new lifestyle suitable for the grown-up woman. (Also see Karavā-Cautha; and Teej.)

304. Yoga

Just as Sāṁkhya is an ancient philosophical system of India, *yoga* is an ancient technique for controlling the mind. This school, however, does not have a metaphysical system of its own but adopts the one provided by Sāṁkhya. The yogic tradition of India is systematically articulated in the *Yoga-Sūtra*, ascribed to Patañjali and usually assigned to the fifth century. The philosophy underlying the text may be summarized as follows: a human being is essentially *puruṣa* (spirit), characterized by pure consciousness, but the empirical human being emerges with its involvement in *prakṛti*. The original point of this involvement is not traceable but its cause can be identified as follows. The first product of *prakṛti*, as noted in the discussion of Sāṁkhya, is *mahat* or *buddhi*. It is called *citta* in Yoga. The pure spirit of *puruṣa* is reflected in it, and the *puruṣa* identifies itself with this reflection in the mind, forgetting its true nature. This *citta* is by itself an inert entity, as it belongs to the realm of *prakṛti* (matter) but appears conscious upon receiving the reflection of the *puruṣa*, just as a plain piece of metal appears as a shining object while reflecting the light of the sun. The *citta* by itself pervades everything and is called *kāraṇa-citta* (*citta*-as-cause) in this state, but becoming associated with a body it contracts and becomes confined to it, and is called *kārya-citta* (*citta*-as-effect). The goal of Yoga is to make the *citta* achieve its unmodified state. That is why Yoga has been famously defined as *citta-vṛtti-nirodha* (cessation of the modification of the mind). As things exist, the pure spirit is caught up in its reflection in the *citta* and identifies itself with it. If, however, the mind could be stilled, then the pure spirit would see its reflection as such, instead of getting caught up in it. Hence the strong emphasis on *vairāgya* (dispassion) in the system. As when water in a lake becomes still, the rash onlooker realizes first that one's body is not shaking, as one thought it was, mistaking one's reflected body for real; and then discriminates between one's own body and the reflected body: The *puruṣa* realizes that it had a misidentified itself with the mind, a process overcome through *viveka* (discrimination) in Yoga. The two realizations that (1) these things are happening to my reflection and not to me (*vairāgya*), and (2) I am not the reflection (*viveka*), are of course closely related. In other words, as the waves of empirical consciousness (*kārya-citta*) subside and calm down, the mind (*citta*) is left in a state of lucidity and stillness, which is the hallmark of its original causal state (*kāraṇa-citta*). Then the *puruṣa* realizes itself as distinct from the body–mind complex, and free by itself. Although the word *yoga* means union, its main goal is to untie *puruṣa* from *prakṛti*. It has been said that the goal of *yoga* is paradoxically *vi-yoga* (disunion between *puruṣa* and *prakṛti*). In the course of normal living the pure spirit, (*puruṣa*), upon identifying itself with the reflection in the *citta*, begins to experience the five afflictions (*kleśa*s) called:

1. ignorance (*avidyā*);
2. egoity (*asmitā*) as a result of identifying with a body–mind complex;
3. likes (*rāga*);
4. dislikes (*dveṣa*); and
5. phobia of death (*abhiniveśa*).

These developments could be avoided if the *citta* could be kept in an unmodified state. Yoga identifies five such modifications (*vṛtti*s) as:

1. valid knowledge (*pramāṇa*);
2. false knowledge (*viparyaya*);
3. verbal knowledge (*vikalpa*);
4. sleep (*nidrā*); and
5. memory (*smṛti*).

Yoga offers an eight-point programme to achieve its goal, and is therefore called *aṣṭāṅga-yoga*: the *yoga* of eight limbs or steps. There steps are listed as:

1. *yama* (restraints);
2. *niyama* (observances);
3. *āsana* (posture);
4. *prāṇāyāma* (breath control);
5. *pratyāhāra* (withdrawal of the senses);
6. *dhāraṇā* (attention–retention);
7. *dhyāna* (meditation); and

8. *samādhi* (meditative trance).

Yama consist of the following five: *ahiṁsā* (non-violence); *satya* (truth); *asteya* (non-stealing); *brahmacarya* (celibacy) and *aparigraha* (non-possession). These are negative in character. By contrast the *niyamas* are positive and also five in number: *śauca* (purity); *santoṣa* (contentment); *tapas* (austerity); *svādhyāya* (scriptural study) and *īśvara-praṇidhāna* (devotion to God). These *yamas* and *niyamas* together have felicitously been described as the ten commandments of *yoga*. That these ethical principles are first to be mentioned seems to imply that there can be no spirituality without morality. The next three limbs: *āsana*, *prāṇāyāma* and *pratyāhāra* deal with steadying the body and the mind, once moral life is stabilized. *Āsana* means posture, and in this form of *yoga*, also called *rāja-yoga*, involves assuming a comfortable position. In another form of *yoga*, called *haṭha-yoga*, a number of *āsanas* are listed because this form of *yoga* concentrates on the body. The system of *yoga* being discussed here focuses on the mind, so the main idea is to transcend body consciousness by assuming a comfortable position, thus enabling one to work with the mind. Mind and breath are closely related in Hindu psychology, so the next step involved in steadying the mind is the regulation of the breath through the practice of *prāṇāyāma*. Once this is achieved, one is instructed to withdraw the mind from the fields of the senses, where it usually roams. This is called *pratyāhara*. The first five limbs of *yoga* are also collectively called *bahiraṅga-sādhana* (external means). The last three stages, which are collectively called *saṁyama*, include *dhāraṇā*, *dhyāna* and *samādhi*. *Dhāraṇā* means holding on to a state of mind and sinking deeper into oneself in meditation (*dhyāna*). Intense meditation induces an almost altered state of consciousness in its abstraction, and this state of consciousness, called *samādhi*, is said to consist of two stages; a lower and preliminary one, in which the mind though absorbed in an object continues to function (*samprajñāta samādhi*), and a final one, in which objective consciousness disappears, the mind ceases to function, and one's true nature as a *puruṣa*, possessing only pure consciousness, stands revealed. The state of *kaivalya* (sublime isolation of spirit from matter), as postulated in Sāṁkhya is then achieved, though in one important respect Yoga differs from classical Sāṁkhya. Classical Sāṁkhya is atheistic but Yoga is theistic. As *yoga* is essentially a technique of mind control, which is necessary for any form of spiritual life, *yoga* has been adopted by almost all schools of Hindu philosophy in some form.

305. Yuga Scheme

Vedic literature contains numerous accounts of creation but classical Hinduism evolved the theory of *yugas* (cosmic cycles), in a scheme which involves vast dimensions of time. The chronology of the *yugas* is presented below:

Yuga or Age	*Dominant Mode of Religiosity*	*Duration (Years)*
Kṛta	*Tapas* (austerity)	1,728,000
Tretā	*Jñāna* (spiritual knowledge)	1,296,000
Dvāpara	*Jaña* (sacrifice)	844,000
Kali	*Dāna* (charity) *Bhakti* (devotion)	432,000
4 *yugas* = 1 *mahāyuga;* 1,000 *mahāyugas* = 1 *kalpa.*		432,000,000

The main thrust of the scheme is that, with each age, the level of virtue and spirituality declines, which necessitates new developments. According to one view, even the caste system and the composition of the Vedas, are to be located in a period after the Kṛta-Yuga. The scheme is mind-boggling in its numbers, but of more immediate relevance is the fact that the Kali-Yuga, which we live, commenced in 3102 BCE and that, in this age, the favoured religious activity is charity, and the favoured religious path is that of devotion. This fact, that the new age has recently commenced, also provided Hindu scholars with a device to effect or regularize changes by arguing that certain practices, while appropriate for previous ages, were no longer so in present Kali-Yuga. This is known as the doctrine of Kalivarjya. Ancient texts mention the right of levirate, for instance, but it was not considered appropriate for the

Kali-Yuga. The view was also developed, that while Kali-Yuga was a depraved age so far as *dharma* was concerned, this dark cloud had a silver lining, which could be minted spiritually. One had to work hard in the previous more virtuous ages to acquire a certain stock of religious merit, but in the depraved Kali-Yuga, even a little goes a long way. (Also see Vyāsa.)

Index